Constituting
International
Political Economy

International Political Economy Yearbook
Volume 10

Kurt Burch, Robert A. Denemark,
Mary Ann Tetreault & Kenneth Thomas
Series Editors

Board of Editors

Constituting International Political Economy

edited by
Kurt Burch
Robert A. Denemark

LYNNE
RIENNER
PUBLISHERS

BOULDER
LONDON

Published in the United States of America in 1997 by
Lynne Rienner Publishers, Inc.
1800 30th Street, Boulder, Colorado 80301

and in the United Kingdom by
Lynne Rienner Publishers, Inc.
3 Henrietta Street, Covent Garden, London WC2E 8LU

Library of Congress Cataloging-in-Publication Data
Constituting international political economy / edited by Kurt Burch
  and Robert A. Denemark.
      p.   cm. — (International political economy yearbook ; v. 10)
    Includes bibliographical references and index.
    ISBN 1-55587-660-9 (alk. paper)
    1. International economic relations.   I. Burch, Kurt, 1958–
II. Denemark, Robert Allen.   III. Series.
HF1410.I579   vol. 10
[HF1359]
337—dc21   97-13955
                                                          CIP

British Cataloguing in Publication Data
A Cataloguing in Publication record for this book
is available from the British Library.

Printed and bound in the United States of America

        The paper used in this publication meets the requirements
  ∞ of the American National Standard for Permanence of
        Paper for Printed Library Materials Z39.48–1984.

    5 4 3 2 1

Contents

PART 4   CONSTRUCTING PRACTICES

PART 5   CONSTRUCTING ALTERNATIVE APPROACHES

PART 6   COMMENTARIES

Preface

Volume 10 of the *IPE Yearbook* marks the arrival of a new editorial team. As our first act—and on behalf of the entire IPE Section of ISA—we admiringly thank William Avery and David Rapkin for their diligent work and valuable efforts. They crafted the *Yearbook* into a prestigious outlet for contemporary IPE research, and they leave a remarkable legacy that we will strive to maintain. We are especially grateful for their counsel and assistance in the transition.

The *IPE Yearbook* has four new coeditors: Kurt Burch, Robert Denemark, Mary Ann Tetreault, and Ken Thomas. We vary in rank, experience, methodological predispositions, and primary interests. Our hope is to bring diverse perspectives to the series and the profession while continuing the *Yearbook*'s tradition of important analyses of substantive issues. Each volume will feature at least two members of the editorial team, one of whom will always have a primary interest in the topic under consideration.

The first named coeditor for each volume charts the project's course and character by contacting representative scholars, wrestles with defining questions, and organizes the thematic coherence of the volume. This coeditor shapes the contributions and the volume with two goals in mind: to deepen the understanding of those readers with specific interest in the topic and to broaden the understanding of those who expect the volume to convey state-of-the-art work. We make these goals our editorial challenge.

To this end, the second coeditor is a full partner acting as ombudsman to the profession, primarily by ensuring that the volume informs not only those keenly interested in the specific topic but also those interested but unfamiliar with its vocabulary and nuances. This editor aids the primary coeditor, but also serves as an advocate for the profession in general. The remaining coeditors help the active pair as necessary, but they focus primarily on planning and coordinating subsequent volumes. As one volume nears completion and another begins, we will change roles. Such rotating will keep the perspectives diverse and the editors fresh.

We thank the IPE Section of the ISA, under the able leadership of Lorraine Eden and Simon Reich, for its continuing support. We hope forthcoming volumes confirm their confidence in us. The Departments of

Political Science at the University of Delaware, Iowa State University, and the University of Missouri at St. Louis help support this endeavor in various ways. Lynne Rienner and her staff are our enthusiastic partners, providing us able assistance and boundless support. We especially appreciate the unwavering support and affection of many friends, teachers, colleagues, and family members.

K. B.
R. A. D.

Kurt Burch

Introduction

The chapters in this volume respond in diverse ways to changes affecting both the global conditions and practices of international political economy (ipe) and the discipline of IPE. The myriad changes reshaping the character of ipe include the formation of trading blocs; the creation of the World Trade Organization; the introduction of free market principles in Eastern Europe and southern China; the heightened perception of the volume and speed of global financial matters; the efforts to introduce democracy and promote liberal social relations; the prospects for restructuring political relations following the Cold War and at the dawn of a new millennium; and, of course, the conditions wrought by corporate and industrial layoffs, dispersed chains of production, slow economic growth in industrial economies, and chronic global poverty.

Simultaneously, the discipline of IPE and its mainstream theories are subject to changes and challenges. Observers and critics challenge conventional IPE theorists to better account for social change. The debates between neorealists and neoliberals affect the nature of theory and apt policy implications. Postpositivist critiques from critical theorists, historical sociologists, feminists, and those employing interpretive frameworks challenge the philosophical, scientific, ideological, and theoretical premises of positivism and realism. Postmodern theory challenges the claims to truth, reality, and knowledge that ground social science generally. Consequently, postmodern theories raise larger questions: Is theory constitutive or explanatory? If theory is constitutive, can it be grounded in foundations, or should (must) it invoke incomparably interpretive claims? Steve Smith (1995:26–27) boldly emphasizes these significant issues:

> In my view [constitutive versus explanatory theory] is the main meta-theoretical issue facing international theory today. The emerging fundamental division in the discipline is between those theories that seek to offer explanatory accounts of international relations, and those that see theory as constitutive of that reality. At base this boils down to a difference over what the social world is like; is it to be seen as scientists think of the "natural" world, that is to say as something outside of our theories,

1

or is the social world what we make of it? . . . Opposed to [constitutive theory] stands virtually all the work contained in the three dominant paradigms of [IR and IPE:] realism, pluralism, and neo-Marxism.

The contributors to this volume advance *constitutive* theory, or *constructivist* accounts (these terms are synonymous), of issues relevant to the discipline of IPE and the social conditions and practices of ipe, although they differ on the philosophical question of foundations. Indeed, as constructivist theorists, the contributors see the relationship between the discipline and the social practices in constitutive terms; that is, the discipline helps structure rules and roles in the ipe, as well as its character and conditions. Inextricably, however, political economy actors reshape the structured, disciplined character of ipe and IPE. The contributors evince unease and anxiety about these relationships, changes, and challenges. They protest, among other ills, chronic and worsening domination, persistent poverty, gender discrimination, and other forms of exploitation, as well as "the myopic and ethnocentric" character and "effective silences" (Smith, 1995:23, 24) of prevailing policy approaches and academic treatments of such subjects. At the same time, the contributors worry that for many people social construction and postpositivism conjure images of relativism and nihilism. Thus, most of the contributors share the hope to remake IPE and ipe to advance different or better social practices and relations.

Three goals motivate this volume:

- To illustrate constructivism or social constitution as a valuable (meta)theoretical approach relevant to IPE and ipe as constituted and constituting constructions
- To illustrate IPE as a worldview, a discipline, and a set of global practices and conditions, and
- To participate in and extend scholarly conversations

Although the editors and the contributors hope the entire volume illustrates the foci, dynamics, and virtues of constructivist analyses, its substantive focus is the reciprocal co-constitution of practices and discipline. However, most contributors address the construction of IPE and the implications that follow. Several chapters consider how social dynamics, policy concerns, and/or philosophical judgments help constitute the discipline of IPE, its premises, foci, and analytic frameworks. Other chapters similarly consider the social construction of patterns and practices in the global political economy. Indeed, several chapters illustrate the incongruence between the nature of the social world as alleged in conventional IPE's premises and the alternative characterizations available from the vantage of other social groups, social behaviors, and approaches.

In raising such issues, the volume poses questions about conventional versus alternative framings of IPE and the need for scholarly conversations about such matters. What insights and consequences might follow from alternative approaches to IPE? What social practices, rules, and roles does conventional IPE constitute? What alternatives (theories, frameworks) arise if diverse outlooks, choices, and social behaviors become either professionally acceptable subjects of inquiry or analytic premises? Beyond the vision or concern of conventional IPE theorists, what alternatives are arising in the changing outlooks, choices, and practices of social actors responding to the burdens and boons of globalization, the challenges of industrial decay and informational abundance, or the social consequences of dispersed production and disposable labor?

This volume offers no uniform set of answers. Rather, it seeks to illustrate and construct alternatives and to spark scholarly and public discussion of such alternatives. Constructivism offers one potentially attractive means of exploring the interplay of discipline and social practices. In turning to constructivism, theorists also turn to the significant debates that animate the social sciences generally. Indeed, by (re)turning IPE scholars to the contextual details of specific situations, constructivism (re)turns those scholars to the tangible concerns confronting people. At the same time, constructivism (re)turns IPE theorists to humanity and the humanities by circling into the wider concerns of social science and social inquiry.

Prominent scholarly themes arising in this book include the nature of theory, the character of constructivism and social constitution, the roles of rationality and rules in accounts of social life, the implications for exploitation and domination of the theoretical premises we entertain, and the construction of conventional IPE and possible alternatives. Other substantive themes include the character of political life and commercial society; the nature of cultural and political-economic hegemony; the treatment of women, children, minorities, and the marginalized in the global political economy; and the character of globalization. Again, we make no effort to draw definitive conclusions. Rather, the individual contributors form conclusions (drawn from other scholarly conversations) for the reader to consider. As a matter of editorial policy, we decided not to try to impose any uniformity or orthodoxy. In keeping with constructivist and interpretive premises, we instead encourage readers to form their own impressions. Yet, we also encourage readers to construct meanings and understandings with an eye to participating thoughtfully in active conversations. Such an approach promotes social construction through shared understanding, not through wholly idiosyncratic methods.

Such conversations advance when one scholar asks of another, "What do you think?" To advance our own discussion, we invited several notable scholars to offer commentaries on the volume as a whole. We restricted the commentators only by imposing a page limit. We did not edit or censor their material, except at their request to check spelling and other such matters. Like all provocative and entertaining conversations, their comments respond to diverse points, themes, and concerns. We hope their comments illuminate readers, enliven conversations, build bridges between subfields, and send the debate spiraling into unanticipated directions.

Although the chapters of this book cover diverse themes that defy simple or rigid classifications, they do fall into several distinct groups. In Part 1, speaking to our first goal, Nicholas Onuf presents his most concise and eloquent statement of constructivism. His "Manifesto" introduces novice readers to the frameworks, motivating concerns, and insights of constructivism, yet familiar readers will encounter fresh ideas and a sharp argument.

Parts 2, 3, and 4 address our second goal. They illustrate the social construction of IPE as a worldview, as a discipline, and as a set of global practices. The chapters by Kurt Burch and Stephen J. Rosow in Part 2 demonstrate the construction of IPE upon often incongruent principles of modernity and liberalism(s). The chapters by Naeem Inayatullah and David L. Blaney, Anne Sisson Runyan, and Nicholas Onuf in Part 3 demonstrate both IPE as a constructed disciplinary discourse and the analytical and political limits that those constructions impose. The chapters in Part 4 turn to the construction of social practices in ipe. Mark Rupert investigates the constitution of "far-right" responses to the consequences of globalization. Wayne S. Cox and Claire Turenne Sjolander consider the constructions of "us" and "other" that arise from the universalizing and fragmenting dynamics accompanying globalization.

The chapters in Part 5 critique constructivism and seek to spark discussion of key issues, thus addressing each of our goals. James C. Roberts and Ralph Pettman contest, respectively, alternative approaches to behaving in the global political economy and studying IPE. Roberts suggests modifying constructivism with rational choice elements, whereas Pettman examines the dramatic limits to rationalist discourse in any vein. Part 6 represents our explicit effort, mentioned above, to maintain scholarly exchange and to make (self-) critique an essential element of scholarly and social life. The section contains the alphabetically ordered commentaries on this volume by Joshua S. Goldstein, James K. Oliver, V. Spike Peterson, and Roger Tooze.

I thank the contributors for their thoughtful work and collective insights. I'm especially delighted by our burgeoning friendships. I thank the commentators for agreeing to participate generously in our social and scholarly enterprise. I thank Bob Denemark for his able partnership, keen eye, and diplomacy. I appreciate Emily Smith's help with office chores and administrative matters and Joann Kingsley's assistance with computer and library matters. Each of these "contributors" substantially shaped the volume you hold.

Part 1

Constructivism

Nicholas Onuf 1

A Constructivist Manifesto

To explain is never anything more than describing a way of making: *it is merely to remake in thought.*

—Paul Valéry, "Man and Sea Shell"
(quoted in Karatani, 1995:24)

Constructivism is a theoretical stance whose name points up its central and distinctive claim. Social relations make people social beings; people as social beings make a whole world, and not just a world of meaning, out of their social relations. Because international relations are always, necessarily, social, this claim has many and diverse implications for International Political Economy (IPE) and International Relations (IR) as fields of scholarship. The most obvious implication is that scholars (people, relations) always begin in the middle. Context is unavoidable. So are beginnings. I begin with the process whereby we (as people, scholars) make the world and the world makes us.

The co-constitution of people and society is a continuous process. General, prescriptive statements, hereafter called *rules,* are always implicated in this process. Rules make people active participants, or *agents,* in society, and they form agents' relations into the stable arrangements, or *institutions,* that give society a recognizable pattern, or *structure.* Any change in a society's rules redefines agents, institutions, and their relation to each other; any such change also changes the rules, including those rules agents use to effectuate or inhibit changes in society.

Recent discussions of "the agent-structure problem" (e.g., Wendt, 1987) have acquainted scholars with the claim that, at any given moment, agents and (what we see as) structure are the products of continuous co-constitution. The practical problem for scholars is deciding where to cut into the process. Beginning with agents tends to preclude adequate consideration of structure, and vice versa. Even scholars who are sensitive to this problem fall prey to it (e.g., Wendt, 1994:385, in calling constructivism "a structural theory of the international system"). The solution to the problem is to emphasize rules, but never rules considered in a vacuum. To begin with rules leads simultaneously in two directions—toward agents and their choices, and toward social arrangements that eventuate from agents' choices.

Giving due regard to all three elements in the equation—agents, rules, and social arrangements, each continuously changing in relation to the other—replaces one practical problem with another. Now the practical problem is the sheer complexity of the social reality that any scholar may wish to investigate. It is no great discovery to say that everything is related to everything else, and no great comfort to know that everyone's starting place is arbitrary. This problem of complexity has two plausible solutions.

One solution is a postpositivist move to interpretation as the only suitable method for investigating the workings of society. Constructivism arose in the context of postpositivist criticism of conventional positivism's assumptions and limitations (Onuf, 1989:36–52). Yet constructivists need not repudiate positivism just because it is liable to criticism. A second solution is a systematic account of both the ways in which rules make agents and institutions what they are in relation to each other and the corresponding ways in which these relations constitute the conditions of *rule* to be found in all societies. Only then is it possible to see in context the many, often incompatible explanations that positivists have advanced for what agents do and how social arrangements work.

If such an account is metatheory (as Wendt, 1991, described my earlier work, 1989), then the measure of its worth is what it does to and for the diverse array of theoretical materials already available to us. I believe that constructivism allows us to form these materials—or at least a significant proportion of them—into a novel and compelling structure, all the while granting them a continuing, even enhanced utility on their own terms. At the same time constructivism exposes positivist assumptions and limitations built into these materials, and it can do so critically and constructively. This at least is my hope for International Relations as a relatively new field whose agents, rules, and institutions are not yet as settled as they will surely become.

Rules make agents of individual human beings by enabling them to act upon the world in which they find themselves. These acts have material and social effects; they make the world what it is materially *and* socially. Agents are never lacking in purpose, motives, or intentions, even if they find it difficult to articulate the reasons for their actions (Giddens, 1979:53–59; 1993:78–84). They use resources, made such through rules, to achieve their intentions. Whether agents articulate their reasons for acting by reference to the opportunities that available resources afford or observers do so for them, we recognize agents' interests in the results.

Although agency does not require the degree of self-consciousness that identity implies, agents are normally sufficiently aware of their identities, singular and collective, that considerations of identity motivate some of their actions. As agents, individual human beings can confer agency on others by enabling the latter to act on their behalf for specified purposes. Individual human beings may also join with others for collective action and enable specified individuals to act on behalf of the collectivity. Such collectivities exhibit material properties in their own right and, as I already suggested, become objects of identification.

Agency is always limited; agents are never free to act upon the world in every conceivable way they might wish to. Some limits are substantially material, and any rule on the subject is beside the point. Rules enabling any agent to act entail limits for other agents. Rules in general limit the range of actions available to agents. If no individual agent has full autonomy, then no collectivity is fully independent, either from the agents enabling it to act as it does or from other collectivities acting as agents. When collectivities operate as agents and through agents within very wide limits, we call them independent states and attribute sovereignty to them. Sovereignty is nevertheless a relative condition—a matter of degree (also see Onuf, 1995:47–48).

To repeat: Agents are free within limits. Their freedom depends on the ability to recognize material and social limits and to evaluate the consequences of ignoring or defying those limits. Agency requires a degree of cognitive competence normally available to individual human beings by virtue of their social existences. Agents exercise their freedom by making choices suiting their preferences. They do so in consideration of their (socially mediated) skills and resources.

Rules offer agents choices of the simplest sort. An agent may follow a given rule, or not. Either choice involves consequences that are more or less easy to calculate. Obviously, rules foster rational choice. As an empirical matter, they present agents with opportunities for clear, calculable choice far more often than interaction with other agents does.

Rules enable agents to make rational choices by prescribing a relation between agents and any given rule's content: Those agents covered by the rule should follow it. A rule necessarily indicates which agents it refers to and what they should do. These agents may act on this information without recognizing that it forms a rule, but any such agent (or well-informed observer) can, in principle, state the rule fully. The form in which a rule must be stated is exactly the same form that a speaker uses to get one or more hearers to respond to whatever that speaker says, thereby achieving some social end (though not, perhaps, the particular end that speaker intended).

When the speaker, hearer, and intention are all particular to the occasion inducing the utterance, we call the speaker's statement a speech act, which takes the following form: Speaker asserts to, demands of, or promises to hearer the existence or achievement of some state of affairs. Speech acts fall into the three categories suggested by the verbs *to assert, to demand,* and *to promise.* They are, respectively, assertive, directive, and commissive speech acts (Searle, 1979:12–20). Whatever the category, particular speech acts are not prescriptive—they have no particular relevance to the next occasion inducing a speech act. A speaker may assert some state of affairs and secure the hearer's assent, or demand something from the hearer and have that demand met, or make the hearer a promise and have the promise accepted, without implications for the extended future.

If, however, some speaker frequently repeats a particular speech act because it succeeds in getting what the speaker wants from hearers, everyone involved begins to think generally about the implications of this repetitive sequence. Convention results, and with it some sense that the speech act itself, and not the speaker, accounts for the way hearers are inclined to respond. If conventions are rules, they are weak rules whose prescriptive effect, or normativity, goes no further than the evidence of regularity in conduct. As agents come to recognize the normativity of their regular conduct for what it is and act accordingly, the convention, or weak rule, is strengthened. Rules retain the form of a speech act while generalizing the relation between speaker and hearer. By combining these properties, rules acquire prescriptive force for themselves. All rules are normative, and all norms (as the term is commonly used) can be stated only in the form of rules.

Any rule in the form of an assertive speech act informs agents about some state of affairs and about likely consequences if they disregard this information. The content of such a rule may be highly general, in which instance we call it a principle (for example, the principle of sovereignty), or it may be very specific (for example, instructions for operating an appliance). However general, a rule in this form is an *instruction-rule.* Offering instruction, the rule is not typically couched in normative terms. Nevertheless, agents always know what they should do because the rule's content tells them something useful about their relation to the world.

Any rule in the form of a directive speech act, or imperative statement, is a *directive-rule.* Such a rule is emphatically normative. By telling agents what they must do, it leaves no doubt as to what they should do. A directive-rule typically specifies the consequences of disregarding the rule, thus aiding agents in choosing rationally whether to follow it.

A commissive speech act, in which the speaker makes a promise that some hearer accepts, gives form to a rule when other agents respond with promises of their own. Once generalized and endowed with normativity, this web of promises yields a *commitment-rule* that agents are likely to rec-

ognize in its specific, highly formal effects. These effects are the complementary rights and duties that agents know they possess with respect to
other agents. Rights may entitle agents holding them to specific benefits or
they may empower agents to act toward other agents in specific ways.
Indeed, rights and duties, powers and limits on powers, make agents of
individual human beings by enabling them to act upon the world.
Instruction-rules and directive-rules also confer agency, perhaps more
directly and (at least as agents in rights-oriented, liberal societies see it)
less "organically" or "naturally" than commitment-rules do.

Speech acts differ in form because they perform different functions for
speakers and hearers—they get things done in three, and only three, ways.
The same three forms hold for rules. They work by instructing, directing,
and committing agents, and we see them as performing different functions
for society. Much scholarship—especially legal scholarship—hints at just
such a functional scheme. Yet philosophers (e.g., Hollis, 1994:152–153)
have devised an alternative scheme that is simpler and highly influential.
On functional grounds, they differentiate between constitutive and regulative rules. This scheme would seem to support a generally constructivist
orientation, but it does so at the cost of much confusion.

For a constructivist, all rules are simultaneously constitutive *and* regulative. Indeed, they are regulative by virtue of their normativity and thus by
definition. Regulation yields constitution as an effect, whether or not this
effect is intended. Given the importance of unintended effects in social
processes, intention is a useful but never decisive criterion for differentiat-
ing rules.

Even if a particular rule is strictly intended to regulate conduct (an
intention it may fail to realize), it will still have an additional unintended
and constitutive effect (either to strengthen or, in the event of regulative
failure, to weaken that rule). The converse holds for rules that are strictly
intended to be constitutive. Many rules are both constitutive and regulative
by intention. The rule that players take turns constitutes the game they are
playing (as one of those games in which players take turns) by regulating
the players' conduct in the game.

Rules differ by function: Agents make and use them to instruct, direct,
or commit themselves and each other. Within functional categories, rules
also differ in the degree to which they have been formalized and the degree
to which they are linked to other rules that are intended to support them.
Rules that have achieved a marked degree of formality and support are
legal. The marks of formality vary from society to society, as do the significance that agents (as opposed to observers) attach to them.

Marked formality lends support to a rule by distinguishing it from
normatively weaker rules. Support also comes from other rules, which
themselves vary in formality and support. For example, the principle of

sovereignty, as a highly formal instruction-rule constituting the society of states, finds support from rules of recognition, which are commitment-rules empowering states, as agents, to bring new members into this society. In turn, rules of recognition find support from instruction-rules that specify the material conditions that must be satisfied before statehood is possible.

Formality and support increase the likelihood that agents will choose to follow a rule by increasing the calculable costs of not doing so. In a complex environment of many closely linked rules, agents will find it rational to follow rules generally because of the unintended consequences and incalculable costs of doing otherwise. They will do so even in the peculiar environment of international relations, where there are very few directive-rules of any formality lending support to or needing support from the many other rules populating that environment.

Rules are linked to other rules in content as well as function. Observers, including agents standing back from the rules they have to deal with all the time, can readily identify the patterns of support and complementary content of linked rules. Rules come in families, we might say. Some sets of rules have rules that document the family pedigree; other sets depend on observers to document family resemblances. Accompanying every set of rules is a body of practices that result from agents' choices in the face of these rules. Rules and related practices are virtually inseparable, because every response to a rule affects the rule and its place in an environment of linked rules.

In the fields of IPE and IR, scholars conventionally call these sets of rules and related practices *regimes.* They could just as well call them *institutions,* for the two terms are conceptually indistinguishable. Regimes consist of principles, rules, norms, and procedures (Krasner, 1982:186). All of these components are rules, differentiated only by degrees of generality (principles and procedures) and formality (rules and norms). Regimes vary in the number and density of the rules making them up, and these rules vary in the properties they exhibit. Regimes also vary in the extent to which some rules work to support other rules. Institutions are no different. They, too, consist of rules that vary in number, density, generality, formality, and arrangement.

Some simple institutions seem to consist of a very few rules that are related in content but lacking in support from other rules. In the context of international relations, the balance of power is an example. The rules constituting and regulating the balance are instruction-rules. They offer guidance to great powers on the consequences of choosing allies and going to war. Yet even this institution is more complex than it seems. Allies have rights and duties; limited war depends on rules for its conduct.

Spheres of influence offer another example of a simple institution, in this instance consisting of informal directive-rules—rules effecting a great power's wishes by directing subordinate states to conduct themselves appropriately. If these rules are accompanied by principled justification, the institution is no longer quite so simple. Treaties are yet another example of a simple institution, apparently consisting solely of formal commitment-rules applicable to the treaty's parties. Supporting all treaties from above, however, is the principle *pacta sunt servanda*—treaties are binding.

Institutions like these are simple only because the observer finds it convenient to extract them from an environment thick with rules, all somehow connected. Agents act as observers when they construe some set of rules, however complex, as a set and thus as an institution. Regimes, one might think (as Krasner [1982:186] seems to), are an observer's construct, linking institutions that agents recognize as such. Yet observers are agents, too, and regimes are institutions to the extent that agents think so. Formal rules both for making rules and for making them formal also make up an institution. In the context of international relations, agents have long recognized this institution as the several sources of international law.

Agents use relatively simple institutions for specific purposes; we think of these institutions as performing distinct functions for agents and other institutions. Depending on what they do, simple institutions such as these give pride of place to rules in one functional category or another. When instruction-rules are dominant, agents find themselves in a *network* of rules and related practices. The balance of power is one such network. By assigning an elevated *status* to a few agents (ideally five roughly equal great powers), the rules constitute the balance of power as an institution, regime, or "system" (this is an observer's construct), whose function is to keep in balance.

When directive-rules are dominant, agents find themselves in a chain of command, a firm, or an *organization*. Spheres of influence are rudimentary, highly informal institutions of this sort. Here the rules assign agents to what, in more formal organizations, we would call an *office*. The function of any organization is, narrowly, whatever the top officer intends it to be. A sphere of influence effectuates the wishes of a leading power over lesser powers.

Finally, when commitment-rules are dominant, agents find themselves in partnership, or *association,* with other agents. In the instance of international relations, the principle of sovereignty and supporting rules of recognition make states formally equal as agents. When states conclude treaties, they do so as equals; they are equally capable of reciprocal commitment, with rights and duties resulting for all parties. In effect, states are formally equal only when they all have the same *role.*

Commitment-rules distribute roles to agents. Agency itself is an ensemble of statuses, offices, and roles. States (and associations of states) can conclude treaties because they alone have this role assigned to them. To use another familiar example, markets function by assigning two roles to all agents—sellers and buyers. All sellers are formally equal, as are all buyers. At least in principle, agents in these roles are free to compete with each other, presumably for the good of them all in association. The function of this and any other association is, again presumably, whatever the agents intend to accomplish by committing themselves to a given distribution of roles. Note, however, that roles need not be equal. For that matter, comparable statuses make their holders equal, just as comparable offices do. Nevertheless, commitment-rules are especially well suited to the task of making large numbers of agents formally equal for specified purposes.

Many institutions combine features of networks, organizations, and associations; they are complex in function and structure. Instruction-, directive-, and commitment-rules all figure in these institutions, if not equally, always in a generally discernible pattern. Institutions always exist for agents' purposes; institutions of any complexity will have general instruction-rules, or principles, telling agents what those purposes are. Support for principles may come from a detailed set of instruction-rules that specify all relevant statuses. Directive-rules may also substantiate principles and support those principles by demanding that officers carry out the directive-rules substantiating them. Where neither status nor office is controlling, commitment-rules lend support by defining multiple, complementary roles for all agents. In effect, agents carry out commitments in support of principles by carrying on as they understand themselves to be entitled or empowered to.

Rules in all three categories often mesh in the support of principles. Alternatively, institutional histories may discount rules in one or even two categories. In the context of international relations, formal directive-rules are notoriously rare. Instead, a considerable bulk of formal commitment-rules, joined with and supported by instruction-rules of varying formality and specificity, support a few highly formal and much noticed principles. Together these rules make the relations of states into a complex institution quite unlike states as complex institutions.

The ruled environment within which any institution acts as an agent is always an institution itself. Society is an inclusive institution, the boundaries of which are more or less distinct to agents and observers. States are societies to which the principle of sovereignty contributes unusually clear boundaries and an unusual measure of agency. The inclusive institution that states constitute as a society and within which they function as primary agents hosts a great variety of additional more or less self-contained institutions, some of which add secondary agents to the society. The aggregate of institutions and their relations, not to mention the vast array of activities that take place within and among all of these institutions, makes the society of states the singular, ever-changing institution that it is.

Institutions consist of rules and related practices. In the limiting case, a single rule is an institution; practically speaking, rules never stand alone. One by one, rules offer agents choices, yet most of the time agents choose to follow the rules. That they do so has the effect of distributing values differentially. These values consist of material and social benefits, including control over resources and over other agents and their activities. As relatively stable sets of rules, institutions always work to the advantage of some agents at the expense of others.

Obviously, those agents who benefit more from the rules will be inclined to follow them. Agents who benefit less are still inclined to follow the rules, if only because of the costs that they would incur from not doing so. Weighing costs and benefits, any agent may indeed choose not to follow any rule, with costs (lost benefits) accruing to other agents. Again weighing costs and benefits, those other agents also have a choice. They may accept the loss of benefit (including a cost to the rule's credibility), or they may present the rule breaker with another, even more costly choice by invoking a rule in support of the broken rule.

As an alternative to breaking the rule, agents who benefit less may choose to pay the costs of changing it and thus the distribution of benefits. Anticipating a loss of benefits from such a change, agents who benefit more may also choose to pay the costs of defending the rule. Furthermore, benefitted agents pay lower costs to change or defend a rule because of their institutional position (status, office, or role, depending on the rules). Clearly, rules have the content they do and institutions endure because agents make rational choices in circumstances that always benefit some agents far more than others. Not least among those benefits is relative control over the content of and support for rules.

To summarize this situation, rules yield rule. Rules make agents and society what they are, and they make rule a necessary condition for agents in society. As a condition, rule is something agents do to and for other agents with rules, *and* it is something that happens to agents when they respond to rules. Specific institutions may constitute a formal apparatus of rule that may seem to limit rule to some agents or agents—we call them rulers—but this apparatus hardly exhausts the modalities of rule in any given social setting. Conversely, there may be few if any institutions to formalize rule, yet rule remains a pervasive condition. Replete with rules but lacking a formal apparatus of rule, the society of states as agents is nevertheless ruled.

Rules in different categories yield different forms of rule. Where instruction-rules prevail and status is conspicuous, ideas, not agents as such, seem to do the ruling (as Marx and Engels [1964:67] pungently observed). As Antonio Gramsci (1971) had taught, this is a condition of *hegemony.* Marx and Engels attributed ruling ideas to the ruling class, Gramsci to its intellectual apologists, all of whom state their ideas in principled, incontrovertible form. They rule by exhortation, inculcation, and example.

Any institution whose principles are supported exclusively by more detailed but equally incontrovertible instruction-rules is purely hegemonic. Caste societies approach this condition. Castes constitute a segmented network, each segment of which is itself a hegemony. So effective is this arrangement that identity is tantamount to rule. Professions offer another example less likely to be found in isolation from other forms of rule. In this case, the application of professional standards constitutes a formal apparatus of rule.

In institutions where directive-rules prevail, these rules are vertically ordered, as are the offices they constitute. Directive-rules that are neither superior nor inferior to each other occupy the same rank and have the same fixed relation of being superior or inferior to directive-rules in adjacent ranks. Superior rules exert directive force over inferior rules because officers at each level deploy resources to execute the rules that their offices require them to. From top to bottom, such an arrangement of rules is commonly called a *hierarchy,* as exemplified by the state as a legal order (see Kelsen, 1961:110–162, for an exhaustive analysis) or by a church (which Weber, 1978:54–56, distinguished as "hierocratic" because agents use "psychic" instead of material resources to carry out their obligations).

When directive-rules are formal (legal), so is hierarchy. Despite appearances, formal hierarchies rarely stand alone. Hegemonic reinforcement yields authority, defined as legitimate control. Thus the authority of military officers flows from their status and office conjoined as rank. Conversely, informal directive-rules can serve to reinforce hegemony that has achieved a high level of formality. Thus postwar Pax Americana depended on the United States as self-proclaimed defender of freedom and guarantor of prosperity (highly formalized status) and self-appointed intervenor for the common good (informal office).

Where commitment-rules prevail, as reflected in a generalized insistence on rights and duties, agents occupy a multiplicity of roles always defined by reference to the roles that other agents occupy. No one role or set of roles even comes close to approximating a formal apparatus of rule. On the contrary, formal commitment-rules mostly seem to function as an adjunct to particular, formal apparatuses of hierarchical rule. They do so by granting limited powers to officers to assist them in performing their official duties and by stipulating rights and duties for all agents, independent of office. In support of liberal and republican principles, the constitutional state exemplifies just such an arrangement.

When roles collectively constitute a condition of rule, this is rule by agents in association, and not by agents whose status or office makes them rulers. Ruled by association, so to speak, agents fail generally to see rule in their roles. Their chief concern is the range of freedom, or number and kind of roles, that rights and duties confer on them. A market, for example, appears to be a domain free of rule. Nevertheless, rational agents are ruled by the play of their rights and duties in such roles as buyers and sellers. The conditions of exchange, as observers describe them, constitute a condition of rule. The invisible hand is still a hand; the rules distributing these rights and duties are no less real for being virtually invisible.

The conventional term for rule by no one agent or collection of agents is *anarchy*. When Frank Klink and I (1989) sought to identify the distinctive properties of rule by association, we rejected this term. In the context of international relations, scholars (e.g., Lake, 1996:5–7) too often define anarchy as the absence of hierarchy and thus an absence of rule. Instead, following Kant, we called the form of rule in which no one seems to rule *heteronomy*.

As autonomy's antonym, the term *heteronomy* describes an attribute of agents, not society. If autonomous agents are free to make their own choices, then heteronomous ones are not. From a constructivist perspective, however, agents always have some autonomy, the range of which is necessarily limited by the (limited) autonomy of other agents. Agents gain autonomy for themselves by making other agents heteronomous, thereby making heteronomy a social condition as well as an agent attribute. The co-constitution of agents and societies ensures as much.

International relations constitutes a condition of heteronomous rule because every state, as agent, claims a significant range of autonomy under the principle of sovereignty. One state's autonomy is a limit on every other's, and heteronomy is the result. Heteronomy is a background condition forming international relations into a ruled institution, or society. Superimposed on and linked to this generalized condition are networks, organizations, and associations varying in scale, duration, and formality. Taken together, the many institutions of international society effectuate a complex mosaic of rule that the term *anarchy* effectively denies.

What Marx said of individual agents is no less true of institutions, societies, and states, because they, too, are agents: "Men make their own history, but they do not make it just as they please; they do not make it under circumstances chosen by themselves, but under circumstances directly encountered, given and transmitted from the past" (Marx, 1934:10). To this I would add: "and often with consequences they do not intend."

Part 2

Constructing
IPE as a Worldview

Kurt Burch 2
Constituting IPE and Modernity

International Political Economy is both a field of study (IPE) and a set of global activities and conditions (ipe). I also interpret IPE as an ideology that characterizes the international system in distinctively modern, typically liberal terms. Indeed, I hold that IPE, liberalism, and modernity share the same ontological framework to such a degree that IPE exemplifies the liberal-modern worldview. In this sense, IPE is a cultural artifact of modernity. Although scholars characterize modernity in different dimensions, the premises of conventional IPE are central.

For example, Walker (1993:13) writes that the "sovereignty of states is often taken to be the most important fact of life in a world of more or less autonomous authorities," thus sovereignty is "the key feature of modern political life" (p. 25). Alternatively, Habermas (1973:51–54) defines the modern era in terms of the separation of politics from economy. I demonstrate in Figure 2.1 that these horizontal and vertical premises construct the categorial premises of modernity. They also construct liberalism and conventional IPE as a grid of social systems (Tooze, 1984:2; Murphy and Tooze, 1991a:2; 1991b) separated by a pair of "cross-hairs" that comprise the ontological framework shared by IPE, liberalism, and modernity (e.g., Gill and Law, 1988:3–4). In this chapter, I explore the social construction of these cross-hairs.[1]

	POLITICAL	ECONOMIC
INTERNATIONAL		
NATIONAL		

Figure 2.1   The Conceptual Framework of the Modern World(view)

In Western Europe primarily in the seventeenth century, myriad social actors constructed and reinforced this ontological grid, a defining element of the modern world(view). Subsequent social theory and IPE address the content, character, and relations of the basic categories and cells. Little dispute arises over the framework itself. Indeed, liberal-modern premises "are absorbed by the individual in so natural and gradual a manner that [one] is not conscious of their being assumptions at all" (Arblaster, 1984:6). "How and why [did] economics and politics bec[o]me separated in the first place" (Tooze, 1984:3)? How did sovereignty become "a fundamental source of truth and meaning" (Ashley, 1988:230)?

Some scholars (e.g., Philpott, 1995) attempt to define *sovereignty* as the conceptual overlap of the intersecting contexts of authority, power, legitimacy, law, supremacy, and territory. I construct no figurative Venn diagrams. Instead, I investigate sovereignty and the conceptual split between *politics* and *economics* through the single, comprehensive subject of *property* and *property rights*. Attention to property rights conceptually and practically coheres the overlapping concerns (e.g., North and Thomas, 1973; Levi, 1987) and illuminates the cross-hairs as the constitutive elements of the ontological framework. For example, sovereignty as a property right conveying authority distinguishes the "inside" state from the "outside" system (Walker, 1993). Property rights also distinguish the economic world from the political by proscribing the use and disposal of possessions, hence production and exchange. In short, by exploring property rights, I "live on borderlines" (Ashley, 1989). As the cross-hairs constitute IPE, liberalism, and modernity, individuals constitute the cross-hairs through property rights in the interplay of social events and circulating ideas. The context is seventeenth-century Europe and the transition to the modern era. The focus throughout this chapter is the ideas, practices, and actors of seventeenth-century Western Europe: the time and place from which coalesced many of the ideas, practices, and actors that have come to dominate the planet.

The chapter is divided into three sections. In the first I orient the posed questions around several definitions. In the second section I illustrate how disputes, practices, and conceptual changes involving property rights constitute state sovereignty. I argue in the third section that social practices and the bifurcation of property into real and mobile forms constituted the conceptual split and ideological premise separating politics from economics, and I follow with a conclusion.

IPE, MODERNITY, AND IDEOLOGY

I investigate the social construction of the defining ideological premises of modernity and IPE. By *social construction* I mean the process by which social agents, social structure, and shared meanings are co-constituted, resulting always in a form of social rule involving a form of domination.[2] As communities of individuals make the world—materially and conceptually—they make sense of it; the making and the making sense are the same. Language is the medium: "The limits of one's language mark the limits of one's world" (Ball, Farr, and Hanson, 1989:2). Moreover, "ideology operates through language and that language is a medium of social action" (Thompson, 1984:5). In this sense I regard concepts, the units of language, as basic ontological elements. Conceptual histories of significant concepts—constitutive principles of society—illuminate changing limits and understandings. Thus, to understand the mutual effects of politics and economics requires an understanding of the concepts *politics* and *economics,* which requires attention to their conceptual separation. I explore their separation, hence the constitution of one of the foundational premises of IPE and modernity, by considering the concepts *property* and *property rights.*

Property rights entail a "system of rules governing the access to and control of . . . resources" (Waldron, 1988:31). Such rules constitute the character of social relations and domination. This is the language of social construction: "Human agents author rules and deploy resources in accordance with those rules so as to secure and ensconce advantages over other agents. . . . Resources are nothing until mobilized through rules; rules are nothing until matched to resources to effectuate rule" (Onuf, 1989:60, 64). *Property,* the resource at issue, is an aggregate of rights relevant to every thing or resource that is or may be owned. Indeed, a property right is "the highest right a person can have to anything" (*Black's Law Dictionary*). In the modern world it is difficult to divorce *property* as "owned object" from "rights to property."[3] This dual character of *property* is a central ideological principle for liberalism and modernity.

By *ideology* I refer to philosophical foundations, not to a doctrinaire program of political change. An ideology comprises the fundamental, socially created meanings sufficiently coherent and comprehensive to constitute a way of life and an outlook on life (Geertz, 1973:12–14; Hamilton, 1987:38). A coherent ideology constitutes a culture and its worldview (McLellan, 1986; Carver, 1995) because ideological-cultural patterns "provide a template or blueprint for the organization of social" activities (Geertz, 1973:216). That is, cultures and ideologies make "politics possible by providing the authoritative concepts that render it meaningful" (Geertz, 1973:218). In this neutral sense, an ideology is a coherent system of thought and practice grounded upon the ontological categories and concepts of a worldview and the epistemological premises about how one understands the world. However, this loose conception of ideology does not help us identify which social groups, hence ideologies, are relevant (Thompson, 1984:126). This problem leads to a critical sense of ideology as a worldview that sustains relations of domination, though often unintentionally (Thompson, 1984:5). Such understandings are often mobilized through legitimation, reification, and rebuttals of critiques that inexorably entwine ideology with language and concepts (Thompson, 1984:chap. 3, especially 127–132).

By *modernity* I refer to the congruence of "the modern era" and "the project of modernity." The development of the state, state system, and capitalism in Western Europe in the sixteenth and seventeenth centuries marks the dramatic social transition to the modern era. Related and equally profound are the development of rationality and a philosophical "quest for certainty." These events constitute the project of modernity, scientific inquiry, and the Enlightenment (Habermas, 1987; Harvey, 1989:10–39; Toulmin, 1990:140–145; Onuf, 1991:425–429). They are reproduced in scholarship. The cross-hairs were constituted in the events precipitating the modern era; the quest for certainty reinforces the cross-hairs' seemingly certain or natural character. Thus, liberalism (Arblaster, 1984; Gray, 1986:90; Rapaczynski, 1987:25–28) and positivist rationality (Bernstein, 1976:3–54; 1983:1–16) are the premier cultural and conceptual embodiments of modernity.

By *liberalism* I refer to the "defining framework" of modern life following the medieval collapse (Marcus and Fischer, 1986:32), the "political theory of modernity" (Gray, 1986:90), "an all-pervading ideology in the Western world" (Arblaster, 1984:8), a "general style of thinking" (Rapaczynski, 1987:6), or an "ideology . . . [offering] a comprehensive view of the world" (Arblaster, 1984:9, 13). As actors reproduce liberal constructs through their practices, the character of liberalism changes over time. That is, "liberalism is not reducible to a set of general and abstract propositions. It is a historical movement of ideas and a political and social practice" (Arblaster, 1984:91). Indeed, these practices make liberalism analogous to a shifting constellation of fundamental concepts, including *freedom, individualism, rights, property, and reason,* among others. "What matters is the world-view through which they are linked to each other and the order in which they are arranged" (Arblaster, 1984:56). The significance of conceptual arrangement or configuration is as true for ideologies generally as it is for liberalism particularly. Indeed, the seventeenth-century "attitude toward [exclusive] property rights has been taken to mark the beginning of liberal political thought and . . . the center of liberalism" (Horne, 1990:5). Importantly, liberalism distinguishes civic interests, pursued in the public sphere of political life, from individual interests that are best attained in the private sphere of economic life (e.g., Walzer, 1984). Thus, liberalism's attention to civil society and commercial society begs questions of political economy.

Gilpin (1975:43) delivers the most widely cited definition of international political economy (ipe): "the reciprocal and dynamic interaction in

international relations of the pursuit of wealth and the pursuit of power."
Conventional IPE is a decidedly Anglo-American study of these mutual
relations that was developed in the 1970s following the erosion of the liberal international economic order. Murphy and Tooze (1991b:12) characterize "IPE as a practice of orthodoxy" that imposes a "common sense" understanding of the world.

> This orthodoxy combines a fairly narrow view of what are the most
> important questions in the field . . . with a view of scholarly "rigor" that is
> not only quite narrow, but, arguably, is also outdated; it ignores significant
> developments in the philosophy of social science in favor of a very simple
> model of the accumulation of knowledge, one rarely employed in other
> branches of the social sciences. (Murphy and Tooze, 1991a:5)

The current IPE orthodoxy or ideology, prevalent since Gilpin's 1975
publication, blends substantive and theoretical concerns about market efficiency arising in neoclassical economics with critiques of comparative
advantage arising in studies of foreign economic policy and the politics of
international economics. It mixes these with questions about interdependence and globalization and with mercantilist efforts to subordinate the
economy to state politics (Caporaso, 1987; Gilpin, 1987). In this mix conventional IPE scholars extend the framework of conventional International
Relations (IR) by defining "economics" as the production and distribution
of wealth, understood as an element of national power.

By this framing, IR/IPE scholars simultaneously reproduce the ontological grid of modernity, justify the special character of the international
system, and argue the priority of international politics, just as material conditions and social events challenge the gridwork. Readers hear Morgenthau
(1956:48) whisper across the decades that "politics exists autonomously"
from other social realms, because "historic evidence points to the primacy
of politics over economics." We hear Waltz (1979:79) shout that "international politics can be conceived of as a domain distinct from the economic,
social, and other international domains." Thus, for many scholars, IPE is
reducible to the "integration" of politics and economics as one might connect the pieces of a jigsaw puzzle (e.g., Gill and Law, 1988:3; Chase-Dunn,
1989:4).[4] Since the cross-hairs are not challenged, IPE advances "without
questioning its, often unstated, foundations" (Murphy and Tooze, 1991a:5).

Yet foundations convey meaning and identification yields power. "It is
the infusion of meaning with power that lends language so freely to the
operations of ideology" because "different individuals or groups have a differential capacity *to make a meaning stick*," whether stated or unstated
(Thompson, 1984:132; emphasis in original). Conventional IPE scholars
reinforce these foundational meanings—they make them stick—by exercising the power of professional status. Robert Keohane (1986:182) offers an

excellent example: He asserts and rebukes when he claims that "the insights of Realism are enduring. They cross ideological lines." His claims are less about realism in IR and IPE (his worldview) than about the world he conceives and constructs.

This world(view) rests atop three defining premises: state-centric organization, rational state behavior, and power seeking. Keohane (1986:163) describes these as the "three most fundamental Realist assumptions." Arblaster (1984:chap. 6) traces identical premises—individual actors, rationality, and interests—as essential to liberalism. Macpherson (1962:3) similarly identifies bourgeois society. By declaration and inference, these premises constitute the character, content, and "spaces" of social life. They comprise a modern worldview exemplified by IPE.

PROPERTY AND SOVEREIGNTY

Richard Bernstein (1983:2) notes that "something is happening that is changing the categorial structure and patterns within which we think and act. . . . [Much] is wrong with the intellectual and cultural matrix." Although Bernstein refers to the modern worldview in the late twentieth century, the sense of upheaval and crisis he invokes was widely shared in Europe in the seventeenth century, which suffered the simultaneous collapse of political and natural order (Pocock, 1957; Aston, 1965; Little, 1969; Tilly, 1975). Reconstructions turned in part on the issues of property and sovereignty.

In political philosophy, law, and history, the meanings of *sovereignty* are mightily contested (e.g., Merriam, 1900; de Jouvenal, 1957; Hinsley, 1986; James, 1986). Yet understood as "final and absolute political authority in the political community" (Hinsley, 1986:26), sovereignty was long ignored by students of IPE and IR. Save Morgenthau (1956:chap. 19), they invoked and stipulated the concept but devoted little attention to the subject until recently.[5] Ruggie (1983) triggered interest when he declared that sovereignty, by "analogous relationship" to private property, is the principle that separates (differentiates) states from one another, and thereby defines the modern era (see also Kratochwil, 1995:25–33). Yet to explore the modern constitutive character of sovereignty requires attention to its medieval idioms and their role in the service of political dispute and justification over authority, property, and social transformation (see Onuf, 1991; Kratochwil, 1995). In this sense sovereignty draws from ancient Greece and Rome the "classical idiom of power and prerogative [and] became the modern idiom of statecraft. It also came to be inseparable from liberalism" (Onuf, 1991:429). More broadly, significant shifts in understandings of property rights constitute the simultaneous seventeenth-century emergence of sovereignty, the state, liberalism, and modernity as a constellation of ideas and practices (e.g., Agnew, 1994).

Before these transitions, European feudal life comprised densely layered, overlapping obligations and rights. Hinsley (1986:75, 77) describes a "medieval proliferation of overlapping and conflicting communities and authorities . . . [yielding] a prolonged bedlam of incomplete and conflicting arguments." Ruggie (1983) describes feudal life as "a form of segmented territorial rule [that] represented a heteronomous organization of territorial rights and claims." Rather than an absolute authority or power, a sovereign was one of many feudal statuses or titles in the "great chain of duties" (de Jouvenal, 1957:171) implicated in the Great Chain of Being.

Sovereign, seigneur, suzerain, sire, sir, sieur (monsieur, monseigneur) are feudal terms sharing etymological roots from Latin, meaning "superiority," "supremacy," or "seniority." As adjectives, these superlatives refer to undisputed rank or status or to unrivaled quality. These characteristics— when wed by practice to power (*potestas,* potency), majestic bearing (*majestas*), and rule—give us the modern sense of sovereignty as supreme authority (Onuf, 1991). Applied to territory, notions of supreme jurisdiction follow, but the concept *territory* suggests more. Sovereign territories were landholdings or estates. Yet the concept *estates* comprises not real estate, but the full range and bundle of rights (*status*) possessed by anyone. One's estate is most clearly manifest in rights over land. Thus, *state* is an etymological hybrid, combining roots from *estate* (land, property, rights) and *status* (authority, standing, rights). In modern idiom the "state" represents the territorially grounded object of the property rights of sovereign monarchs. The set of such specific rights was called *dominium* (thus *domain* and *domination*), *proprietas* (property), or simply *sovereignty.* In this sense, Kratochwil (1995:25) concludes that sovereignty represents "the quality of a claim to authority" and is therefore "inherently limited."

As a practical matter, early modern rulers endured severely limited authority. They were poorly equipped and positioned to be obeyed. They lacked substantial physical resources and personal influence along the overlapping edges of fading feudal loyalties. For example, European rulers could rarely avoid convening advisory assemblies. "The crown had never been sovereign by itself, for before the days of parliament there was no real sovereignty at all: sovereignty was only achieved by the energy of the crown in parliament" (quoted by de Jouvenal, 1957:177). Thus, whereas sovereigns were many, sovereignty was rare.

Public finances greatly strained rulers and encouraged centralized authority. Upon becoming monarch, the ruler acquired a specific estate (property rights and assets) from which to satisfy public functions, but the resources rarely sufficed (de Jouvenal, 1957:178–180; Wilson, 1977:131–132; see also Howat, 1974; Kenyon, 1978). With only limited rights and authority, monarchs confronted foreign foes, institutional rivals, and powerful domestic agents. The monarch had to invite subsidies, but those asked to contribute negotiated for favorable conditions or reciprocal rights.

The interlaced practices of royal families, privileged elites, and restless merchants transformed the monarchy into the Crown, then into the crown state, when rulers transferred property rights to the bourgeoisie as part of an institutional alliance. Royal property rights and political need allowed rulers to dispense commercially advantageous property rights in politically beneficial ways through grants and monopolies (Burch, 1994). What followed is the modern inclination to "unbundle" property rights from a relatively narrow but eminently workable conception of *title* versus *possession* to the multiple and overlapping property rights that currently construct social life. The decisive (rhetorical and political) move allied bourgeois elements with those advocating a centralized, more resolute sovereignty. Members of the bourgeoisie, now more free of feudal bonds and therefore better able to participate in the commercial revolution, now sought to protect their property and rights by buttressing public authority as a weapon against remaining feudal ties (de Jouvenal, 1957:181). Real property set the foundation for the claims by states' rulers to be territorial rights-bearers—that is, landholding sovereigns. Mobile property and natural law underscored merchants' claims to be rights-bearers, too—that is, citizens possessing personal sovereignty and liberty. Not surprisingly, the stage was set for an era-shattering clash of powers, prerogatives, and rights.

The result was two forms of sovereignty and two forms of property. Monarchs exercise sovereignty over a state; individuals exercise limited personal sovereignty over themselves and their possessions. Indeed, in the view of many, a ruler may exercise sovereignty over a subject population of citizens on the condition that the monarch respect private, personal property (*potestas in re*) and personal liberty (*potestas in se ipsum*).[6] As Kratochwil (1995:25) notes, "Sovereignty became a distinct institution when the claim to supreme authority was coupled with a specific rule of allocation for exercising this authority." To rule requires rules or implicit norms recognizing property (rights) as landed *and* mobile. Most important, claims to the absolute, exclusive character of personal liberty and property—and the economic system it constitutes—delimits the supreme quality of "royal prerogative," the sovereign rights to authority held uniquely by the monarch. In this sense it becomes clear that absolute or unqualified sovereignty as a matter of political authority never existed. Instead, these were *claims* of rights and authority; they were political ploys or practices.

The quality of a claim to authority depends directly on the quality of the property rights held by the claimant. How might one reasonably claim absolute sovereign authority? How might others entertain the claims?

As a property right, "sovereignty" is the highest, most complete right of ownership (dominion), combining both perfect title and possession. Such rights are variously called *proprietas plena* or *plenitudo potestatis* or "full property." To call the rights "absolute sovereignty" in the seventeenth century connoted not absolute power or authority, but absolute (pure, uncontested) *claims to property.* "Absolute sovereignty" is a redundancy intended to clarify and emphasize a legal claim to land or property. However, to translate these property rights into rights of authority, governance, and rule required unique conceptual and historical circumstances. Such circumstances arose in the seventeenth century. Moreover, these circumstances created incentives for vesting royal authority with greatly enhanced political power and status. Only in this situation do the *political* connotations of absolute sovereignty emerge, though the rights and powers remain far from absolute.

The significant crises of the century generated a widespread need to reconstruct authority: "From 1620 on the state of Europe was one of general crisis" involving prolonged economic upheavals, widening poverty, sociopolitical chaos, violent religious intolerance, and science as a "defensive counter-revolution" (Toulmin, 1990:17). Indeed, scholars now view the century "as having been among the most uncomfortable, and even frantic, years in all European history," most nearly comparable to "Lebanon in the 1980s" (Toulmin, 1990:16, 17). Reconstructions centralized authority. Legal discourse became the means for discussing and enacting social change: "Throughout the century virtually every important controversy was formulated, and every position justified, in legal language" (Nenner, 1977:ix; also Little, 1969/1984:vii). Through legal discourse, social forces justified concentrated authority. Property and property rights provided the specific vocabulary and the substantive focus (see Tuck, 1979). In justifying sovereign *political* authority in terms of relatively exclusive (rather than conditional) *property* rights, imperial notions of sovereign authority and liberalized notions of exclusive rights entered the lexicon. Ultimately, property claims of absolute sovereignty (the quality of a property claim) encouraged and metamorphosed into political claims of nearly absolute sovereign authority and political supremacy (a condition of rule).

However, guarded recognition of supreme authority on the basis of "absolute sovereignty" was a socially advantageous fiction. The claim to sovereign political authority, sufficiently well grounded in property rights, satisfied many domestic groups and interests. Fundamentally, however, claims to absolute sovereignty satisfied the craving to create a stable, workable, tolerable social order. Hegemonic claims—whether advanced by warring families, religious groups, or philosophical factions—proved insufficiently compelling or popular to become truly dominant ideas. Profound social disaster followed. However, burgeoning heteronomous ideas were also insufficiently rooted but were rapidly blooming among commercial classes. Only hierarchy remained. It was feasible, drew from well-established idioms, and could be erected upon existing social rules, especially property rights. Better still, the hierarchical form, though nominally absolute, would never be so in practice. As noted earlier, monarchs had to recognize the personal, exclusive rights of individuals. In so doing, monarchs exchanged reciprocal promises (heteronomy) with the proto-bourgeoisie. Moreover, the essence of the promises legitimized the developing liberal worldview and its practices as a potentially hegemonic set of ideas. Thus, actors constructed the specific hierarchy of absolute sovereignty in part to occlude inchoate hegemonic ideas and relations. This configuration rules today in liberal-modernity.

In England in particular, political authority had collapsed by the mid-1600s, yet God had not revealed alternatives. Each individual had to "rediscover in the depths of his own being the means of reconstituting and obeying" social authority (Pocock, 1985:55; also Pocock, 1975:348; 1977:15; 1980:10–11). A retreat to theology promised renewed sectarian conflict, yet anticlerical sentiments motivated Hobbes and Harrington to craft chillingly secular conceptions of natural politics. This titanic clash of worldviews pitted feudal remnants and apocalyptic theology against revitalized republican (Greek) conceptions, imperial (Roman) traditions, and inchoate liberal-modern ideas (Pocock, 1975; Onuf, 1991). Reconstituting authority necessarily begged questions about the "title" (property rights) by which political personality was constituted. On what basis (*status,* standing) could authority be claimed or recognized? On what basis should individuals obey? What property rights (civil liberties) would citizens possess? Monarchs possessed the proverbial nine-tenths of the law—that is, the absolute sovereignty to their personal, landed possessions. The adage illustrates the centrally important legal principle "that every claimant must succeed by the strength of his own title, and not by the weakness of his antagonist's" (*Black's Law Dictionary*). As monarchs possessed the strongest titles, their success seemed most likely, hence also the success of the larger effort to reconstitute authority, reconstruct society, and protect heteronomously liberal relations. Bourgeois citizens exacted an exchange. "Unless men inherited or acquired property, it was hard to see how they acquired an obligation to obey the laws of society. . . . [F]reedom must have a material base: that a man must own himself if he were not to be owned by another" (Pocock, 1977:27).

The cumulative, conflicting efforts to reconstruct political authority by myriad actors—policymakers, public officials, feudal nobles, merchants, bankers, financiers, entrepreneurs, lawyers, judges, philosophers, theologians, millenarians, citizens, and others—were efforts to reconstitute society as a whole. As a result, the state emerged as an agent of order and reason in both political and cosmic senses because seventeenth-century individuals in Europe generally conceived "authority and magistracy [as] part of a natural and cosmic order" mirrored in national social life (Pocock, 1985:55). Said in seventeenth-century terms: "What God is to Nature, the King is to the State" (Toulmin, 1990:69–71, 126–128, quotation on p. 127). In this sense, "the history of sovereignty is linked with the history of administration" and state-building (de Jouvenal, 1957:179), and so with cosmic renewal.

Only in the context of the state does sovereignty—embodying a fusion of ideas from different idioms—become a constitutive principle. At the dawn of the seventeenth century, a prominent French jurist declared that "sovereignty is entirely inseparable from the state. . . . Sovereignty is the summit of authority, by means of which the state is created and maintained" (quoted in de Jouvenal, 1957:180). To this degree, states and sovereignty are distinctively and solely modern (Onuf, 1991:426). In the transition to modernity wrought by profound material and conceptual change, actors construct states, sovereignty, "possessive individualism" (Macpherson, 1962), reconstituted authority (Pocock, 1975), and liberalism. As a set, these features constitute much of modernity. Thus, sovereignty is central to "reorganizing reality" as modernity (Bartelson, 1995:chap. 6). Knowledgeable, conflicting actors constituted the elements through practices derived from bifurcating property rights. In short, "properties are the foundation of constitutions" and constituting (quoted in Macpherson, 1962:139).

In the social tumult of the seventeenth century, arguments from Grotius and Pufendorf for exclusive property rights and justifications from Bodin and Hobbes for unchallengeable law-making authority set in place the elements for the institutionalization of depersonalized sovereignty and the emergence of modern relations. Hobbes's citizens fear not the Leviathan, but the social chaos unleashed by ruthlessly self-centered, atheistic individuals unfettered by convention, custom, or authority. Political necessity demands that to centralize reconstructed authority into the institutions of the sovereign state requires the expansion and protection of personal sovereignty and individual liberty. Simultaneously and inextricably, to establish and defend personal liberty requires a powerful authority. Bourgeois individualism and commercial society require the order that follows from the law (commands) of an unassailably sovereign authority. Thus, "sovereign authorities" guarantee general and specific (property) rights in return for support, deference, and contributions by landowners and merchants to coffers and war efforts. Hence, both sovereign authority and individual liberty are reciprocally truncated, though tentatively and suspiciously. In this rhetorical move, "sovereignty in itself"—a sovereignty not possessed by a sovereign—enters the stage (de Jouvenal, 1957:198). With it, "the rights of the ruler, no less than those of the community, succumbed to the doctrine of the sovereignty of the state itself" (Hinsley, 1986:126). Thus, the modern era and worldview arrive because sovereignty in itself constitutes the state and the state system.

By the seventeenth century, the subject of politics is no longer the cultivation of the "good life" but is instead the achievement of security and prosperity within an orderly, rational society (Habermas, 1973:43). Modern "politics" becomes (domestic) "domination" in which "society" subsumes "polity" and "economy." As a result, "the *dominium* of the princes becomes sovereign and the *societas* [is] privatized under the administration of territorial states" (p. 49). These changes occur in part because the "point of departure of the Moderns is how human beings could technically master the threatening evils of nature" (p. 51), notably physical attack, starvation, and cosmic uncertainty. "This practical necessity requiring technical solutions marks the beginnings of *modern* social philosophy," traceable to Machiavelli and More but manifest in Hobbes, Locke, William of Orange, and Louis XIV (Habermas, 1973:50–51).

This view of property rights and concomitant social relations suggests that the origins of the modern state as a territorial entity are based not solely upon sovereignty (Ruggie, 1983; Kratochwil, 1995) but upon specific property rights, of which sovereignty is a distinct set. Sovereign property rights simultaneously yield states and the state system as a matter of definition and social practice (Kratochwil, 1995:25). The conditions and social practice of sovereignty in itself construct and rule modernity as they divide discrete national realms of sovereign authority. Yet this is only part of the story; the political system of authority was itself separated from a system of exchange (of rights). Again, property rights help us see the split.

PROPERTY AND THE SPLIT
BETWEEN POLITICS AND ECONOMICS

> *Political economy requires analysis of the way in which ideas about what constitutes* the political *and* the economic *have emerged historically.*
>
> —Stephen Gill and David Law (1988:xviii)

In Western Europe prior to 1600 there was no clear distinction between the state system and capitalism or between political and economic activity; they were a unity. By approximately 1700, however, commercial expansion, transferable entitlements, and the diversity of social practices created distinctly real and mobile forms of property, hence novel applications of property rights (Pocock, 1957; Burch 1994). During the 1600s, states and a

Constituting IPE & Modernity*

Constituting IPE & Modernity 33

Constituting IPE & Modernity 33

state system developed and capitalism's distinct socioeconomic relations emerged from politics. At one extreme are the early Dutch and English joint stock companies, founded in the 1550s, and the establishment of the Dutch central bank in 1605; at the other extreme is the founding of the Bank of England in 1694 and the failed French attempt in 1719 to create a central bank modeled on the English example.

Attempts to define, control, and constitute property rights were key. Monarchs extended property rights to other actors in order to reinforce royal rule and domination. Rulers also realized that the institutional needs of burgeoning states required resources that were effectively attained by promoting mobile property and capitalist exchange. Simultaneously, beneficiaries profited from the social stability provided by effective rule. Bargains were struck.

The bifurcation in property (rights) established the conceptual division between the state system (real, tangible property) and the capitalist system (mobile, intangible property). Upon this conceptual foundation, and with the development and recognition in practice of mobile property, capitalism becomes a system of fluid exchange. "The perception of credit in many ways preceded and controlled the perception of the market" (Pocock, 1985:69). The framework of property rights contributes to the constitution and singular coherence of capitalism and the interstate system (Chase-Dunn, 1981; Burch, 1994); differences between real and mobile property contribute to the differences between the two systems. Crucial to this development is the interplay of ideas and practice.

As a matter of ideas, seventeenth-century disputes over property were inextricable from contemporaneous disputes over rights generally, whether expressed as natural versus positive rights or contingent versus exclusive rights. Sparking the controversies was the growth of market society and capitalist relations, and with them "massive revolutions" (Shapiro, 1986:71) in law, roles of the state, morality, authority, commerce, philosophy, and worldviews. England was the crucible (Tuck, 1979:81; Shapiro, 1986:71 and 23–79 more generally). Partisans in the English civil war used elements of Grotius's earlier advocacy of a strong (property) rights theory to defend absolutism, individual property, and resistance to absolute rule.

One doctrine, the jurisprudential tradition of legal interpretation, encouraged in two ways the emergence of (so-called) distinctly economic activity. First, the juristic view conceives social life as relations between individuals and objects. "Rights" characterize the relations. Indeed, the concept of rights thoroughly imbues the liberal, modern worldview (e.g., Arblaster, 1984; Shapiro, 1986; Rapaczynski, 1987). Matters of rights quickly transformed into conceptions of "use," with decidedly economic connotations. These bleed directly into production, exchange, and accumulation, thus promoting trade, profit, and savings. Second, the juristic tradition's emphasis on property rights ultimately undermined political participation as the key social activity. This emphasis augured the crucial separation of political and economic realms, making "property a juridical term before it was an economic one" (Pocock, 1985:56). Thus, "putting boundaries round the political theory of property poses special difficulties, because property as a social institution is a legal, economic, and political phenomenon" (Reeve, 1986:10). In this sense Walzer (1984:315) writes that "liberalism is a world of walls," echoing Marx's (1844/1964:103) comment that "private property rests altogether on partitioning." The social world was not always divided so. Property rights play a key role in maintaining and bridging these walls.

To shift metaphors, property was a wedge that split the spheres of society yet also a tie that bound them. New conceptions of property rights transformed the "political" world and laid the foundation for an "economic" realm that burst forth from household or manorial production to become society's prime mover. "Economics" related individuals to objects in the service of marketable production in a manner that eclipsed the political relations among people (Pocock, 1985:105). Market society vanquished the classical view of participatory politics and replaced it with alienated politics (Marx, 1844/1964). Actors no longer understood politics as the relations among (equal) individuals in a civic community. Instead, politics entailed the hierarchical relations of authorities to subjects or of owners to owned. This situation was entirely analogous to the property relations between individuals and possessed objects. The new economics was crafting a social world in its own image, though in the liberties of market society the hierarchical shadow of domination never faded.

As a matter of practice, by promoting mobile property rights sovereign authority could, through rules and rule, marshal resources to establish social order and challenge foreign foes. Systemic competition and domestic pressure spurred bureaucratic development in both England and France. The exercise of sovereign property rights catalyzed the drive to both global capitalism and the competitive state system as it also became the means of directing the state toward acquisitive and aggressive ends. Acquiring material and monetary resources posed a particular difficulty, so policymakers fostered institutions that could accomplish these tasks. Again, the practice and ideas involved property.

Rulers use rights over mobile property to service competition with other states; such competition creates opportunities to accumulate capital. Monarchs specifically solicited, promoted, and often created companies to redress the problem of chronic national insolvency in the period 1500–1800. "Given the relative backwardness of the British economy and the serious problems that stood in the way of efficient tax collection, government tax revenue was plainly never going to expand sufficiently to cover more than a part of its expenditure" (Wilson, 1977:131–132). The chronic poverty of national treasuries encouraged state leaders to encourage but co-opt successful companies. Merchants understood the circumstances so looked to profit by, for example, extending high-interest loans to the Crown.

In turn, the Crown extended property rights—as grants, monopolies, charters, use rights, exemptions, and many other benefits—primarily to induce companies to bear most of the investment risk, to act on behalf of foreign policy interests, and to meet national infrastructural and consumption needs. For example, the British Crown granted companies monopoly property rights to build bridges, roads, and waterways, to mine ores, and to produce a range of goods, from paper and soap to weapons and uniforms (Scott, 1912/1968, vol. III). Against European foes, rulers used trading companies to advance colonial claims and consumed the credit extended by newly created central banks to finance military operations (e.g., Polanyi, 1957; McNeill, 1982; Andrews, 1984). In general, in exchange for property rights, the Crown attained goals, promoted social order, and received necessary resources, goods, services, and specie.

Thus, joint stock companies date to as early as 1450; they became prominent by the 1550s and were prime movers by roughly the 1650s. Cruder means of acquiring resources existed, too. In Britain, where citizens' rights were better situated in law and practice, pirating appropriated the resources of rival states (Thomson, 1994). In France, where individual liberties were weakly advanced, various forms of coercion appropriated citizens' resources at the expense of individual rights but to the advantage of sovereign power. Thus, Louis XIV created "devil's brigades" to collect taxes and confiscate resources, primarily for infrastructural development and international competition. Similarly, England developed in the last half of the seventeenth century an institutional infrastructure that appeared more modern than medieval. The English state comprised an institutional-legal order inextricably wed to joint stock companies that received monopoly concessions.

Thus, the development of central banks, joint stock companies, and an institutional-legal infrastructure in England, France, and the Netherlands occurred at similar times and under similar circumstances during the seventeenth century. Whether told as stories of state building, interstate rivalry, capitalist expansion, or colonization, these experiences were understood and conducted in terms of property rights. Indeed, the uncertain seventeenth-century distinction between statecraft and economic activity illustrates the degree to which the separation of politics from economics contains an ideological premise that coalesced in the following century. After 1700 the development of liberal thought and modern practices further encouraged the view of politics and economics as distinct realms.

From this view, seventeenth-century actors constructed—through the discourse and rules of property—the seeming separation of economics from politics and their separate characteristics. The practices, and later the corresponding fields, can be distinguished by the character of the property rights appropriate to each. The emergence of distinctive economic rights heralded the arrival of the modern era and liberal market society.

CONCLUSION

Through the development of relatively exclusive property rights (over specifically unbundled titles, uses, and dispositions) and their bifurcation into real and mobile forms, individuals' choices constituted sovereignty and the split between politics and economics. These concepts form the ontological cross-hairs of the prevailing worldview. The cross-hairs constitute the foundations for modernity, cohere in the ideology of liberalism, and are exemplified by conventional IPE. The conceptual bifurcation of property links the unfolding of the modern era and the development of liberal ideology as inextricably entwined episodes implicated in the simultaneously inextricable emergence of sovereignty and the economy (market) in the seventeenth century. In the wake emerged the practices and the conceptual framework for constituting the state, the state system, and capitalism. As social rules, the property rights appropriate in each system are a medium by which actors conduct the practices of sovereignty, political/economic "bordering," liberalism, modernity, and IPE.[7] Unique forms of social rule and social and material domination result. Thus, the relations, actors, and rules of the modern world and the international order are constituted as a modern set.

Property rights, as social rules, simultaneously constitute social conditions and regulate activities. Actors make choices by deciding to obey, modify, or condemn a rule. Seventeenth-century actors—whether monarchs, elites, clergy, merchants, or other—had to decide whether or how to obey the diverse rules invoked to reconstruct society: royal prerogative, papal infallibility, parliamentary sovereignty, the "ancient constitution" (see Pocock, 1957), and the "Law of Reason" (Locke 1690/1965:348, par. 57). Actors' choices always, if imperceptibly, affect rules and thus reshape society and the condition of rule (Onuf, 1994b).

With the emergence of state sovereignty, domestic rule becomes decidedly hierarchical because a monarch commands. Since rulers assert sovereignty, interstate relations become hegemonic—that is, subject to a prevailing worldview or set of ideas—especially to the extent that sovereignty becomes a dominant idea. Yet the appearance of hegemony hides international hierarchies commanded by great powers, not by hegemonic actors, as the currently mistaken vocabulary puts it. Simultaneously, heteronomous relations prevail among agents exchanging rights in a market, because contracting parties promise. As noted at the outset of this chapter, property rights are rules and practices that constitute systems of rule and domination (e.g., Waldron, 1988:31; Onuf, 1989).

Similarly, sovereignty and the split between politics and economics are also social conditions and practices (Walker, 1993:154). Thus, the edifice of conventional IPE is also a social practice. Defense and reinforcement of the constitutive cross-hairs buttress both a discipline and a worldview. Yet the ideological stamp of conventional IPE goes generally unrecognized amid the striking durability of the foundational ontological grid. Mainstream IPE and IR lack theories of the state, capitalism, and the global system. They also typically lack history, interpretation, socially contingent behavior, and attention to the emergence of historical structures. Gilpin (1987:10, n. 1) boldly declares ahistorical, stipulative foundations: "State and market, whatever their respective origins, have independent existences, have logics of their own, and interact with one another." The presumption that liberalism comprehends and coordinates the structures of states and capitalism reinforces their acceptance as the defining elements of the system.

Alternatively, as Walker (1993:21) notes, "if the early-modern principle of state sovereignty that still guides contemporary political thought is so problematic, . . . it is necessary to attend to the questions to which that principle was merely an historically specific response." I do so in this chapter by investigating the property rights debates impinging on sovereignty and the conceptual bifurcation of property. I seek to constitute sovereignty and the politics-economics split through social construction. However, most IPE and IR theorists offer parthenogenesis rather than generative theories. Rather than explain or understand, most IPE and IR theorists stipulate and describe in ideological terms. Mainstream IPE is less a discipline or subject than an ideological architecture constructed largely of property rights claims. The world is as individuals and groups define and construct it through their worldviews and practices.

As an ideology, the premises of conventional IPE precisely duplicate the ontological foundations of modernity (e.g., Weber, 1958; Habermas, 1987:1–2; Toulmin, 1990:7–13) and liberalism (Seidman, 1983:14–18; Gray, 1986:7–15, 62–72). In one sense, the cross-hairs constituting IPE's ontological framework situate the state, state system, capitalist economic activity, and domestic society. Prominent seventeenth-century actors hailed this framework as rational and virtuous: "The comprehensive system of ideas about nature and humanity that formed the scaffolding of Modernity was thus a social and political as well as a scientific device: it was seen as conferring Divine legitimacy on the political order of the sovereign nation-

state" (Toulmin, 1990:128). Thus emerge our modern sense of domestic
and international politics, a separate system of economic relations, and the
centrality of reason and certainty as the measures of human practice.
Similarly, liberal notions of individual liberties and rights develop, protected (or usurped) by sovereign authority from foreign threats and domestic foes but exchangeable as fluid property rights in the economic realm of
market society.

Although these social systems appear "natural," they were seventeenth-century constructions built atop the fiction of absolute sovereignty,
at least of the unassailably absolutist variety imagined by Bodin, Hobbes,
and Western European political theorists who conclude, with John Austin,
that the law is whatever the sovereign commands or utters. Similarly, from
the landed confines of traditional politics, actors constituted a seemingly
natural economic world of fluid commerce. "The intellectual scaffolding of
Modernity was thus a set of provisional and speculative half-truths"
(Toulmin, 1990:116–117). Individuals now conceive the world in these
terms. One consequence has been the displacement of republican virtue and
"right reason." In toppling one form of domination, other forms have
emerged.

Indeed, deeply implicated in these practices, as with all rule-based phenomena, is exploitation and domination. Imperial rapine, colonial impoverishment, capitalist underdevelopment, domestic coercion, and the daily
miseries of cheating and theft each testify to the omnipresence of modern
exploitation justified and exacted through systems of rules that simultaneously privilege and dispossess as they constitute conditions and regulate
behavior. Property rights exemplify such rules, as conventional IPE exemplifies liberal-modernity. Liberal-modern domination is one version of a
wider condition. So constructed, IPE is also a political practice involving
property rights and domination.

To challenge mainstream IPE is to challenge a world(view).
Worldviews are essentially unassailable, however. Instead, actual practices
offer compelling challenges. For example, human rights advocates press
their claims in the vocabulary of (property) rights (Hannum, 1990).
Governments seek to protect their "sovereign integrity" and extend their
sovereign property rights in the same vocabulary (Weber, 1995).
Oppressive and suspicious governments use property rights objections to
protest international plans to intervene in their countries to offer humani-
tarian aid, engage in peacekeeping operations, or end violence (Lyons and
Mastanduno, 1995). Despite the prominence of appeals to property rights,
defeated or ignored governments often see their property rights reshaped.
Germany was carved up after World War II. More recently, in 1989, U.S.
troops forcibly "kidnapped" or "arrested" Manuel Noriega, the Panamanian
head of state. Similarly, since 1991, Iraq has endured a no-fly zone imposed

on its allegedly sovereign territory. Note, however, that NATO forces will not violate Serbian sovereignty to arrest Slobodan Milosevic for war crimes, nor did U.S. aircraft "trespass" in Libyan airspace to deliver equipment to Operation Desert Storm or relief supplies to Rwanda. In the 1980s the U.S. Airforce did down a Libyan military jet and bomb targets in Libya, but proudly declared that U.S. planes had not entered Libyan territory. Clearly the rules and principles are flexibly arbitrary. Yet even by the premises of power politics evident in conventional IPE, political practice reconstitutes the cross-hairs of modernity. Attention to property rights helps track those practices, and the consequent conditions, of the categories, concepts, and cross-hairs of modernity and IPE.

NOTES

1. This chapter extends previous work (Burch, 1994) and anticipates Burch (1997).

2. I distinguish the structure-oriented constructivism (SOC) of Alexander Wendt (e.g., 1987, 1992, 1994, 1995) from the rule-oriented constructivism (ROC) of Nicholas Onuf (see Onuf's "Manifesto" and citations in this volume). Wendt (1995:71–72, minus parenthetical comments) declares that social constructivism "involves two basic claims: that the fundamental structures of international politics are social rather than strictly material, and that these structures shape actors' identities and interests, rather than just their behavior." Onuf (1989:63) asserts that the regulative and constitutive character of rules "is the necessary starting point for a constructivist social theory" because rules identify individuals as agents and arrange agents' choices and subsequent relations into institutions that structure society.

3. I draw the definitions and etymologies in this chapter from *The Oxford English Dictionary* and *Black's Law Dictionary.*

4. Similar definitions of political economy are legion. Gill and Law (1988:xviii) refer to "an integrated field that encompasses politics, economics, and international relations"; Goldstein (1988:1, 4–5) refers to the "close connection between economics and politics at the international level" because "politics [is] coequal with economics . . . [but] is, however, constrained by economic forces and certainly not autonomous from economics"; Frieden and Lake (1991:1) note that there is an "interplay of economics and politics in the world arena . . . for politics and markets are in a constant state of mutual interaction"; and Lairson and Skidmore (1993:4) observe "the connections between politics and economics." Even Sherman (1987:5, 40), a self-styled "radical political economist," describes his topic as the relationship between "economics" and "social and political institutions."

Several notable titles reflect the twin concerns: Frieden and Lake (1991), *Perspectives on Global Power and Wealth;* Lairson and Skidmore (1993), *IPE: The Struggle for Power and Wealth;* Kindleberger (1970), *Power and Money: The Politics of International Economics and the Economics of International Politics;* Lindblom (1977), *Politics and Markets;* Bowles and Gintis (1987), *Democracy and Capitalism;* Freeman (1989), *Democracy and Markets;* and Strange (1988), *States and Markets.* Strange resists the framing that her title suggests, focusing instead on structural power, but she reintroduces the foundational distinction at a critical stage of the argument. See also Stopford and Strange (1991), *Rival States, Rival Firms;* Schwartz (1994), *State versus Markets;* and Boyer and Drache (1996), *States Against Markets.*

Only Robert Cox (1987), in *Production, Power, and World Order,* introduces the distinction with an economic concept preceding a political one, perhaps a consequence of his Marxian roots. Such ideological distinctions carry stigma or status, as Marxians and those similarly affiliated are typically relegated to the margins of the discipline.

Cox (1989), Gill and Law (1988), and Frieden and Lake (1991) employ realist, Marxist, and liberal categories. Gilpin (1975) identifies mercantilist, radical, and liberal perspectives. Unlike others, Gilpin (e.g., 1981:110) is careful to specify the distinctively "modern" character of international relations, although the market-based reasoning of acquisitive individuals "is not historically or culturally bound" (1981:xii).

Other valuable surveys include Strange (1984), *Paths to International Political Economy;* Staniland (1985), *What Is Political Economy?;* Murphy and Tooze (1991), *The New International Political Economy;* and Rosow et al. (1994), *The Global Economy as Political Space.*

5. For example, Krasner (1988), Onuf (1991), Burch (1994), Bartelson (1995), Fowler and Bunck (1995), Inayatullah and Blaney (1995), and Philpott (1995) address the concept of sovereignty. Jackson (1990), Walker and Mendlovitz (1990), Camilleri and Falk (1992), Spruyt (1994), Lyons and Mastanduno (1995), Weber (1995), and Kuehls (1996) address the character of sovereignty and sovereign practices in specific contexts.

6. As defined in *Black's,* the conditional promise is manifest in the concept of *eminent domain,* "the power to take private property for public use." "Eminent domain is the highest and most exact idea of property remaining in the government," yet it cannot occur without "just compensation" to the owner. That is, the sovereign (state) remains supreme but must recognize and respect private property rights.

7. On sovereignty as a social practice, see Ruggie (1983), Walker (1993:154), and Weber (1995). On the social practice of creating and maintaining the border between politics and economics, see Ashley (1983) and Burch (1994). On liberalism as a social practice, see Arblaster (1984:91). On modernity as a social practice, see Harvey (1989:38, 63, 111–113) and Giddens (1990:1). On IR and IPE as "knowledgeable practice," see Ashley (1989:287).

Stephen J. Rosow **3**

Echoes of Commercial Society: Liberal Political Theory in Mainstream IPE

Theories and academic disciplines are historical creatures. They arise at particular times and places, and one may offer contextual explanations for their emergence and dominant forms. International Political Economy (IPE) is no exception. Its history as a discipline is well recorded. Less well studied is the conceptual genealogy of its dominant forms and theories. In this chapter I address the latter. Specifically, I interpret how IPE's mainstream forms are embedded in the history of liberal political theory.

While few deny IPE's roots in liberal political and social theory, IPE theorists resist situating themselves within liberalism. Scholars in IPE often trace lineages to Adam Smith and David Ricardo and occasionally to Hobbes and Locke as well. Moreover, the academic field of IPE emerged in the early 1970s in the wake of the liberal state's concerns with developments in the world economy: multinational corporations, the return to full convertibility of European currencies, shifting terms of U.S. trade, unequal development, the oil crisis, and the rise of Japanese economic power. Although not all academic responses to these developments were liberal, liberal responses did predominate and set the terms of IPE as a discipline.

Nevertheless, IPE thinks of itself as a discipline that needs no political theory: It either (or both) casts itself as a purely behavioral science, drawing on game theory or a rational choice version of neoclassical economic theory, or draws on images of the international realm as "anarchy" and therefore in principle incapable of a political theory. In short, whereas IPE seems firmly embedded in a particular political theory, it creates the appearance of having no political theory at all.

IPE emerges speaking truth to power—that is, to the liberal state. Critical theories in IPE, such as various Marxian approaches, emerged to rival liberal explanations of the world economy, yet they were marginalized within the academic discipline (e.g., Hymer, 1979; van der Pjil, 1984; and

41

Gill, 1993). I argue that similarly marginalized are politically robust forms
of liberalism, including those forms recently associated with radical democratic political theory.[1]

In this chapter I tell a three-part story of mainstream IPE's liberal political theory. First, I address the construction of economic liberalism as the
dominant understanding of liberalism in IPE. Also, I examine how IPE theorists invoke a utilitarian social contract theory to complement economic
liberalism when it becomes difficult to believe IPE's economic liberal view
of commercial society. Such difficulties arise during depressions, turmoil,
dislocation, or periods of structural change. Last, I look at the tendency of
mainstream IPE's liberal politics to oscillate between IPE's celebrations of
global commercial society, on the one hand, and, on the other, a politically
thin industrial policy derived from utilitarian-managerial views.

I interpret the movement of mainstream IPE within liberal political
theory. Since IPE does not explain its own embeddedness in liberalism, my
interpretation constructs and situates IPE in two ways. In the chapter's first
section, I construct IPE from what its theorists say about liberalism and, in
part, from what its theorists imply but do not say. I also illustrate how economic liberalism explicitly dominates understandings of liberalism in IPE.
In the second section, I unpack the starting point of IPE's definition of liberalism in an economic liberal interpretation of Adam Smith. In the third
and fourth sections, I turn to political implications of IPE's liberalism(s). I
then conclude.

IPE'S LIBERALISM

When IPE scholars address liberalism they tell a particular story. Robert
Gilpin's influential and popular textbook outlines it:

> The liberal perspective on political economy is embodied in the discipline
> of economics as it has developed in Great Britain, the United States, and
> Western Europe. From Adam Smith to its contemporary proponents, liber-
> al thinkers have shared a coherent set of assumptions and beliefs about the
> nature of human beings, society, and economic activities. . . . Liberalism
> may, in fact, be defined as a doctrine and set of principles for organizing
> and managing a market economy in order to achieve maximum efficiency,
> economic growth, and individual welfare. (Gilpin, 1987:27)

Gilpin's narration signals economic liberalism as the dominant liberalism
of IPE and then moves smoothly to a utilitarian account of the liberal state.
Gilpin does not support either claim. He neither defends his implicit claim
that the origin of liberalism is in an economic liberal interpretation of
Adam Smith nor secures an alliance between Adam Smith and a utilitarian

conception of the state as "organizing and managing a market economy." Nevertheless, this version of liberalism is sufficiently embedded in the practice of mainstream IPE that Gilpin can cite it as an uncontested definition of IPE's dominant school.

However, during the past fifteen years, liberal political theorists have challenged such economistic understandings of the liberal tradition. Scholars have long contested the degree of reliance of political versions of liberalism upon economic liberalism, and vice versa. Recent debates among liberal political theorists revolve around the moral and social content of liberalism, often explicitly challenging the complementarity of political (and democratic) forms of liberalism and economic liberalism (cf. Laclau and Mouffe, 1985; Keane, 1988, 1991; Rosenblum, 1989; Avineri and de Shalit, 1992; Mouffe, 1992). In short, contemporary political theory compellingly demonstrates the need to argue the content of liberalism; contemporary IPE assumes that content. In assuming that liberalism possesses an economistic character, IPE constructs the parameters of liberal politics. These constructions marginalize alternative possibilities that demean economic liberalism's privileged place or invite into IPE more robust forms of political liberalism.

In contrast to Gilpin's conflation of economic liberalism and IPE, historians of liberalism typically posit different origins to liberalism. "Essential to any correct understanding of liberalism, accordingly, is a clear insight into its historicity, its origins in a definite cultural and political circumstance and its background in the context of European individualism in the early modern period" (Gray, 1986:ix). First, Gilpin's story assumes too much and excludes an important prehistory. Second, although Gilpin claims to find liberalism's origin in Adam Smith, scholars introduce myriad interpretations of Adam Smith (Winch, 1978; Xenos, 1989; Seligman, 1992; Shapiro, 1994). Thus, the conceptual foundations of liberalism are more complex than Gilpin's definition implies.

I argue that IPE scholars reduce liberalism to a single (economic) meaning that unfolds in the wake of *The Wealth of Nations*. However, to reduce liberalism in this way is to reduce the interpretation of civil society in modern states to an echo of commercial practice, an echo that reverberates in contemporary liberal IPE. This conception reduces the possibilities of liberal civil society to bourgeois civility, to an echo of self-interest, egoism, private property, and the profit motive. By reducing the meaning of liberalism in this way, Gilpin's definition naturalizes the goals of "maximum efficiency, economic growth, and individual welfare."

By launching a history of liberal political economy in this way to frame IPE as a discipline, mainstream IPE theorists valorize renditions of "commercial society" by Smith and others of the Scottish Enlightenment. Yet mainstream IPE theorists do not defend such valorization. Mainstream

IPE does not acknowledge that its definition of liberal political economy involves *an interpretation* of commercial society. Moreover, this interpretation is subject to alternatives and in need of defense. Instead, however, conventional IPE assumes as complete and unproblematic the interpretations of commercial society constructed by Smith and others. Below I detail mainstream IPE's interpretation of commercial society and its consequent construction of a particular kind of politics.

INTERPRETING IPE'S STORY OF LIBERALISM

> *The search for descent is not the erecting of foundations: on the contrary, it disturbs what was previously considered immobile; it fragments what was thought unified; it shows the heterogeneity of what was imagined consistent with itself.*

> —Michel Foucault (1977:147)

> *But since every historical phenomenon, human attitudes as much as social institutions, did actually once "develop," how can modes of thought prove either simple or adequate in explaining these phenomena if, by a kind of artificial abstraction, they isolate the phenomena from their natural, historical flow, deprive them of their character as movement and process, and try to understand them as static formations without regard to the way in which they have come into being and change?*

> —Norbert Elias (1978:xv)

IPE considers the history of liberalism as settled and secure, as unified and static. The IPE story constructs Adam Smith as the originating founder of liberalism. The contexts, circumstances, and intellectual forebears that molded Smith's thought go unexamined (cf. Hirschman, 1977). Thus, a crucial philosophical and political content of his theory remains obscured, carried through liberal IPE only as an echo.

Smith becomes in this interpretation the paragon analyst of the market as a self-regulating mechanism. Through the market an invisible hand creates public wealth out of the individual interests of its participants. The market is an engine of economic growth for the nation, and the state exists to grease and maintain the market machine. Further, this version of "Adam Smith" constructs the old regime as a mercantilist state. By meddling in the laws of the marketplace, the old regime impoverishes rather than enriches the state and restricts the gainful employment and fulfillment of its subjects.

In this interpretation, civil society and the state oppose each other.

Indeed, civil society dominates and restricts the autonomy of the state. Thus, politics is recast as a managerial and utilitarian enterprise. That which is deemed important to human life occurs not in the political realm but in the market—that is, in the pursuit of individual interests. The subject is depoliticized. This construction of social life recasts the state as a functional and instrumental unit dependent on a separate civil society. In this view, the structure of civil society follows naturally from the pursuit by individuals of private gain.

It is controversial to read Smith as casting the distinction between state and civil society as an opposition that in turn recasts politics as the management of the market. Smith's theory supports diverse interpretations of the meaning and implications of a distinction between state and civil society. Also, Smith leaves much unsaid about that distinction in his work. IPE's story interprets and constructs Smith as the first element in a continuous and unproblematic tradition from Adam Smith through the liberal utilitarians (such as Jeremy Bentham and James Mill) to contemporary IPE. The last sentence of Gilpin's definition secures this lineage and its relationship to IPE. This interpretation separates the economy from its embeddedness in social and political practice—a foreign thought to Adam Smith and his contemporaries. By separating the economy from other social practices, IPE looks to a future of industrial mass production in need of fine-tuning and social management by the state. However, Smith assumes capitalism entails primarily a commercial society, not an industrial one. Smith explains the workings of modern industry by situating his analysis within a political theory of the economy as a commercial society.

Underlying the belief in the market as a machine is a normative conception of the economy that looks to commerce as the dominant form of capitalist accumulation. When and how did the conception of an economy as a commercial society arise? The image of the market as a natural and unproblematic condition to which individuals willingly surrender is an invention of the eighteenth century. It follows, writes Smith, that individuals have a "natural propensity to truck, barter, and exchange one thing for another." Although markets may be ubiquitous in human history, a market economy is neither natural nor self-evident (Polanyi, 1957). How did the complexity and multiplicity of commercial practices in early modern Europe make possible a singular discursive formation reducible to the term *the market*? How did the various commercial practices of early modern states and the merchant and manufacturing classes (Tigar and Levy, 1977; Burke, 1988) congeal into a system that Smith and others endowed with world historical significance? In short, how did "the market" transform into "commercial society"? This prehistory of IPE's economic liberalism reveals alternative political possibilities that mainstream IPE obscures.

This prehistory is told in several ways by critical political economists and political theorists: in terms of bourgeois relations to the absolutist state (Anderson, 1974), in terms of the emergence of modern property rights (Burch, 1994), and in terms of the growth of Atlantic Republicanism (Pocock, 1975). Others address the importance of the emergence of a "consumer society," understood as a general marketization of early modern life (McKendrick et al., 1982). Thus, the story of how IPE embeds itself in liberal political theory requires a prehistory. Different accounts suggest that the market has different ancestries and politics, whether as an ideology of class dominance, as a foundation of political liberty, as a modern reworking of the politics of republican virtue, or as the beginnings of a mass society.

The eighteenth-century language of commercial society suggests a broader focus and a broader conception of social order than the economic liberal and utilitarian conceptions considered unproblematic by IPE's definition of liberalism. Commerce in eighteenth-century social theory signaled general dilemmas for human beings and the possibility of an ordered and stable social life. Observers considered the increasing prominence of commerce in European social life a problem to critique or a condition to defend. Enlightenment thinkers sharply contested the relationship of commerce to a "civilized" life of virtue. All set commerce within a broader conception and problematique of social and moral order.

Observers initially interpreted commercial society against the background of the unity of the medieval Christian worldview. To thinkers in the seventeenth and eighteenth centuries, commerce intensified the contingency of the individual subject. In medieval economies one's position and status at birth endured for life, though, certainly, episodes of hardship and economic collapse undermined the assurance of one's fixed status. Yet such radical contingency was not a general condition until the advent of a market society and the construction of the subject as an individual of civil society (Xenos, 1989). In a world reduced to individual motives and perceptions, the assurances of a natural hierarchy in a God-given order paled. Hobbes and other social contract theorists were wary of enlisting commercial practice as a surrogate for a natural hierarchical order. They sought instead a conventional, civil, and political hierarchy to promote whatever security the contingent world of human interactions would allow. They believed that rational individuals would authorize such conventional sovereignty over the political or civil society. Scottish philosophers and political economists such as Hume and Smith constructed their interpretation of commercial society to challenge the strong Hobbesian claim that commercial society was inadequate for general social order.

However, IPE's definition of liberalism ignores this controversy. Mainstream IPE assumes that the idea of the market as a commercial society formed unproblematically and was an established fact by the time

Adam Smith writes. Mainstream IPE theorists assume that Smith describes a system that already exists. This assumption effaces Smith's political theory of commerce and leads IPE either to shun a historical account of the emergence of the concept of market society or to shirk the moral and political consequences of depicting commercial society as a representation of civil society. IPE presents the market as operating outside the assurance of the moral and social order that Smith considered central to it.

Yet Smith and others of the Scottish Enlightenment are not simply describing a system already in existence. Rather, they advocate a certain political economy and moral order because these systems lead to a valuable kind of civilization. Moreover, this civilization is to be spread globally through interstate commerce. The discourse of commercial society that sits at the beginning of IPE's story of economic liberalism is inseparable from an account of the moral and political implications of commercial society. Indeed, this discourse (and its implications) introduced the idea of commercial society as a world economy.

The Scottish Enlightenment conceived capitalist commercial society as a world economy endowed with special normative significance. Commercial society appeared to them as a lawlike mechanism and a moral universe. This was a representation of the economy with great political significance. Commercial society represented progress by reassuring those who experienced primarily the contingencies of the market, but not its elegance as a rational machine. The market was both a causal nexus (a creation of Newtonian science) and a representation of a natural sequence of human time (a "developmental stage"), a conception that had roots in the early modern discourse of universal history (Rosow, 1994). Moreover, commercial society represented a civil society accessible to the entire human race. Unlike the sovereign powers and civil-political society of social contract theory, commercial society was available to all, so for many thinkers it represented a higher stage of human development.

The novel idea of a global economic civilization situated individuals in the undefined and infinite space of a market economy reaching in all directions simultaneously, opening new spaces constantly. In the theory of stages of development, individuals are first located in their immediate material conditions, then within the boundaries of a state that protects them, and finally within a global commercial society represented as a moral unity rather than as a collection of random effects of the practices of economically powerful actors. Such a conception of a global commercial society is carried over into later theory in IPE, such as the formalized trade theory of comparative advantage. Concepts such as comparative advantage then not only signify "empirical" facts about differential resource allocations in the world economy but also convey a conception of a unity of the human world through the world economy. As part of such a unity, the places and everyday lives in which people find themselves are re-endowed with some natural meaning and significance.

The eighteenth-century political economists described the global commercial society as a sociological and moral unity. They naturalized the market as both a rational system and a transcendental order at the center of which was a conception of commerce as a structural, social, and moral unity. Subsequent theory in political economy likewise configures as a unity the multiplicity of commercial practices of the world economy, but such theory hides its commitments to some conception of transcendental order.

The idea of commercial society discursively orders the randomness and contingencies of expanding capitalist markets. Individuals are not lost and adrift as long as they attune themselves to the imperatives and rhythms of the commercial society (or to the "information society" or to some other metaphorical unity of the local and the global). Economic liberalism has invoked several metaphors to replace the assurance lost by the end of "commercial society" as the eighteenth century understood it. Such metaphors unify the character of the world economy and its future. These include "information society" and "new balance of power" rooted in national "competitiveness," which configures "competition" as a dynamic that converges actors into a singular system. These metaphors invoke an irresistible power or logic to which all must submit.

When necessary, advocates of economic liberalism draw on actors' commitments to interpretations of commercial society as a transcendent order, yet those advocates do not argue for such interpretations or commitments. By invoking and interpreting Adam Smith as an economic liberal and as the originator of liberal IPE, mainstream IPE theorists also introduce global civil society as a commercial society. However, mainstream IPE valorizes a concept of global civil society as a commercial society without seeing any need to defend it. By doing so, I now suggest, mainstream IPE thins out the possibilities for politics, liberal or otherwise, within IPE.

THE NEOLIBERAL/NEOCONSERVATIVE
POLITICS OF LIBERAL IPE

The implication of the historical/conceptual interpretation I offer above is that liberal IPE, in addition to its commitments to a market economy, commits itself to some version of a global capitalist civil society. Eighteenth-century thinkers understood this implication and defended a conception of global civil society as a "commercial society." They looked back to the age when commerce dominated capitalism and to a historical process in which the practices of late medieval and early modern commerce were seen by contemporaries as unified in a market economy on a global scale. This conception of a global commercial society was central to their analysis of the market. These thinkers also recognized notions of a global commercial society as an *interpretation* of a modern global civil society. Observers pointedly contested such interpretations by posing alternatives, including the political conceptions of sovereignty in social contract theory and the republicanism of the continental natural law tradition (Onuf, 1997).

I regard the politics of mainstream IPE's liberalism as an echo of the eighteenth-century interpretation of civil society as a commercial society. Conventional IPE theorists fit the new conditions of industrialization and the contemporary global division of labor into the earlier eighteenth-century model, which is lifted out of the particular philosophical and political contexts that defined it.

This uncritical revival in IPE of a neoliberal conception of global civil society as a commercial society has been accompanied recently by a neoconservative politics. Arguments circulate that reducing state interference in the economy—now not only for states at an advanced stage of development but for all states—will unleash a moral and wealth-producing civil society. The historical agents defining and driving this global civil society are the large, globally competitive corporations. Their vehicle is the search for profit through the sale of technologically advanced commodities across the globe.

The processes of global corporate competition define the new commercial culture, often loosely congealed in the term *globalization*. Neoconservatives present these dynamics as embodiments of a particular system of virtue, which they assume to be consistent with a global commercial economy. Rather than draw on the eighteenth century's Enlightenment conception of the virtues of commercial society, however, the current conception draws more on the values of Victorian England. These values accompanied the introduction of machine-driven industrialization and mass production, to which contemporary global production is heir, though distinct. Global commercial society reaffirms the "traditional" values of individual initiative and reward, a privatized family, respect for rightful authority, and respect for all individuals as economic subjects of the market—that is, to the extent individuals are capable of buying and selling in the market and adapting their skills, norms, and personal behavior to new means and relations of production. The new commercial culture reduces rationality to the microrationality of self-interest and reduces civility to the anxious repression of the fixed social (masculine) norms of "hard work," individual merit, and private families.[2]

The neoliberal politics of the new commercial society are both stark and celebratory. They starkly embrace the contingency of the market, seeing virtue in what Strange (1986) calls "casino" capitalism. The natural propensity to truck and barter becomes an ontological and moral imperative: The market economy and the new commercial society result from human nature; individuals have no choice but to conform to its imperatives. Observers attribute the decline of socialism to a failed attempt to reform human nature; this failure confirms the market as the natural way to be (Fukuyama, 1992). Neoconservative conceptions of the new commercial society similarly rule out radical-democratic alternatives because of their allegedly utopian and antimarket conceptions of human nature.

The starkness of this neoconservative vision—that one must submit to the imperatives of the global commercial society or be swept away by history—is warmed by a neoliberal celebration. Neoliberals hail the universal benefits of the new civilization of advanced technology and globally mass-produced goods and services. Celebrations of the new commercial society absorb the disruptions and dislocations that follow the dizzying pace of change in labor and financial markets. In some visions the commerce and the materialism of the new global civil society create unity and peace by overcoming differences of race, class, language, and religion through the spread of global commodities.[3] Other visions celebrate global civil society as a new wave of progressive technological sophistication that will unite the world order in an "Information Society" or an "Electronic Age" if only the market is left to work out its own ineluctable logic. Even if the sovereignty of the state must give way to the world economy, the result will reinstitute the commercial society that was eroded by the Keynesian "liberal" state (the contemporary echo of the absolutist qua mercantilist state). "Liberal" states constrained commercial society in part by ceding authority to sources of power outside the state, such as the UN.

Such reassurance, of course, does not always work. The neoconservative politics of reassurance never produces the Smithian "harmony of interests" it promises. Thus, the sovereign impulse to manage capitalist civil society will be great unless new information and computer-based, flexible mass production eliminate poverty and violence, since neoliberal policies intensify both in practice. Encouragements to manage capitalist civil society arise not only from those disenfranchised by neoliberal policies but also from those multinational corporations and global financial institutions seeking greater stability and predictability in world markets.

Some critical leverage over global civil society is necessary within this liberal politics. Neoliberalism seems to lead to an alternative. Indeed, many liberal scholars in IPE remain skeptical of the beneficence of the new global civil society. They appeal to some version of neorealism coupled to a managerial and utilitarian politics, just as Gilpin (1987:27) does in his definition of liberalism. Others appeal to Keynesian-style managerial liberalism. Still others return to pale versions of social contract theory.

IPE'S CRITICAL LIBERAL POLITICS

Mainstream IPE's story of liberalism allows little critical leverage on global civil society. Neorealism levels criticisms that arise in its politics of commercial society, which introduces a liberal utilitarian theory of state sovereignty. Global civil society becomes a commercial society in need of management by sovereign power, rather than a society that inherently engenders a reassuring civilization and moral order. The virtues of a commercial society are only to be realized through careful, technical management by sovereign agents. In this interpretation, states are the primary agents, but multinational corporations, international organizations, and nongovernmental organizations also authorize international institutions and regimes to manage the anarchy.

Neorealism complements economic liberalism with a conception of global civil society as a Hobbesian state of nature. This conception adds an element of international relations to the story of liberal IPE's roots in liberal economics. Neorealists position their interpretation of international political economy (in both IR and IPE) as a middle ground between the neoliberalism that promotes a "one-world" harmony of interests and a realism that ignores the autonomy of the laws of the world economy. In so doing, neorealists unquestioningly accept the basic structure and features of the world economy as a liberal commercial society.[4]

Neorealist IPE depoliticizes social contract theory to introduce a limited element of *political* liberalism to global civil society. Neorealism's aim is not to respond to the conditions of the absolutist state, which was the context of initial liberal appeals to sovereignty in seventeenth-century social contract theory, so neorealism does not advance the political liberalism of rights, toleration, or the rule of law. Neorealist scholars take for granted these features of global civil society, rather than regard them as historical elements that need to be demonstrated. Neorealist theorists assume that these political features follow from the state's management of the technical aspects of global and national markets. Because these features are taken for granted, neorealism's liberalism in IPE refigures the contractarian appeal to sovereignty in utilitarian form, thereby reinventing social contract theory in a particularly depoliticized way. In this reconfiguration, neorealist IPE retains the predominance of the market and constitutes the state as a supplement to it.

Several versions of a utilitarian managerial liberalism circulate in IPE. In spite of significant differences between the versions, they all seek to adjust national economies to the global civil society rather than surrender to it, as neoliberal/neoconservative theories do. Gilpin advances a strict, statist version of utilitarian management that is similar to Keynes's. Neoinstitutionalists and regime theorists promote functionalist management to address externalities and "market failures" and to adjust global markets to local needs. Such suggestions harken the 1950s' strategies to supplement Bretton Woods with functionalist international organizations. Both of these positions assume that states manage civil society and imply that the benefits of civil society depend upon and can be realized through adherence to strategies of economic management. Neither offers a critical analysis of global civil society as an echo of commercial society. In this respect, each is true to the reductionist history of liberalism that lies embedded in the mainstream definition of liberal IPE.

In neorealist liberalism, contests over the worth of global civil society dissolve into utilitarian contests over technical strategies of state management. On the one hand, this outcome deflects from mainstream debates in IPE those political alternatives that challenge the neorealist interpretation of civil society. On the other, it makes neorealist IPE vulnerable if state management does not succeed, for whatever reasons, in countering the dislocations and dissatisfactions of citizens in the global civil society.

A more recent version of neorealist liberalism in IPE argues for an active industrial policy through a neocorporatist relation of state and civil society. Such a theory revives mercantilist theory and modifies it in light of the new conditions of global accumulation. The neocorporatist strategy is not so much to protect industries directly but to use the state to promote the national interest as interpreted in utilitarian and liberal terms. This means the state must aid key industries to compete for global market shares. Like Keynesian and functionalist liberalisms, neocorporatism also accepts as given the political theory of commercial society, though it questions the makeup of civil society more than the other theories do. Nevertheless, the neocorporatist concept of national competitiveness echoes the political theory of commercial society while deflecting any need to analyze and critique it.

These arguments appeal in utilitarian fashion to statist industrial policy. Hart (1992:5) makes the point:

> I argue that some state-societal arrangements are conducive to the creation and diffusion of new technologies and others are not. Differences in the state-societal arrangements among the five major industrial countries examined here emerge when one studies the distribution of power among government, business, and labor. I argue that the distribution of power among those three social actors is the basic underpinning of state-societal arrangements.

Hart denudes liberalism of any traditionally politically liberal features: no concern with rights, equality, or empowerment. The only hint of political liberalism is the vague implication that the pluralistic play of corporate groups somehow renders the state responsive to its subjects. The invocation of sovereign power is a utilitarian means to maximize "the creation and diffusion of new technologies" (Hart, 1992:5). The form of state-society complex that Hart supports may look very much like a contractarian liberal one, but citizens accept social contracts because they promote social welfare and political rights and protections. However, Hart's utilitarian, statist, industrial liberalism advances political advantage, not social welfare; and its connection to individual political rights and protections is ambiguous at best.

Neorealist industrial policy may also appeal directly to a new social contract, appearing to fold a somewhat more robust political liberalism into a neorealist liberal IPE. Yet again, this occurs under the watchful eye of an unargued conception of global civil society conceived of, first, through economic liberalism and, second, through a utilitarian conception of the state.

The *Cuomo Commission Report* (1988), for example, appeals to the metaphor of a new social contract as a part of industrial policy. Yet this appeal responds to the seeming inevitability of a global civil society driven by a new system of comparative advantage expressed in a discourse of national "competitiveness." The report refers to a new social contract between labor, management, and the state to ensure the competitiveness of the national economy. The state will provide training in the new technologies and will maintain welfare state functions in return for significant changes in the Fordist work rules of industrial capitalism. The contract also stipulates a semidemocratized workplace by assigning workers more responsibility for decisionmaking on the line, but not for overall decisionmaking involving the firm. This limited version of economic democracy advances utilitarian aims by taking for granted the structure and value of the new global civil society. Moreover, it takes for granted the liberal version of state sovereignty in which people authorize the state but do not participate directly in governing. In this view, democratization is limited in scope and does not enhance the political values democratization might bring, hence little is said about the need for broader forms of democratization. Instead, this version of democratization seeks to enlist the workers' support for the struggles of the new global civil society. Such limited calls for economic democracy insulate multinational corporations from direct public control and commit the state to the contradictory imperatives of supporting the structural needs and interests of the corporations and the citizenry.

I cannot address here all of the strategies by which contemporary liberal states confront these contradictory imperatives. One discursive strategy, however, reworks the identity of its citizens to constitute them as "consumers" rather than "workers." In effect, this strategy further depoliticizes liberal citizenship and returns liberal politics to the neoliberalism/neoconservatism of a reassuring commercial society. Citizens in a global economy may have lost any significant control over their work lives, but they can be assured of a comfortable life through increased consumption in the global marketplace. This strategy, in turn, means that the state must ensure low prices, encourage monetarist policies, and limit government services in order to cut taxes.

As people experience deprivations and oppressions rooted in global processes and markets over which states have little direct control—as the theory of industrial policy argues—they are likely to be dissatisfied with the limited effects of industrial policy. This dissatisfaction may encourage disaffection from the state by citizens who come to regard it as weak, irrelevant to their everyday lives, and a social burden rather than a utilitarian manager. Others may turn toward stronger forms of democracy, seeking more deeply political strategies to confront global corporations and their effects than the managerial strategies of industrial policy. Moreover, these democratic strategies are likely to turn toward transnational and nonterritorial political movements and coalitions. Both responses will likely undermine national industrial policies—as well as Keynesian and neofunctionalist versions of neorealist liberalism—thereby leading the state to discipline and limit these politics.

The way IPE defines and embodies liberal political theory provides little critical leverage on this cycle. To persist in economic liberalism in a global context puts faith in some new form of commercial society to work its magic globally. To persist in a utilitarian liberal attempt to manage the global economy puts a faith in sovereignty that is difficult to sustain, since global markets give multinational corporations power to circumvent state regulation. Economic liberalism leads one to consider statist-utilitarian efforts to manage the global economy, which thereby reinforces notions of economic liberalism, and so on in an incessant cycle. Neither conception or interpretation analyzes the underpinnings of global civil society or conceives those underpinnings as reshaped by a new version of capitalist commercial society.

CONCLUSION

In conclusion, it is worth asking whether IPE must oscillate between a utilitarian social contract liberalism (which strips it of most of its political liberalism and limits democratization) and a neoliberal/neoconservative liberalism (which retransforms the market into a pure commercial society).

One consequence of conventional IPE's economic and utilitarian orientations to liberalism is the decentering of political liberalism—that is, the dethroning of concerns for rights, distributive justice, and democratization. Whereas liberalism can be defined and its history told in alternative ways that position these issues more centrally within liberalism, mainstream IPE focuses attention elsewhere. Mainstream IPE theorists rarely explicitly raise such issues. Thus, mainstream IPE moves between a conservative celebration of a global commercial society and a utilitarian managerialism.

Mainstream IPE's discourse of liberalism also limits IPE theorists' critical leverage over global civil society. IPE theory does not question or contest global commercial society as a valuable, complete achievement by the time of Adam Smith. Nor does IPE theory challenge whether or how Smith founded liberal political economy, despite evidence that Smith and his compatriots in late Enlightenment political economy felt compelled to defend conceptions of global commercial society against alternative conceptions of a good life. These premises lead liberal IPE theory away from investigations of its history and philosophical underpinnings. These premises also lead IPE theorists away from investigating forms of politics—liberal and otherwise—that contest the makeup and value of a global commercial society.

These may be good reasons for turning away from liberalism in IPE and moving toward alternatives such as Gramscian theories (Gill and Law, 1988; Gill, 1993); world-systems theory (Wallerstein, 1979); feminist IPE (Tickner, 1992b; Peterson and Sisson-Runyan, 1993); or versions of IPE rooted in radical democratic political theories (Gordon, 1988; Held, 1991; Carnoy et al., 1993). For those committed to liberalism, the challenge my analysis poses is to fold more robust political liberalisms into the basic categories of IPE, perhaps along the lines that Charles Beitz (1979) suggested almost twenty years ago. Whether alternative accounts of liberal political theory can more adequately address global civil society must remain an open question.

NOTES

I wish to thank Kurt Burch, Bob Denemark, and the participants in discussions on the constitution of IPE at the ISA annual meeting in San Diego, April 1996.

1. Mainstream IPE often marginalizes critical theories because they challenge the defining assumption that sets off (conventional) IPE as a separate discipline: the categorical separation of domestic and international political economies. For Marxists, for instance, IPE hardly seems necessary, since its investigations of the global political economy would be folded into a more general critique of political economy.

2. The mainstream story of liberalism ignores how the separation of civil society from the state redefines the role of women as private. This story or interpretation defines civil society in terms of only one set of interests, which modern societies typically restrict to men acting in public. Thus, mainstream IPE either ignores or marginalizes feminist concerns. Among prominent nonfeminist IPE theorists, Wallerstein (1983:23–26) offers an alternative way to fold feminist concerns more directly into IPE.

3. The anxieties and contingencies of the market are reassuringly transformed into a unified celebration of commercial society through advertisements. A commercial for Hanes underwear, for example, assimilates the myriad differences of race, color, class, religion, and history to three simple identities: "small, medium, and large." The theme of children in globalist advertising would seem to effect the transformation of the market to commercial society most poignantly, as in the now famous Coca-Cola Christmas advertisements: "We'd like to teach the world to sing in perfect harmony."

4. This interpretation of the discipline of International Relations and the relation of IPE to it is contested by various critical theories (see George, 1994).

Part 3

Constructing
IPE as a Discipline

Naeem Inayatullah
David L. Blaney

4

Economic Anxiety: Reification, De-Reification, and the Politics of IPE

We focus in this chapter on an especially puzzling aspect of the contemporary IPE literature: that two prominent yet often opposed figures—Robert Gilpin and Richard Ashley—similarly treat the economy as a special source of anxiety and as a special object and source of reification. In constructing the economy without regard for the meaning and purpose it holds for actors, Gilpin and Ashley thereby detach political inquiry from broader questions of social theory and ethics. Drawing on the work of Hegel, Marx, and Polanyi, we point to more productive lines of thought that help transform anxiety into a more nuanced reading of the economy and its role in modern society. This more nuanced reading allows us to rethink the politics of IPE.

We have organized our argument into four parts. First, we stake out a position on the role of reification and de-reification in social life, against which we read the work of various scholars. Second, we discuss the economic anxiety that binds the work of Gilpin and Ashley, despite their important differences. For Gilpin, the economy, reified as a technical and relentlessly expansive logic, generates an anxiety that makes him an apologist for hegemonic domination. In contrast, Ashley constructs a challenge to domination but similarly reifies a technically rational economy. Ashley constructs this reified and reifying economy as the "other," against which he cements the identity of an essentially de-reifying politics. Third, we briefly examine the work of Hegel, Marx, and Polanyi as alternatives to economic anxiety. Although each scholar criticizes modern society and appreciates the dangers of capitalism, each avoids constructing the economy as a special source of anxiety. In contrast to Gilpin and Ashley, Hegel, Marx, and Polanyi depict a richer picture of the meanings and purposes structuring the economy and surrounding political economy. Fourth, we suggest that IPE can regain a theoretical rigor and an emancipatory

59

relevance to issues of freedom, equality, and justice by conceiving itself as participating in a deeper tradition of dialectical social theory and criticism.

REIFICATION AND DE-REIFICATION IN SOCIAL LIFE

The economy is a structuring of meaning and purpose (Blaney and Inayatullah, forthcoming). By this definition we mean to indicate that, on the one hand, the economy is produced and reproduced by knowledgeable practice. Social actors constitute the economy because they know how to conduct the mutual relations of economic life; that is, they know how to "go on," how to proceed in sometimes new and ambiguous circumstances, and how to alter those circumstances (Wittgenstein, 1958:151, 179; Giddens, 1979:5, 67; Lamb, 1979:chaps. 1–2). To put it differently, the economy, like any complex set of social practices, is instantiated or constituted by social actors engaged in "making sense" of the world in which they live (Thomason, 1982).

On the other hand, we might say that the economy as a social practice also imposes its sense on actors. The production and reproduction of the economy across time and space constitutes social actors as it also structures the meanings and purposes that make up the economy. Rules, norms, and tacit understandings structure these meanings and purposes. Indeed, these purposes and meanings become part of the mostly tacit "interpretive scheme" by which actors make sense of and inhabit the economic world. These schemes or frameworks reliably guide action to the point that actors can take them mostly for granted.

We stress this "mostly tacit" feature of social action because it allows us to introduce the crucial role that reification plays in social life in general: "Without institutional channels, and without taken-for-granted reifications, the social world would be devoid of substantive content. There would be no established guidelines and, for that matter, nothing meaningful to react *against*" (Thomason, 1982:107). Thus, this unquestioned structuring of meaning and purpose makes practical consciousness effective by allowing actors to "locate the meaningful ground" of their conduct. Where such unquestioned structuring is absent, actors will find it difficult to see their actions as operating within a meaningful and predictable context. Only with difficulty can they see themselves as agents or originators of relatively meaningful actions or plans (Thomason, 1982:81–85). Thus, actors simultaneously establish their agency and are established as agents via social arrangements. These arrangements *seem* taken for granted.

At the same time, this process of establishing the agency of actors by attributing to social practices an objective "thing-like" quality poses a danger: "Once we attribute to our institutions a kind of taken-for-granted facticity, our social world becomes a structure of dominations. We are constrained and channelled by our own constructions" (Thomason, 1982:107). Yet this does not mean that any set of social practices, including economic life, is fixed. Instead, "certain de-reifying practices must also operate to counteract the stultifying, thing-like status which social reality tends to assume" (Thomason, 1982:108).

Making sense of the structures of the social world thereby involves more than just manipulating a reified background and foreground. Making sense also involves the possibility of making new senses, of reconstituting the social world. The process of making sense is not, then, merely learning to bend to fixed structures of meaning, as powerful and necessary as this compulsion may appear. Rather, "going on" with knowledgeable practice is demanding, creative, constructive, and serendipitous. That is, we declare that a "dialectic of reification and de-reification" operates in social life. Human beings at once *make* the world out of the social materials at hand, just as they must figure out what to *make* of a world already present.

> A positively dialectical conception of man's relationship to social reality must combine these active and passive senses. We "make" social reality not only by actively constituting an otherwise chaotic "raw material" but also, *and at the same time and in the same process,* by passively just discovering the sense which must already have been "out there" before our efforts. Similarly, what may seem to be only a passive discovery of already "given" features of our world is also, *and even for this very reason,* an active and creative construction of that same social world. The sense we *make* of social reality transforms and constitutes *a* world at the same time as it just interprets *the* world. We "make" our world by "making sense" of it, and we make sense of our world by making it. The two are completely intertwined (Thomason, 1982:168; see also Giddens, 1979:5–7; 1984).

Reification and de-reification are crucial and interconnected moments in actors' efforts to participate in, reproduce, and transform any set of social practices.

Despite this understanding of social life, theorists commonly conceive economic life as governed by laws operating behind actors' backs; that is, theorists often argue that economic laws work through actors but without their knowledge. In contemporary IPE, reified economic laws either drive theoretical analysis (e.g., Gilpin) or are treated as a background against which a de-reifying politics is championed (e.g., Ashley). In neither case do actors constitute the economy through their tacit and discursive knowledge of social practice. A dialectical process of reification and de-reification should be the focal point of our understanding of the economy. What is puzzling is the extent to which this insight is lost on contemporary IPE and the special anxiety that lack of insight generates about the economy.

ECONOMIC ANXIETY AND
STRANGE BEDFELLOWS: GILPIN AND ASHLEY

Such anxiety about the economy motivates the work of both Robert Gilpin and Richard Ashley. Gilpin fears the economy. On the one hand, its homogenizing logic threatens the pluralistic nature of international politics as a society of sovereign states. On the other hand, its redistributive and pluralizing processes of uneven economic development threaten the position of the hegemon and thereby international order. Gilpin combats this potential disordering of political life by justifying continuing hegemonic domination in relation to a reified picture of economic life.

Ashley follows a similar practice, despite his explicitly de-reificationist stance. For Ashley the economy is also a special source of anxiety because it is treated as a (or the) source of reification and social closure: The economy freezes the current order, solidifying and perhaps universalizing a particular historical moment. By reifying and freezing the entire social order, the economy destroys political life. Although Ashley explicitly rejects such reifications, this picture of a reified and reifying economy plays a crucial role for Ashley; it is posited as the "other" of an intrinsically and essentially de-reifying politics.

We claim that Gilpin's and Ashley's constructions, though different in numerous respects, converge in a reified picture of the economy. Each theorist denies to the set of social practices comprising the economy the constitutive characteristics of all social life.

Robert Gilpin: Economic Anxiety and Tragic Choices

Gilpin mourns the fact that the rise of IPE as a disciplinary subfield has overemphasized the role of economics in international relations. He seeks a theory that neither ignores the role of politics nor reduces it to economic underpinnings. He claims that his theory of international political economy maintains politics and economics in a reciprocally dynamic relationship. Although Gilpin claims to draw eclectically on the traditions of liberalism, Marxism, and mercantilism, his deepest commitments are to political realism (Gilpin, 1981:311–330; 1987:85). Realist assumptions—of competitive and potentially hostile states within a structure of anarchy—create an initial anxiety for Gilpin. They make it difficult to understand the formation and maintenance of an international economy. Thus, Gilpin's realism establishes for himself and for IPE an anxiety about the very presence of an international economy (Gilpin, 1975:39, 72, 77, 234, 259).

Gilpin addresses this anxiety by suggesting that states are "induced" to cooperate in the formation and maintenance of an international economy by the benefits—wealth!—attendant on participating in an international division of labor (Gilpin, 1975:39–40). Yet since states may opt to maximize individual gains in the short run at the expense of international economic order, Gilpin argues that hegemony alone reliably secures the political support and management required for an international economy. As the hegemon pursues its own interests, over time it generates public goods and stabilizes the rules of international economic life. In other words, Gilpin's story of the formation and maintenance of an international economy relies on a narrative of a self-perpetuating hegemon.

However, Gilpin recognizes that a narrative of static hegemony is inconsistent with the historical record of the rise and fall of great powers. Gilpin requires a force beyond the control of hegemonic political power to explain this disordering of international life. The international economy begins to emerge in Gilpin's analysis at this point, less as a function of political activity and more as an autonomous and determining influence on social life. Accordingly, the international economy assumes the status of a set of iron laws, governed by certain natural and technical imperatives. A new narrative comes to dominate Gilpin's claims: a depiction of the spontaneous emergence of markets and the maintenance of economic activity without central direction, all traceable to the natural disposition of the human species to exchange (Gilpin, 1987:27–28, 77–78, 81–82). But the story Gilpin tells deviates from the one scholars associate with classical and neoclassical economics because he bends the logic of economy—as a self-regulating market and a technical imperative—to the needs of his theory. Rather than producing social and political order, as in the conventional story, economic laws erode that order:

> Although a favorable political environment is required for the release and development of market forces, the international market tends to operate according to a logic of its own. . . . In time, the market produces profound shifts in the location of economic activities and affects the international redistribution of economic and industrial power. The unleashing of market forces transforms the political framework itself, undermines the hegemonic power, and creates a new political environment to which the world must eventually adjust. With the inevitable shift in the international distribution of economic and military power from the core to rising nations in the periphery and elsewhere, the capacity of the hegemon to maintain the system decreases. Capitalism and the market system thus tend to destroy the foundations on which they must ultimately depend. (Gilpin, 1987:77–78)

If earlier international economic life was an anxiety-creating puzzle to be explained by political forces, now economic life appears as a second but altered and deepened source of anxiety: The autonomous logic of economy creates "a diffusion of industry and technology" that profoundly shapes and disorders world politics (Gilpin, 1975:42).

It is difficult to overemphasize Gilpin's sense of anxiety about the economy. Economic development homogenizes global conditions, threatening to produce a stateless and boundary-less world. Although he treats the state and the state system as given, unalterable features of the global political landscape, Gilpin fears that economic development will disrupt these basic units of political organization. However, he also constructs an even more anxiety-producing alternative scenario.

By restoring the state to its dominant and determining position as an immutable feature of international politics, Gilpin suggests that the state system will necessarily subordinate the forces of the international economy. Where hegemony is absent or fragile, political sovereignty will constrain the scope of economic life, as it did following the decline of the Roman Empire. Here, Gilpin pictures the devolution of the global (in the historical case, Roman) economy into a series of autarkic and relatively backward economies. In the absence of the hegemony that the economy disrupts, we are faced with the kind of tragic consequences realism consistently offers us: Unalterable anarchy confronting the relentless logic of the economy inevitably produces the suboptimal outcome of an autarkic dark age (Gilpin, 1975:42–43; 1987:406).

This tragic outcome depends on a certain picture of the economy, one that is formal, technical, and overly abstract. Gilpin treats the market as an especially efficient mechanism for allocating resources toward generating wealth. To the extent that Gilpin explains the rise of the market mechanism, he points to its relative efficiency (Gilpin, 1987:10). Gilpin assumes that efficiency adequately explains markets because he does not ask why the dictates of efficiency would play a historical role in choosing among possible institutions. Nor does he discuss any other features of the market that might influence its appeal.[1] To address such issues would fracture his assumption of a "natural" instrumental logic that generates ever more efficient techniques of exploiting nature and producing wealth (Gilpin, 1981:116). Given this reasoning, the logic of the economy appears not as a historical invention but as a naturalized, trans-historical, universal quality of social life. The market, to the extent it embodies this economic logic, is a mere vehicle of this natural imperative. Notably, this conceptual move drains the economy of all meaning and purpose apart from its instrumental function.

To be fair, we must acknowledge that Gilpin thickens his conception of the market when he contrasts it with the state as an alternative allocative mechanism. He notes the usual distinction between impersonal price signals and budgetary authority, but he highlights as crucial their differing relationships to space. The state cannot exist unless it successfully fences off and claims something like absolute sovereignty over a distinct territory.

The market, by contrast, multiplies wealth partly but crucially by extending its laws across geographical space, regardless of the boundaries demarcated by sovereign states (Gilpin, 1987:8–9, 11).

This spatial distinction suggests that states and markets possess different purposes and meanings, but Gilpin does not explore this theme beyond the idea that IPE is defined by the investigation of how politics and economics—state and market—"interact" (Gilpin, 1987:10–12). Although he refers to a "debate" raging "for centuries over the nature and consequences of the clash of the fundamentally opposed logic of markets and that of states" (Gilpin, 1987:12), he reduces the issues addressed to the problem of economic cooperation among states under conditions of anarchy.

Lost from this view are the particular structuring of purpose and meaning that makes state and market possible and the processes shaping their interconnection and interaction. One mines Gilpin's work in vain for a discussion of the meaning of freedom, its relation to the private interest and the public good, or the distinction between economy and polity. Gilpin also overlooks the importance of wealth to freedom, individuality, equality, and inequality. Indeed, Gilpin's sense of international political economy holds little connection to the historical and theoretical foundations of political economy (see Caporaso and Levine, 1992; Levine, 1977, 1988, 1995). Perhaps we should not be surprised: Gilpin accounts for the development and durability of both the state and the market in terms of efficiency (Gilpin, 1987:10). By treating the state and the market in instrumental terms, Gilpin cannot discern the structuring of meanings and purposes that constitute the social practices of state and market.

With the economy empty of historical meaning and purpose, Gilpin centers his narrative of anxiety and tragic choices upon a naturalized economy. The economy assumes a taken-for-granted quality; Gilpin reifies the economy, but there is no de-reifying moment: The economy serves natural imperatives, possesses an intrinsically universal quality, pushes inexorably across space, and endures across time. Confronted by two unchanging features of world politics—the structure of anarchy and the universalizing logic of the economy—Gilpin's economic anxiety constructs a tragic choice upon the implicit moralism of his realist stance; that is, global relations yield inevitably either to hegemonic domination or to an impoverishing autarky.

Gilpin concedes in this world of tragic ethical choices as constructed by a realist IPE the practical inevitability and ethical necessity of hegemonic domination. With political economy uncluttered by the richer purposes and meanings associated with political and economic life and with the political agenda unencumbered by the deeper issues surrounding the relationship of polity and economy, our tragic ethical choice remains unclouded by troubling problems of human freedom, individuality, and equality. Thus, as Gilpin constructs his dismal political message, he also constructs a reified but barrenly instrumental economy.

Richard Ashley: "Othering" Economic Anxiety

It is odd to think of Richard Ashley as reifying the economy. His stated task in "Three Modes of Economism" (1983) is precisely to de-reify economic logic. However, Ashley does not de-reify the logic so much as he fixes it in order to construct *politics* as intrinsically and essentially de-reifying. For Ashley, the logic of economy lacks social purpose, thematic tension or ambiguity, and creative contestation, which contrasts the logic of economy against the creative and generative possibilities suggested by politics. Thus, the identity of politics is established against the "otherness" of the economy. Politics is constructed and empowered by reifying the economy as a technical rationality drained of social meaning and historical purpose.

Ashley's definition of economy presupposes a distinction between "social system" (society) and "environment" (nature): The environment is a source of objects subject to "manipulation and control" for social reproduction (Ashley, 1983:474). Ashley informs his definition of the logic of economy with familiar neoclassical propositions that render the economy in instrumental terms (Ashley, 1983:474–475). He thereby follows Gilpin in identifying "efficient allocation of resources" as the central and exclusive logic of economy.

Ashley recognizes that this "objective logic of the economy" is relatively empty, drained of all but the most minimal of social meaning and purpose. To say that the logic of economy preserves the economic viability of a social system is to say very little. After all, nature's wide limits allow a broad range of cultural projects (Berger and Luckmann, 1966:46–52; Sahlins, 1976a:viii, 209; 1976b:65–66).

Ashley conceives an economic anxiety that Gilpin did not. He fears that the logic of economy is also "an abstract theoretical contrivance" that with the rise of modern capitalism has led to the "conscious contemplation" of choices in instrumental terms: "Economic behavior" has become "self-consciously understood by women and men in just these transparent terms, i.e., in terms of a logic of economy" (Ashley, 1983:475). When the logic of economy has such a hold on our minds, we are led to accept the social world as "given" or "politically neutral" (Ashley, 1983:473). Thus, technical rationality prevails. As "the premier justificatory framework for human action," it presupposes

> the essential givenness and internal consistency of the decisionmaker and his values or goals, by regarding as given the definition of a problem (the

gap between desirable and actual system conditions) to be solved, and by treating as unproblematic a distinction between values to be served and options to be taken[;] the algorithm exactly reproduces the logic of economy's presupposition of given boundaries between (a) fixed and apolitically defined system structures to be reproduced . . . and (b) a manipulable environment to be objectified and controlled in the interest of reproducing those structures. Like the logic of economy, technical rationality reflects not at all on the truth content of values or ends, and never on the structures or boundaries of the agent, but only on the efficiency of means. In short technical rationality is the unreflective logic of economy *par excellence*. (Ashley, 1983:475–476)

For Ashley the logic of economy and the social practice of capitalism are special sources of reification. Thus, "the period of historical economism we are now experiencing is a very dangerous time" (Ashley, 1983:490).

Although we share Ashley's sense of the dangers of technical rationality, we find it puzzling that he unproblematically attributes the predominance of "technical rational logic" to the rise and development of capitalism. Although Ashley's immediate purpose is not to explain the rise of capitalism, he nonetheless fails to provide a compelling account of the thicker logic of capitalist culture (cf. Hirschman, 1977). Rather, he remains satisfied to depict the economy as a social practice that is reducible to and reified as the logic of technical rationality. We see this economizing of the economy as a "fourth mode of economism" beyond the three Ashley identifies.

We claim that this fourth mode is crucial to Ashley's picture of the logic of politics. Reified in this mode, the economy becomes a special source of anxiety against which Ashley constructs politics. More precisely, Ashley builds on a series of bifurcations between the economy and politics. As Gillian Youngs (1994:15) suggests:

In broad terms Ashley's arguments can be interpreted as a profound warning against uncritical approaches to economistic commitments embedded in theory. For him the political realm offers salvation in very practical senses. He posits the "logic of politics" as prior to and "richer" than "the logic of economy." The former sets the dynamic and ongoing social context for the latter's expression of specific circumstances at particular points in time. Thus, the "logic of politics" allows for the consideration of transcendence whereas the "logic of economy" deals with "given" sets of social relations and values.

A crucial part of this bifurcation of danger/salvation turns on the opposition between an *asocial* economy and a *social* politics. The economy appears as a fixed, technical relation between society and nature, not as a social relationship within a social system. By contrast, "political logic addresses itself to relations within a social system," a "shared sociality" making "possible the coordination of mutual understandings and shared expectations in an open-ended process" (Ashley, 1983:477–478, emphasis removed). Thus, whereas the reifications presupposed in the logic of economy offer merely "power and domination," the political logic always involves some measure of voluntary compliance and the possibility of change (Ashley, 1983:476–477).

In this final contrast, political logic avoids becoming merely "power and domination" because it involves "an intrinsically dialectical logic, at once depending upon, anticipating, and calling into question the dominant social order" (Ashley, 1983:478). Ashley elaborates this dialectic as involving processes of both reification and de-reification. Although "political logics presuppose the possibility of some background social consensus of shared understandings and expectations," such logics also "always involve questioning the truth content of the dominant, habit-linked order" (Ashley, 1983:478–479). Yet for Ashley the same dialectical questioning does not occur in the social practices of a capitalist economy. He thereby disallows the possibility of resistance and change within the economic realm. We are forced to choose between politics or economics.

> Having considered "the logic of politics" and "the logic of economy" side-by-side, there should be no question that the former is the richer and has the greater generative potential. Indeed, it is possible to argue that whereas attempts to translate political logic into economic logic require the near-complete trivialization of the former, political logic is capable of fully grasping economic logic with no distortion whatsoever. The one-sided subject-object relation invoked by the logic of the economy is but a moment abstracted from the open-ended and recursive logic of politics. (Ashley, 1983:479–480)

Ashley offers an unambiguous choice between a logically closed set of reifications and a process of perpetual de-reification.

However, this view of the logic of the economy, instantiated as a "historical economism" (Ashley, 1983:485), at once stunts our theorizing of political economy and, in the name of constructing unlimited political possibilities, distorts the character of our political options. First, Ashley's bifurcations create serious analytical problems. He distortedly and aridly conceives economic life as somehow devoid of the structuring of meaning and purpose that makes knowledgeable practice possible. To put it starkly, the economy is not granted the status of a social practice, since Ashley reduces economic practice to the asociality of technical rationality. He does not conceive this apparently (social?) asociality as a consequence of the rich structuring of social meaning and purpose that makes the economy possible (see Rosenberg, 1994:chap. 5; Inayatullah and Blaney, 1995; Blaney and Inayatullah, forthcoming).

Second, and curiously, economic anxiety leads Ashley to construct politics and economics as a choice between two logics. In contrast, political economy presumes that the logics of economics and politics are constitutively interwoven. By locating the reifications that support the existing social system exclusively on one side of a political/economy dichotomy, Ashley elevates politics mostly above these reifications and purifies it as a tool of salvation. Choosing the political (and de-reification) necessarily dissolves the economic, since reification is its distinguishing characteristic. However, where reifications *occur in an interweaving of politics and economics,* such simple conclusions become suspect and the easy resort to politics as salvation is ruled out. The situation requires a more careful analysis.

CONVERTING ANXIETY INTO AMBIGUITY

The economic anxiety we find in Gilpin and Ashley is not surprising given the dislocation, exploitation, and domination associated with the rise and continuing evolution of capitalism. Nevertheless, such acute anxiety is not necessary, even as part of a serious critique of capitalism. Although Gilpin and Ashley clearly have different purposes—one strives to legitimate structures of dominance, the other to challenge them—their anxiety about the economy is partly explained by a common resort to neoclassical economics as a characterization of economic life. Neoclassical economics describes a natural and universal logic and prescribes technical rationality as the economic project. However, a richer, more critical tradition of political economic thinking exists. Hegel, Marx, and Polanyi help overcome a specific anxiety about the economy. They address the larger questions of social theory: wealth and poverty, freedom and bondage, individual and society, progress and regression. In their work, the economy provokes anxiety and ambiguity about these central questions.

Hegel and Marx: The Antinomies of Capitalism

Hegel conceives the economy as an explicitly ethical institution. The capitalist economy within modern bourgeois society crucially promotes individuality, equality, and, more generally, freedom. Hegel favors the market as an institution because it promotes plural interests and fosters individual actors, thereby resisting the subordination of the individual to the whole. However, Hegel also recognizes that the market produces poverty, fosters alienation, and threatens social disintegration. The state, the needs of the family, and the requirements of civil society each necessarily circumscribe the market in response. Although Hegel seeks to reconcile individual freedom with social imperatives, he retains a nuanced understanding of the role of market economy in modern society (Heiman, 1971; Ver Eecke, 1980, 1987; Riedel, 1984).

For Hegel, civil society, including the economy, promotes individual expression and self-seeking. It also recognizes and protects that individuality (Hegel, 1991:182, 183, 187; Avineri, 1972:141–143; Stillman, 1987:68–70). That is, civil society constitutes individuals as self-determining subjects who, in turn, re-create civil society as a set of social institutions uniquely capable of realizing and protecting individual freedom. At the same time, civil society potentially threatens the integrity of the community and the individual. Unleashed from the political, ethical, and religious strictures of earlier eras, individuals may act as atomized, narrowly self-interested actors, who may rend the very fabric of modern society (Avineri, 1972:chap. 5). Although the division of labor established by the economy generates wealth, it also creates poverty and dependence. The working class suffers a loss of the "feeling of right, integrity and honor" and becomes unable "to feel and enjoy the wider freedoms, and particularly the spiritual advantages, of civil society" (Hegel, 1991:241–244). Further, modern production and exchange relations create an alienation from self, nature, and others that must be overcome in public life.[2] However, modern society is unable to conceive or execute a solution to poverty, Hegel argues (1991:244 addition). For Hegel, like Ashley, these conditions are integral, not incidental, to civil society (Avineri, 1972:90–98, 109, 136–137, 147–148, 153–154; Plant, 1987:118, 123; Westphal, 1987:227–228).

Despite this shared belief, Hegel's picture of the economy remains more nuanced than Ashley's. For both scholars, the logic of the economy cannot stand alone; it is embedded within a wider set of social institutions comprising a historically specific ethical order.[3] Unlike Ashley, Hegel renders self-seeking and instrumental rationality as less dangerous because they are necessarily embedded and circumscribed in a larger social whole (Gallagher, 1987:173). Whereas the logic of economy is purely technical for Ashley (and Gilpin for that matter), Hegel declares that unleashed self-interest, a hallmark of modernity, is laden with ethical value: subjectivity, self-expression, and social recognition. Yet, rather than being a special and inherent source of reification, life in civil society is a potentially educative experience: Individuals may come to learn that the pursuit of self is possible only in relations of mutual dependence entailing the recognition of the rights and needs of others (Pelczynski, 1971:17; Stillman, 1987:77; Ver Eecke, 1987:150).

In these terms Hegel's discussion of the economy departs substantially from Gilpin's and Ashley's. Hegel stresses that the logic of economy is delimited historically. It arises with modern society in relation to other components of society to shape and reflect that historical context. The economy promotes both progress and privation. Thus, for Hegel, the

economy and modern society represent neither an unambiguous historical achievement nor a special source of anxiety. In this state of tension,
political economy may find a space for moving beyond economic
anxiety.

Students usually read Marx as the preeminent theorist of economic
anxiety, yet our reading suggests that Marx's evaluation of capitalism is
more ambiguous than conventional views suggest (Inayatullah and Blaney,
1995; cf. Sayer, 1991). Although a ruthless critic of capitalism, Marx also
insightfully analyzes the relative achievements of capitalism and thus
avoids simplistic versions of economic anxiety.

For Marx (1973:540–542), the unprecedented release of human productive capacities by capitalism was historically momentous. Capitalism
creates a stock of wealth and develops the means of wealth production necessary to fuel social progress and the possibility of communism (Marx,
1973:325). At the same time, these productive advances promise individual
freedom and equality. "Equality and freedom are thus not only respected in
exchange based on exchange values, but, also, the exchange of exchange
values is the productive, real basis of all equality and freedom" (Marx,
1973:245). Freedom and inequality become the basis of economic and
social life (Marx, 1973:158, 245, 472–474; Gould, 1978). Although capitalism constructs an aspiration for and the material possibility of a "free individuality" (Marx, 1973:158), it delivers the opposite. The apparent individual freedom and equality disappear as one uncovers the real relations of
capitalist society: The personal independence made possible in bourgeois
society is founded on an "objective dependence" of the worker on the capitalist (Marx, 1973:507–508). Thus, the "exclusive realm of Freedom,
Equality, Property, and Bentham" offers different experiences for workers
and capitalists: "The one [the capitalist] smirks self-importantly and is
intent on business; the other [the laborer] is timid and holds back, like
someone who has brought his own hide to the market and now has nothing
else to expect but a tanning" (Marx, 1977:280).

Marx sees, with Hegel, that capitalism expands human possibilities and
"the development of a rich individuality" (Marx, 1973:325), but only at a
tragic cost in poverty, alienation, and domination. Marx vividly accounts:
"In bourgeois economics—and the epoch to which it corresponds—this
complete working out of the human content appears as a complete empty-
ing out, this universal objectification as total alienation, and the tearing
down of all limited one-sided aims as sacrifice of the human end-in-itself to
an entirely external end" (Marx, 1973:488).

Marx's work poses an interpretive problem because of the delicate balance it strikes. Although he is no apologist for capitalist society, Marx recognizes that bourgeois society offers advances over previous modes of life
because it promotes the aspirations and material possibilities of equality
and freedom. Yet it also produces history's cruelest and most complete

exploitation and alienation. Thus in Marx's view, bourgeois society both supports and inverts the narrative of progress (Marx, 1973:84; 1977:169–171; Inayatullah and Blaney, 1995). This nuanced picture allows Marx to negotiate a middle ground between a romantic rejection of bourgeois society and the shameless apologetics he attributed to the economists of his day. We assert that this middle ground suggests an escape from the grasp of economic anxiety.

Marx's work offers a stance toward the economy that is clearly distinguishable from the economic anxiety of either Gilpin or Ashley. Gilpin's abstract characterization of the economy constructs a perpetual economic anxiety that he uses as an equally shameless apology for domination. Both Marx and Ashley condemn (bourgeois) economists for constructing a project of alienation that empties social life of human meaning and purpose. Yet for Marx, the capitalist economy still serves an important historical purpose by connecting wealth with human individuality and freedom. This connection should not be obscured by impoverishing the economy as a simple embodiment of technical rationality. Whereas Ashley's economic anxiety leads him to reify the economy as technical rationality, Marx's critical stance toward capitalism involves a richer appreciation of the structuring of meaning and purpose that it embodies yet also thwarts.

Karl Polanyi: Political Economy as "Double Movement"

Polanyi, Hegel, and Marx each argue that society erodes as individuals reduce economic activity to self-seeking exchange. Polanyi specifically addresses the creation of the "self-regulating market," that is, "the institutional separation of society into an economic and political sphere" (Polanyi, 1957:71). Polanyi means to distinguish this specifically modern conception of the market from the economy as a general human concern. The economy is an abstraction referring to the requirement that every society must interact with nature in order to provide for its needs. Thus, the economy exists only as "embedded" in a particular set of social institutions, whether that set is the familiar relations of the household, the reciprocities of clan and village, or the rights and duties of nation and state (Polanyi, 1957:chaps. 4–5). In contrast with neoclassical economics, Polanyi argues that the logic of economy cannot exist as social practice. Nonetheless, the modern effort to create a self-regulating market involves disembedding the economy, constituting a purely economic *logic* as defining social life, and consequently inverting the relation of economy and society: "The control of the economic system by the market is of overwhelming consequence to the whole organization of society; it means no less than the running of society as an adjunct to the market. Instead of economy being embedded in social relations, social relations are embedded in the economic system" (Polanyi, 1957:57; see also pp. 30 and 71).

Arguing along lines suggested by Hegel, Marx, and Ashley, Polanyi readily concedes the dangers of the market and its economic logic: "The self-adjusting market implied a stark utopia. Such an institution could not exist for any length of time without annihilating the human and natural substance of society; it would have physically destroyed man and transformed his surroundings into wilderness. Inevitably, society took measures to protect itself" (Polanyi, 1957:3-4). Efforts to institutionalize a disembedded economy sparked a "spontaneous reaction" that re-embeds and circumscribes the logic of economy. This "double movement" was crucial to the institutionalization of the market in modern society (Polanyi, 1957:76, 83, 132, 149–150).

Polanyi's account of the "double movement" turns on his idea of "fictitious commodities." The market subjects labor, land, and money to the market as if they were "produced for sale on the market" like other commodities. But labor, land, and money are not produced in this sense:

> Labor is only another name for human activity which goes with life itself, which in its turn is not produced for sale but for entirely different reasons, nor can that activity be detached from the rest of life, be stored or mobilized; land is only another name for nature, which is not produced by man; actual money, finally, is merely a token of purchasing power which, as a rule, is not produced at all, but comes into being through the mechanism of banking or state finance (Polanyi, 1957:72).

Whether fictitious or not, the commodification of these three elements is nonetheless necessary for the self-regulating market, though the consequences are dire. Polanyi (1957:73) conveys his passion in comments about the commodification of labor:

> The alleged commodity "labor power" cannot be shoved about, used indiscriminately, or even left unused, without affecting also the human individual who happens to be the bearer of this particular commodity. In disposing of man's labor power the system would incidentally dispose of the physical, psychological, and moral entity "man" attached to that tag. Robbed of the protective covering of cultural institutions, human beings would perish from the effects of social exposure; they would die as the victims of acute social dislocation through vice, perversion, and starvation.

Similarly, if land were commodified, "nature would be reduced to its elements, neighborhoods and landscapes defiled, rivers polluted, military safety jeopardized, the power to produce food and raw materials destroyed" (Polanyi, 1957:74). The fluctuation and erosion of purchasing power for individuals and business make the commodification of money a similar disaster.

Although Polanyi paints a foreboding picture of this "stark utopia," he is not simply an enemy of the market in modern society. In fact, he notes that suppressing the role of the market creates economic irrationalities and impoverishes masses of people (Polanyi, 1957:chap. 8). Rather, Polanyi believes that the market promotes the "baffling paradoxes" characteristic of bourgeois society, where "poverty seemed to go with plenty," and "hope" and "progress" coexist with "despair" and "dislocation" (Polanyi, 1957:84–85). Indeed, the "freedom to exploit one's own fellows" is connected to "freedoms that we prize highly" (quoted in Stanfield, 1986:141; see also Polanyi, 1957:252, 255–256).

Rather than simply opposing economy to politics, Polanyi opposes the idea of a self-regulating, disembedded economy to a vision of a modern society with an embedded economy. Thus, Polanyi's "socialist" politics seeks to "transcend the self-regulating market by consciously subordinating it to a democratic society" (Polanyi, 1957:234). Polanyi envisions mass participation and decisionmaking devoted to learning the limits and purposes of the market and politics (Stanfield, 1986:149).

We can draw the contrast with Gilpin and Ashley more clearly. For Polanyi, the economy can never be the embodiment of a purely abstract rationality, nor can it successfully subordinate social life to the dictates of technical rationality, as Gilpin and Ashley take for granted. Rather, the economy must always be seen in its actual social embeddedness. Although a devastating critique of the market motivates a certain form of politics for Polanyi, it is also a point of contrast with Gilpin and Ashley. For Polanyi, the economy motivates an effort to "balance" freedoms in a democratic process; it is not an apology for domination, as in Gilpin. In contrast to Ashley, this democratic politics continues to operate within a complex political economy. There is no effort to construct an intrinsically creative and generative political life in relation to an intrinsically reifying economy. For Polanyi (e.g., 1957:254), the economy, like all social institutions, is an embodiment "of human meaning and purpose." Thus, the democratic political economy emerging in the "double movement" necessarily involves an ongoing process of making sense of the meanings and purposes of economy and polity: the meaning of labor, land, and money; the purposes served by economy and polity; and the boundaries between them. As Polanyi (1957:254) writes: "We cannot achieve the freedom we seek, unless we comprehend the true significance of freedom in a complex society."

ECONOMIC ANXIETY AND THE POLITICS OF IPE

Both Gilpin and Ashley make sense of the economy in ways that inhibit the kind of meaningful democratic political economy that Polanyi recommends. Gilpin's anxiety about the inexorable laws of the global economy produces a conservative politics, built on the claim that a wealth-producing global division of labor requires hegemonic domination. Gilpin thereby forecloses a deeper, critical agenda for IPE. Ashley imagines an infinitely generative politics, but only at the cost of impoverishing economic life as the reified and reifying "other" against which he constructs this romantic vision. However, this romantic vision fails to consider the processes of knowledgeable actors as they practice and re-create the economy. As do all romantics, Ashley severs a critical politics from an inquiry into the deeper meanings and purposes of economic life and the concrete possibilities of social reform and transformation. Thus, Ashley's claims, despite their critical edge, inspire a political quietism that, like Gilpin's, favors the status quo.

Since Gilpin and Ashley treat the economy as an abstract, ahistorical, and technical instrument, they divert us from exploring the rich structures of meaning and purpose that make possible the economy as a set of social practices. As we have argued earlier in the chapter, these meanings and purposes are constructed by knowledgeable actors, but these structures in turn constitute knowledgeable actors. Thus, we argue that IPE must *begin* by exploring the understandings of actors—an exploration of who they are and how they live. By beginning with this hermeneutic task, theorists can avoid the temptation to resort to a language of economic laws that inexorably shape the lives of human beings without their knowledge. In this way, economic practice becomes knowledgeable; actors know and negotiate the rules, forces, and tensions of modern economic life. Knowledgeable practice at once reproduces the "laws" of contemporary capitalism and is also the basis for reflection on and the transformation of those laws. For "theorists" and "laypersons"—and all of us beings are always in some measure both—IPE is thereby necessarily an exploration of who we might be and how we might live differently. Theoretical inquiry needs to own up to its status as political and social intervention.

We argue equally that the politics of IPE must move beyond either an unthinking valorization of economic laws or a denigration of economics *tout court*. Inspired by Hegel, Marx, and Polanyi, we embrace a critical but self-limiting politics (see Marsh, 1974; Cohen, 1985) that recognizes the importance of reification and de-reification, a politics we link with dialectical social theory. Politics thereby emerges from the particular traditions and practices of a community yet also challenges those traditions. Put differently, we share the view of Ashley, Walzer (1988:chap. 1), and others that international political economists must be social critics. IPE theorists confront social meanings, relationships, and practices by conducting intrinsically ethical inquiries that (may) affirm or challenge our most basic commitments and taken-for-granted social practices. As social critics, they (should) highlight the social practices that thwart our highest aspirations, generate ethical dilemmas, and precipitate often tragic consequences. The sense of unease we feel with our world requires that we find new ways of going on.

However, Ashley leads us astray by constructing an infinitely generative and abstract politics counterpoised against a reified and reifying economy. When one instead locates politics within a meaningful and purposeful political economy, not only does one discover the need to de-reify and circumscribe the logic of economy, but also one encounters the limits of politics in the meanings and purposes of the economy in modern society. For example, to consider the purposes of wealth (does it serve human freedom?) and the continuing need for wealth generation (in the struggle against poverty?), we need to face questions of the social role of self-interest and private capital accumulation as the generators of not only wealth and autonomy but other, less desirable social consequences, such as poverty and alienation. Likewise, if we hope to restrain or transform the role of the market, we should pay due heed to the consequences for the self-determination of individuals in private life and in relation to their various associations and identifications. IPE theorists must acknowledge and challenge the limits set by the preconditions of IPE and the global political economy in the structures of social meanings and purposes.

Ashley's generative politics ignores the limits and thus obscures the meanings and purposes of the economy. To identify and investigate those limits requires that analysts attend to the contradictory structures of purpose and meaning constituting political economy. Only by such critical inquiry can thoughtful advocates convert mere economic anxiety into deliberations on the merits of political economy as a global mode of social life.

NOTES

This paper was originally prepared for the annual meeting of the International Studies Association, San Diego, California, April 16–20, 1996. We wish to thank the participants of that panel, especially Nicholas Onuf, for suggestions and comments. Also, we can only praise Kurt Burch for his skills as an editor and organizer. Finally, we need to thank David Levine, who, though he hasn't read this chapter, has mightily shaped its content.

1. Thus, Gilpin (1987:27) explicitly severs liberal economic theory from its concerns with individuality, freedom, and equality. His reading of Marxist thought is similarly sterile and technical (1987:35–36).

2. Avineri (1972:89–94) highlights the parallel between Marx's theory of alienated labor and Hegel's early analysis of capitalist society (see also Heiman, 1971). Indeed, Avineri names Hegel "one of the earliest radical critics of the modern industrial system."

3. We intentionally foreshadow a theme discussed more forcefully by Polanyi. This connection between Hegel and Polanyi is the centerpiece of Gallagher 1987. On the embeddedness of the economy in Hegel, also see Riedel (1984:chap. 6), Arthur (1987), and Plant (1987).

Anne Sisson Runyan 5

Of Markets and Men: The (Re)Making(s) of IPE

"REAL MEN" (RE)MAKING IPE

The most often told story of IPE is about men, states, and markets. Even in contemporary retellings of this story in standard IPE textbooks, the "making" of IPE as a field is routinely traced to such men as Machiavelli and Hobbes, then Smith and Ricardo, and, finally, Marx, as progenitors of all IPE perspectives. This is typically followed by the "makings" of IPE. This is the narrative of the supposedly "real" international political economy, which according to past and present "makers" of IPE, is about "the exercise of power" as embodied by the state, "the allocation of resources" as embodied by the market, and the forces of production "reflected in the political conflicts emanating from tensions between people involved in production—owners of capital and providers of labor" (Schram, 1995: 51, 53).

Yet is this grand narrative of (white) men, states, and markets the "real" IPE to which we must attend? Or is it, as social welfare theorist Sanford Schram (1995:52–53) argues, "what is at the margin, off-stage, and not part of the public transcript" that "may be critical for understanding the 'actually existing political economy'"? To arrive at this claim, Schram engages in a refreshing mixture of both field- and self-examination. He recounts the inferiority complex he felt as a white male student of political economy who was, in his mind and based on the dominant parameters of the field, perversely interested in poverty and welfare. His self-doubt about this seemingly errant preoccupation stemmed from three senses of inadequacy brought on by the demands of the "real man's" study of political economy (Schram, 1995:51).

The first source of his feelings of inadequacy about himself and his subject came from the prevailing disciplinary assumption that the poor constitute an "'underclass'—that is, those below the class structure of society" (Schram, 1995:51), and thus living outside of heroic class struggle. The second source of his shame arose from the dominant assumption that

79

welfare is a site of reproduction "concerned only with the secondary, marginal, residual activities associated with the private realm of family relations" and, thus, peripheral, at best, to the forces of production in "market-
centered societies" (Schram, 1995:51). Third, if white male decisionmakers
generate all the "action" in political economy, why was he focusing on
"activities that were salient primarily for marginal people of color"
(Schram, 1995:52)?

Schram does not explicitly theorize how the masculinist constructs and
commitments of a "real man's" political economy led to his sense of displacement from the center of the study of political economy. However, he
does recognize that his own "unreflective acceptance of the economic, gender, and race biases concerning what was commonly taken as central to our
political economy" led him to accept for some time that his concerns about
poverty and welfare were, indeed, marginal at best (Schram, 1995:53). To
his credit, he sought neither refuge nor recentering by abandoning his study
of poverty and social welfare but rather came to see that

> what is on the bottom is arguably what we need to understand if we are to
> see how such political economies create hierarchies of power, privilege,
> and purpose. Knowing how it is that some come to be seen as being on the
> margin or on the bottom can tell us much about how the discursive consti-
> tution of social relations contributes to deciding meaning and value, iden-
> tity and other, inclusion and exclusion, "us" and "them." The outside is
> inside; the marginal, central; the bottom, the top for providing the strate-
> gic view that allows for understanding the systemic forces at work in get-
> ting people to help reproduce the life the way it is through their daily
> actions and exchanges. (Schram, 1995:53–54)

For Schram, this view is not a rationale for justifying the focus of his
work either to himself or to the powers that be in political economy. Such a
move would seek to stabilize his masculinity by insisting on being at the
center of explanatory power. Rather, this view represents a political commitment not only to the nonmarginalization, but also to the nontrivializa-
tion of "the ongoing political contestations where those in need resist the
structures of power in their daily lives" (Schram, 1995:52). From this
angle, Schram resists traditional readings of political economy policy
issues—whether neoconservative or neo-Marxist—that disregard or trivial-
ize social welfare needs. For example, he effectively "inverts" neoconservative and neoliberal reasoning by countering it with the everyday life struggles of the poor.

> What was called "welfare fraud" was often not recognized as an honest
> attempt to make ends meet in the face of horrendous bureaucratic obsta-
> cles. What was called "lack of work effort" was often not seen as an
> expression of commitment to family and children. What was called "wel-

fare dependency" was often not appreciated as an attempt to escape difficult circumstances, leave an abusive spouse, take control over one's own
life, and protect one's children. (Schram, 1995:53)

But Schram also challenges neo-Marxist emphases on production and labor
that consistently downplay the provision of social needs when he argues
that "what was 'nannygate' was a problem of child care, not the problem of
the exploitation of low-wage labor" (Schram, 1995:53).

THE REPRESSED POLITICS OF RECIPROCAL EXCHANGE

Schram "inverts political economy" by beginning with "domestic" social
needs and putting women and children first. This perspective locates his
approach to political economy firmly within feminist critiques of International Political Economy. Feminists identify the "actual existing political
economy," whether "domestic" or "international," as the "provision of
basic needs" done by women, which "takes place outside of the market, in
households or in the subsistence sector of Third World economies"
(Tickner, 1991:193). Prevailing IPE accounts render invisible or marginal
such basic "providing." This marginal framing of basic needs and household subsistence relies heavily on neoclassical separations of the economic
from the political, separations of the economic from the social and familial,
and caricatures of rational economic man.

Critiques of neoclassical economic constructions are, of course, not
unique to feminists. As feminist economist Ann L. Jennings (1993:111–
112) argues, institutional economics of the late nineteenth and early twentieth centuries lay the ground for feminist arguments. Such institutionalists
as Thorstein Veblen and Karl Polanyi employed cultural analyses that led
them to reject separate sphere arguments as "cultural defenses of existing
social distinctions" and as "notions of functional necessity in the ways
human needs are met, except in the very narrow sense that existing social
values may create cultural blindness to alternative arrangements and interpretations" (Jennings, 1993:114). Their belief that "processes and meanings" are not universal but are rather "mutually and historically determined" (Jennings, 1993:114) produced their critiques of neoclassical
assumptions about human nature and the economy.

According to Jennings, Veblen countered conventional assumptions by
arguing that "men's market activities" were "wasteful." So, too, were the
housewifery, consumer, and ornamental activities to which nineteenth-century bourgeois women were consigned in the newly emergent market economy. In Veblen's view, the "social provisioning process," in which women
play significant roles, constitutes the "real economy" (Jennings, 1993:113).

Polanyi also challenged the classical and neoclassical political economist idea, well entrenched in modernist IPE, that the market is the economy. He argued that prior to the rise of the "market pattern," economies were embedded in and subsumed by social organizations. In these organizations the principles and practices of "reciprocity" and "redistribution" in *both* local and long-distance trade took precedence over "exchange" as means to meet social needs (Polanyi, 1957:47–53). The rise of the market pattern brought not only the bifurcation of politics and economics by the nine-teenth century but also "the dominance of the principle of the market over other social principles" (Nicholson, 1986:187).

Polanyi traces the freeing of "labor, land, and money" from state con-trol to produce a market economy that subsumes society to it. However, he neglects to track the separation of the economy from the family and the resulting diminution of the family as a significant governing institution over economic activities (Nicholson, 1986:186–187). Feminist political theorist Linda Nicholson points out that in "kinship-organized" societies—the type that Polanyi invokes as predecessors to the market society—"sexu-al and economic relations are integrally linked" because rules determining how and by whom food and objects are made are always developed "'in connection' with those rules regulating marriage and sexuality" (Nicholson 1986:195). Polanyi's failure to explore these relationships as well as Marx's earlier failure to acknowledge them further reified "the belief in the separability of productive and reproductive activities" (Nicholson, 1986:195). This belief, Nicholson (1986:193) argues, is itself "a product of a society which gives priority to food and object creation over other life activities."

Several problems arise from this bifurcation and devaluation. The first problem, as Nicholson observes, is that political economists can dismiss gender relations as separate from and less influential than class relations. This dismissal bars any exploration of the "historical conflicts over other socially necessary activities, such as childbearing and childrearing" as well as the historical relationships between these arguably more primary activi-ties and the arguably more secondary activities of food and object produc-tion (Nicholson, 1986:193). In this regard, Nicholson (1986:193) asks "Does it even make sense to attempt to separate the changes involved, prior to the time when these activities were themselves differentiated, i.e., prior to the time when the 'economy' became differentiated from the 'family'?" Moreover, given that it was kinship that served as the primary "means of organizing the production and distribution of goods" prior to the rise of the "principle of exchange," Nicholson argues that gender relations historically constitute class relations (Nicholson, 1986:195).

The second problem associated with the nonsensical bifurcation of reproduction and production is that both Polanyi and Marx fail to account for the fact that "not all labor becomes subordinate to the laws of the market" (Nicholson, 1986:187). Although domestic and reproductive labor primarily performed by women is affected by market forces, it is still not organized completely by them. Indeed, feminist economist Irene van Staveren (1995) argues that the three circuits of the economy that Polanyi identified are still present. She acknowledges that the *exchange* circuit most associated with the global market economy now dominates the circuits of *redistribution,* associated with state taxation and subsidies, and *reciprocity,* or the "care circuit," of the economy. However, the reciprocal economy—where women predominate as volunteer workers in the community and as unremunerated caretakers of children and the elderly—still represents a huge portion of economic activity. For example, UN Development Program figures from 1995 estimates that women's unpaid work is worth an additional $11 trillion on top of women and men's paid labor ($23 trillion) (van Staveren, 1995:101, 103). Exchange came to dominate through

> colonising processes that were formerly part of care or redistribution (such as neighborly help or food subsidies) or undermining caring and redistributive processes (for example by commercialising the positive cost-benefit parts of a process and leaving the not recoverable costs to the other circuits, such as in the cases of caring for the chronically ill, or public services such as drinking water for the poor). (van Staveren, 1995:102)

However, care work is not diminishing, but rather, in many cases, increasing even as women become more involved in market relations.

Although Polanyi significantly underestimated the continued power of familial gender relations as an organizing force of a large proportion of the economy, he did remind us that the word *economy* is derived from the Greek *oeconomia,* which refers to the household and consists of "production for one's own use" (Polanyi, 1957:53). Ecofeminist and physicist Vandana Shiva makes a similar point when she notes that both of the terms *economy* and *ecology* (or *oecologies*) come from the same Greek root *oikos,* "the daily operations and maintenance" of the household (Shiva, 1995:6). She argues that the rise of market dominance has meant a shift away from a "home economy metaphor" that does not rest on a "hierarchical divide between domestic production and commodity production for exchange and trade" nor on a "divide between nature's economy, the sustenance economy and the market economy" (Shiva, 1995:6). This has been supplanted by a "trade economy metaphor" in which "something only has value if it is traded" and "nature's economy is valueless" (Shiva, 1995:11). Feminist economist Diane Elson refers to this shift as a split between "the commodity economy, the one everybody thinks of as 'The

Economy,'" and the "care economy." This split privileges the "making of money" over the "meeting of needs," and it places those most "bound up with the care economy" at a disadvantage in the commodity economy (Elson, 1995:14).

This split is related to the third problem of the shifting definitions of public and private from the seventeenth through the nineteenth centuries. This laid the ideological foundation for the bifurcation of production from reproduction and the devaluation of the economic realm of reciprocity. As Jennings (1993:120) observes, the initial public/private split associated with the rise of liberal political theory in the seventeenth century was designed to oppose state to family in order to privilege the state as a site of "political rights, access, and prerogatives." By the nineteenth century, however, "the main target of the new 'political economists' was state control over economic affairs" in order to limit the state to "pursuits that private, self-interested entrepreneurs could not undertake themselves" (Jennings, 1993:120). Thus, the crucial ideological divide between public and private also separated the state from the market. The effect of this "double dualism" was that "while markets became 'public' with respect to the 'private' family in the nineteenth century, they retained their 'private' status vis-à-vis the 'public' state. In both cases, public/private distinctions privileged the market . . . because the market had become both public and private" (Jennings, 1993:121). Moreover, the "boundary between the state and the economy" remained much less rigid than "the boundary between the family and the economy," thereby allowing state elites still fairly wide latitude to intervene in the market economy. Families and women who were assumed to have no other role but a familiar one became defined as "non-economic" (Jennings, 1993:125).

This ideological construction did not obliterate the other circuits of the economy, but enabled the market to become parasitic on them. With the massive "care" circuit rendered invisible and the "redistribution" circuit of the welfare state being undermined in the age of globalization, the discounted "care" labor of women is counted on to deal with the socioeconomic fallout that is "not so much caused by market failures" as by "a serious failure of markets" (van Staveren, 1995: 103).

THE REPRESSED PSYCHOLOGY OF MARKET EXCHANGE

In order to discount economic relations of reciprocity, (neo)classical economists and political economists have advanced a notion of human nature that discounts care and social need as motivating factors and elevates exchange and profit as the only animating forces that compel economic activity. Polanyi problematizes this characterization when he questions Adam

Smith's claims about "primitive man's alleged predilection for gainful occupations" and also challenges the "natural" progression of "primeval man . . . bent on barter and truck" to a market economy based on an overwhelming penchant for exchange and, thus, needful of a rationalized division of labor (Polanyi, 1957:44–45). To achieve this hegemonic representation of rational economic man, traditional gender ideology has had to be turned on its head. In this story, it is men's work that is deemed "natural" and "unchanging." The production and exchange of objects is "naturalized" and made transhistorical in order to universalize a particular historical economic formation and practice. This move to obliterate reproductive practices and relations from the repertoire of human needs, wants, and motivations is necessary, according to feminist economist Susan Feiner, to hide the role that these practices and relations play in the ideological constitution of neoclassical economics.

In order to make the case that the particular preoccupations and persuasive power of neoclassical economics have much more than is apparent to do with reproductive than productive practices, Feiner subjects neoclassical economic theory to a feminist psychoanalytic critique derived from the object relations school. Since economics presents itself as "'the study of the allocation of scarce resources to the infinity of human wants'" (quoted in Feiner, 1995:157), it cannot avoid addressing its psychological claims about human wants. Nor should economics be able to escape or deflect critical readings of its own psychology. Moreover, Feiner (1995:153) contends that "the intensity with which many people, inside and outside the circle of trained academic economists, defend one or more aspects of the neoclassical approach, despite startling incongruities between the economy which neoclassicism describes and the economies of our lives" demands inquiry that explores beneath the surface of typically insufficient rationalistic explanations (Feiner, 1995:153). It is the symbolic and affective dimensions of such theories that most propel their persuasive character and hegemonic power. Although Feiner admonishes readers that economic theories cannot be reduced to psychoanalytic explanations of the type she employs, feminist psychoanalytic readings help unpack the power of economic theories.

Feminist object relations theory, first popularized by Nancy Chodorow in her highly influential work *The Reproduction of Mothering* (1978), places in the foreground a basic reality conveniently eclipsed by almost all "male-stream" political and economic theorists: We are all born of women. This still remains the case despite the advent of in vitro technologies and even cloning. For the most part, it is also the case that it is with a mother— whether "natural," surrogate, or adoptive—that a child first forms a relationship, initially in the womb and later outside it. In the view of feminist object relations theorists, this initial mother-child relation is central to the ways a child appropriates, internalizes, and organizes early experiences in their family—from the fantasies they have, the defenses they use, the way they channel and redirect drives in this object-relational context. A person subsequently imposes this intrapsychic structure, and the fantasies, defenses, and relational modes and preoccupations that go along with it, onto external social situations. This reexternalization (or mutual externalization) is a major constituting feature of social and interpersonal situations themselves. (Chodorow, 1978:206)

Most significantly, the newborn is completely dependent on "its primary caretaker—usually its mother" for its basic and urgent needs "for food, warmth, and nurturing" (Feiner, 1995:157). Of course, as much as mothers may try to anticipate and meet the needs of babies, it is impossible always to do so immediately or in the right ways. "One of the primary fears of infancy and early childhood is that demands will not create their own supplies. To the extent that children experience mothers withholding (after all, a child must first cry to let her needs be known) then food, love, security and nurturing are not immediately available" (Feiner, 1995:160).

According to Chodorow, these early frustrations are particularly internalized by males. She contends that in capitalist patriarchal societies males are required to separate themselves from their mothers. Male dependency on women, particularly of the intense type involved in the mother-child relationship, is inconsistent with the "idealized" masculinity that male children must aspire to achieve. Such idealizations arise from relatively infrequent contact with flesh-and-blood fathers, who are typically more distant caretakers in male-dominated societies (Chodorow, 1978:181).

To repress the mother-son relationship, however, does not eradicate "the desire to recreate relationships from the past" at the unconscious level (Feiner, 1995:152). Feiner posits that such a re-creation occurs in the construction of neoclassical economics wherein the market takes the place of the mother. The market is supposed to provide for male subjects all that real-life mothers cannot.

The notion of the free market can be seen as an expression of a wish. In its theoretic and cultural elaboration, the market functions as a substitute for the perfect mother who is unfailing in her capacity (and willingness) to meet all needs and wants. The idealized market (the home of "homoeconomicus") of neoclassical economic theory mirrors the fantasy mother of the unconscious. (Feiner, 1995:156)

However, for the neoclassical masculine subject to remain unthreatened by the "market-as-mother" in order to repress his early dependency on an actual mother, the market must remain "distant":

The very mechanisms through which the market accomplishes the meetings of wants [are] impersonal, cold, and objective. This image is the antithesis of a caring mother and so denies the reality of warmth, emotional contact and passion as essential to human satisfactions. . . . The meeting of needs and the satisfaction of desire require nothing but exchange. "Homoeconomicus" always gets what he wants, but he gets it without affective connection. (Feiner, 1995:160)

Thus, both infantile frustration and masculinity anxiety are relieved by the neoclassical projection of the market-as-mother, which, ironically, "functions psychologically to infantilize subjects, since every action produces only what the subject wants" (Feiner, 1995:161). Exchange must preclude sharing in order to protect the subject's denial of dependency and contingency. Thus, "it is not the market which meets needs but it is rather the neoclassical representation of the market which meets needs" (Feiner, 1995:162).

To gauge the power of this representation to thwart efforts to meet needs, it is useful to return to Schram and his story of the rise and fall of the U.S. poverty line. This story begins with the research of Mollie Orshansky, who began work as a "home economist" in the Social Security Administration in 1958. Joining those who were pejoratively known as "the 'ladies who studied poverty'" (quoted in Schram, 1995:78), Orshansky was "the author of what thirty years ago was to become the government's official poverty line" (Schram, 1995:78). By the early 1960s, Orshansky had developed a "relational concept of poverty" that did not "measure economic destitution, but [instead] how much money an 'average' family would need to achieve the lowest healthful level of the prevailing standard of living. As the standard and cost of necessities on which it was based changed, it would be necessary for the poverty standard to change" (Schram, 1995:83). By the 1970s, however, both the Johnson and Nixon administrations had refused to adjust the poverty line on the basis required by Orshanky's formula: a continual sensitivity "to the costs of buying necessities and the proportion of those necessities constituted by food." Instead, male macroeconomists "had taken over, and they relied on one of their most significant achievements—the measurement of price increases (i.e., the CPI)—to tell them how to adjust the poverty level each year" (Schram, 1995:81). Lost in this shift from a relational to an abstract way of "think[ing] about poverty in terms of aggregates" was any sensitivity to the "specifics of day-to-day coping practices" (Schram, 1995:81). Had the U.S. federal government retained Orshansky's approach, the poverty line in 1990 "for a family of four would have been $22,300 rather than the official standard of $13,360" (Schram, 1995:82). In light of recent attempts in the United States to recalculate the CPI to further reduce entitlements,

Schram's conclusion that bottom-up "home economists" are the "real" economists becomes even more compelling.

REMAKING A "REAL"
INTERNATIONAL POLITICAL ECONOMY

(Neo)liberal globalization advocates appear to be relying on the neoclassical fantasy that relieves infantile frustration by insisting that "exchange makes all exchangers better off, all desires are met perfectly, and there is no trading outside equilibrium" (Feiner, 1995:161). (Neo)realist protectionists appear to be relieving masculine anxiety that results from "the memory of infantile dependence on (m)other" (Feiner 1995:161) when they elevate autonomy to such a degree that acknowledging (inter)dependency and engaging in sharing constitutes a major security threat. Even (neo)Marxists deny dependency on the "care circuit" by marginalizing reproductive work and relying on the forces of production to meet all needs and desires.

The problem with all these "approaches" is that they ultimately share the same approach—the denial that men and markets are, in some of the deepest and broadest historical senses, "of woman born." This denial enables the ideological bifurcation of familial and social practices that embody reciprocity from the practices of external trade. IPE conveniently ignores familial and social practices as domestic and affective relations outside its purview. Similarly, IPE turns external trade into a purely unique, modern, statist, and "international" phenomenon that may affect social life, defined in domestic terms, but that operates above and outside it.

The one exception to this view in mainstream IPE is the invocation of "diffuse reciprocity" by Robert Keohane. Keohane describes how international regimes replace "tit for tat" actions by self-interested states with "social norms and a widespread pattern of obligation" (Keohane, 1989:247; also quoted in Sylvester, 1994:125). He goes on to argue that the "norms on which diffuse reciprocity rests may reflect empathy of people toward one another, and could therefore be consistent with what Carol Gilligan refers to as an 'ethic of care' and what Joan Tronto discusses as a conception of identity describable as 'the connected self'" (Keohane, 1989:247; also in Sylvester, 1994:125).

Feminist international relations theorist Christine Sylvester balks at this characterization by pointing out that no such empathy appears to operate in male regimist treatment of female underlings employed in the lowest paying and most vulnerable jobs within international institutions (Sylvester, 1994:126). Nor does such empathy extend to the more vulnerable women and children throughout the world on the receiving end of regimist policies (Runyan, 1996). Instead regimes and male regimists appear more as "opportunists" who "can refuse to cooperate" whenever power hierarchies, relations, and privileges are at stake (Sylvester, 1994:127).

By censoring the life story of the historical relationship between reciprocity and external trade, IPE becomes a story of estrangement that finds care in the bodies of cold, calculating, and opportunistic international institutions (regime-as-mother?). IPE is beginning to be concerned with the current disruption of the post-war domestic social contract between state and society brought on by globalizing forces. However, its repressed memory of the earlier disruption(s) that not only separated social relations from the market but also subsumed them to it keeps it searching in all the wrong places in hopes of finding the right relationships. The masculinist-economistic basis of IPE prevents it from acknowledging that all manner of physical, social, and spiritual needs and desires cannot be reduced to nor fulfilled by the machinations of states and markets. Mutual respect, care, and welfare can only arise through struggles for nonhierarchical social relations. Focusing on such struggles can reconstitute IPE by disrupting its reliance on the gender-based, infantile fantasies of neoclassical economics. It can also constitute for everyone political economies worth living in.

Nicholas Onuf **6**

Hegemony's Hegemony in IPE

The term *International Political Economy* refers to a set of material and social conditions that we feel warranted in treating as a distinctive and coherent whole worthy of study in its own right. Who is this "we"? When did "we" begin to think this way? For what end, by what means, and to what effect?

The "we" in question is the set of scholars who began to use the term during the 1970s and continue to do so. At first, many of us were from the United States, trained as political scientists, identified with International Relations (IR) as a field of study, and broadly liberal in the way we thought about economics. A generation later, we are surely more varied in background and allegiances. Nevertheless, the field of International Political Economy (IPE) is deeply affected by its beginnings.

IPE began when scholars, already dissatisfied with the presumptive identity of security concerns and international politics, belatedly recognized that international economic relations have political implications. More to the point, we realized that the United States had used its great power to set up liberal international institutions to expedite trade and finance in the postwar world, just as Great Britain had in the nineteenth century, and that these institutions thereafter contributed significantly to the power and prosperity of the United States, just as they had for Britain. These institutions also contributed to the peace and prosperity of the liberal world, a condition that soon came to be known as "hegemony" (the Greek term for "leadership").

In this chapter I use the term *hegemony* more abstractly to describe a form of rule that manifests itself in a great variety of social arrangements. This use of the term depends on a general theoretical stance that I have developed elsewhere (Onuf, 1989) and recapitulate in Chapter 1 of this volume ("A Constructivist Manifesto"). I reprise some of its elements in this chapter, which is divided into two parts.

The first part examines the hegemonial features of IPE as a self-defining world of scholarship—a world no less real for being notional. Scholars in all fields have increasingly come to think of themselves in professional terms. I argue that professionalization fosters hegemonial rule. Ideas rule, but not just any(one's) ideas.

In the case of IPE, its ruling ideas—about preponderant power and its relation to peace and prosperity—providentially appeared in 1973. Thereafter, everyone identifying with the field was professionally obliged to refine, test, extend, and rearrange these ideas. We could not disavow them, however, and stay in the field. Ideas rule by telling us who we are and what is important. Hegemony is important for what it says about the field and its abiding concerns. Ruling ideas are persistent, not precise.

The second part of this chapter shifts from the world of ideas to the world of states. One of the ruling ideas in the field is that Great Britain and the United States created in successive centuries conditions for peace and prosperity reaching far beyond their boundaries. Immensely powerful *and* liberal, the two countries created these conditions in much the same way, that is, the way liberals always proceed when they can: by developing institutions that benefit everyone. Liberals do so on the generally well-taken guess that they will benefit at least as much as everyone else.

I first try to show that prevailing ideas about nineteenth-century Great Britain are seriously misleading. Early in that century, the United States, not Great Britain, fostered international institutional developments that we now think of as liberal. I then show that so-called British hegemony was instead an instance of informal hierarchy, though it was reinforced by hegemony. I use the term *hierarchy* to describe a second form that rule may take in any society, including the society that states constitute through their relations.

The developments that the United States did much to augment in the nineteenth century reflect a third form of rule that had already emerged as a pervasive condition ruling the relations of states. I call this third form of rule *heteronomy*. Institutionalizing heteronomy was one way for the United States to resist British power, and it was consistent with U.S. institutional history. The United States joined Great Britain's informal hierarchy later in the nineteenth century and assumed responsibility for hierarchical rule after World War II. In both situations, the United States actively promoted institution building consistent with the heteronomous character of international relations. It did so with favorable consequences for the growth of international trade and finance, its own prosperity, and cordial relations among the chief beneficiaries of hierarchical rule within a more generally heteronomous setting.

Hegemony, hierarchy, and heteronomy correspond to three categories of rules and institutions, which in turn correspond to the three general ways that people can speak to social effect. First, we can assert, deny, or otherwise comment on states of affairs (on the world). Second, we can direct other people to bring about some state of affairs (some change in the world). Third, we can promise to bring about some change in the world ourselves.

Speaking to social effect can and often does eventuate in the formation of rules that tell people what to do and what to expect when we (fail to) follow those rules. Three ways of speaking to social effect give rise to rules that work the same three ways that speech does. I call them instruction-rules, directive-rules, and commitment-rules. Instruction-rules tell us what the world is like and how we fit in. Directive-rules tell us what other agents want us to do. Commitment-rules tell us what we can do to and expect from each other. Varying in formality, rules in all three categories exist everywhere. Collectively, they make us the agents that we are.

At the same time, rules make up the institutions that we find all around ourselves. Liberal scholars have always emphasized rules and institutions. One might conclude that the theoretical stance that I propound here is little more than liberal institutionalism tricked out in the fashionable language of social construction. Against liberal sentiments, I claim that agents participate unequally in the formation of rules and that they are unequally affected in the distribution of benefits that arises from following rules. The beneficiaries of this condition use their advantages to keep the rules in their favor; those whom it prejudicially affects are at a disadvantage in changing the rules. The resulting institutions yield rule as a generally stable but never fixed condition of asymmetric effects.

Both the pervasiveness and the asymmetries of rule discomfit liberals. The social theory that I draw on reaches beyond liberalism to focus on domination and exploitation (Giddens, 1981:49–68). Such terms as these might seem to suggest that some people take advantage of others without regard to rules. Obviously, this happens. Yet any persistent pattern of domination and exploitation brings on rules affirming and supporting these activities. Changing rules may mitigate the particular effects of rule, but rule, as such, always involves some manner and degree of domination and exploitation.

Each of the categories of rules that I have identified yields a distinctive condition of rule. When instruction-rules establish statuses and routinize activities, we know how we fit in, and hegemony is the result. When directive-rules organize our activities into a chain of command, hierarchy is the result. When commitment-rules confer rights and duties on us, we know individually what we are free to do, just as we know what others are free to do.

More precisely, we expect others to acknowledge what we are free to do, just as we know that others expect us to do the same. This generally reciprocal set of limitations on our individual autonomy yields heteronomy as a condition of rule. In practice, rule is likely to result from mixing rules in all three categories. Nevertheless, an observer can always identify the elements of rule and tell which is dominant.

HEGEMONY IN THE WORLD OF IDEAS

The Professionalization of Scholarship

Among the many institutions of modern society are those that produce and distribute scholarship. In my terms (and from an "American" point of view), three sorts of institutions combine to rule the world of scholarship. First, networks of scholars demarcate fields by deciding among themselves what to study and how to do it. Status considerations significantly affect the degree to which any given scholar's participation makes a difference. Ruling ideas are the ones that scholars of the highest status advance. This is hegemony at work.

Second, scholars, at least in the United States, are typically officers of instruction involved in the training and certification of new scholars. The internal organization of universities reflects and supports the demarcation of scholarly fields. As organizations, universities acquire and dispense status by appointing influential scholars as officers. Hierarchical arrangements reinforce the multiple hegemonies represented by fields of scholarship.

Third, scholars are nominally equal. Each has a right to produce scholarship and a correlative duty to consume the scholarship of others. In principle, ideas freely compete for attention. Funding, publication, citation, and awards are the indices of success. Nevertheless, access to this market is severely restricted. Influential scholars control sources of funding, sit on editorial boards, and dispense awards. They often reject ideas incompatible with their own, insist on exclusionary standards, and discount the advice of scholars whose status is lower. In effect, they extol the free exchange of ideas while they exercise strict control. As a result, they mask hegemony and its organizational support in the appearance of heteronomy, itself fictively represented in the language of autonomy.

In recent decades, the world of scholarship has rapidly professionalized. Scholars have become more self-conscious about training and certification. We accelerated the long-term process of institutionalizing fields by forming professional associations, founding journals, and organizing university departments. Whether by ranking ourselves, our departments and universities, our journals and presses, or our fields, we assigned status to everyone and everything in the world of scholarship. We also secured an extraordinary measure of self-rule and privileged access to resources.

In this context, IR emerged, after World War II, as a professionalized field of scholarship. The field's early debates reflected the pressure to professionalize, and its ruling ideas reflected the position of the United States in the world. Success meant the triumph of realism over liberal-institutionalism (dismissed as idealism for its naïveté) and science over traditional, largely descriptive treatments of international relations (dismissed as journalism and dilettantism). By the 1970s, scholars committed to realism and positivist science had fenced off the field, in the process disallowing claims that scholars in other fields had anything beyond method to contribute and discouraging talk of the field's "interdisciplinary" potential.

At the same time, scholars in the field needed, somewhat paradoxically, to vindicate their new institutional identity by claiming for the field a long, distinguished tradition of scholarship. Thucydides and Machiavelli were said to have anticipated realism's substantive concerns and even a skeptical attitude later formalized as science. Hobbes was no less important for having divided politics into two states of affairs: the state of peace under the state and the state of war in nature and (even if Hobbes never said so explicitly) among states. This division warranted two formally equal fields of scholarship—political science and IR—nevertheless related by heritage and a commitment to science.

The Year 1973

Even as IR came into its own as a field of scholarship, its boundaries were called into question. During the 1970s, realist scholars began to see the power the United States had deployed since World War II by virtue of its position in the world economy. The United States had used its power to set the rules for trade and finance: This was *political* economy. The rules themselves favored economic growth through trade: This was *liberal* economy. The international institutions that these rules created were a benefit to the United States and every other country in the liberal world.

It took an economist, Charles Kindleberger, to make these "realities" clear. Kindleberger's assessment of the Great Depression and its causes (1973) had an immediate impact on scholars already unsettled by changes in the world economy. First came the failure of institutional arrangements for monetary relations, which was soon followed by a dramatic increase in oil prices and a worldwide recession. Political events also played a part. As the United States extricated itself from Vietnam, there seemed less to military capabilities than met the scientifically trained eye. If scholars were ready to reconsider some of their standing assumptions, Kindleberger (1973:28) made it easy by proposing a theory of leadership: "The international economic and monetary system needs leadership, a country which is prepared, consciously or unconsciously, under some system of rules that it has internalized, to set standards of conduct for other countries; and to seek to get others to follow them, to take on an undue share of the burdens of the system."

Thus stated, Kindleberger's theory is incomplete. A need not met has dire consequences, in this case, a Great Depression resulting from the lack of leadership. Why would any state's agents assume "undue" burdens for the greater good? The theory of collective goods, already familiar to scholars in the field (Olson, 1965; Ruggie, 1972), provides an obvious answer: Producing benefits for oneself, even if they cannot be denied to others, is better than not having any benefits at all. The United States assumed leadership after World War II, as Great Britain had in the preceding century, because benefits outweighed burdens. Perhaps reluctantly, any leader facing undue burdens will give up leading.

Kindleberger has received most of the credit for establishing the practical and theoretical significance of U.S. leadership in the world economy, but credit also belongs to David Calleo, a Europeanist with a background in political theory, and his student Benjamin Rowland (1973). Like Kindleberger, Calleo and Rowland saw the United States as benefiting from liberal-institutional arrangements. Unlike Kindleberger, they saw other states acceding to these arrangements, not because they benefited but because they had to.

Nationalist in temper and mercantilist in policy, most states resist "outside intrusions."

> Thus, when a powerful state presses "interdependence" and "openness" on its enfeebled neighbors, they are inclined to see imperialism and to resist it if they can. Hence, as the predominance of the superpowers recedes and the world becomes more plural, nation-states are likely to disport themselves in a new independence. Collective international institutions which depend primarily on hegemony will have trouble surviving once hegemony is gone. (Calleo and Rowland, 1973:6)

Given the unmistakable parallel between the United States after World War II and nineteenth-century Great Britain, Calleo and Rowland (1973:11–13) linked hegemony and imperialism as "liberal imperialism," carried out through policies and institutions designed to secure free trade. According to Calleo and Rowland, hegemony may take other institutional forms, such as formal empire and federation. Frequently buttressing the former is "a centralizing ideology designed to legitimize the overlordship of the hegemonic power" (p. 8). In the latter case, "the trappings of federalism are used to soften, legitimize and thus consolidate an imperial hegemony that continues" (p. 10).

Calleo and Rowland's theory of hegemony and Kindleberger's theory of leadership are closely related. A dominant state institutionalizes rule for its own benefit. In some measure, other states also benefit, especially if the dominant state and the institutions it fosters are liberal. When such a state loses its dominant position, institutions will suffer and benefits will disappear.

Calleo and Rowland's version of the theory is broader than Kindleberger's, and their classification of institutional forms is more complicated. Does hegemony take different institutional forms, or is hegemony just one form that drastically unequal relations can take? Indeed, 1973 saw the publication of a classificatory scheme predicated on the latter possibility. In this work, political scientist James R. Kurth characterized U.S.–Latin American relations as hegemonial. He also wondered why these relations had not taken some other form.

In a survey of "relations between great powers and small countries" since 1648, Kurth (1973:281) identified three recurring institutional forms, or "systems": "(1) suzeraintal systems (ceremonial subordination of the small countries coupled with normal nonintervention within them), (2) colonial systems (formal annexation and direct administration of the small countries), and (3) hegemonial systems (formal independence of the small countries but foreign interventions, alliances, aid or advisors)."

Kurth also classified all countries in terms of their economic and social development. Once all were traditional; some, and then all, began to modernize; some have become modern. Based on the evidence, he concluded that traditional great powers prefer suzerainty. Modernizing great powers prefer colonial relations with traditional or modernizing small countries, although they occasionally resort to hegemony (Kurth identified four instances). Modern great powers prefer the flexibility of hegemony in their relations with small powers (nine instances; Kurth, 1973:284–285, fig. 1).

Kurth's treatment of unequal relations brought politics and economy together, but not in a way that either realists or liberals could readily accept. Kurth (1973:294, fig. 2) saw the world economy as a background condition that promoted uneven development. The United States used its extraordinary advantages to multiply spheres of influence, and it used familiar political techniques—intervention, alliances, and aid—to do so. Liberal international institutions figure as little in Kurth's assessment of U.S. hegemonies as the world economy does. Indeed, Kurth lists four U.S. hegemonies: Latin America, East Asia, the Middle East, and Western Europe. To use Kurth's (1973:290) description of U.S. hegemony over Latin America, such spheres of influence are capable of being "formalized, routinized, and institutionalized" without becoming administrative units in a full-blown empire.

Kurth's hegemony is the informal political control that great powers exercise over small countries; greater power means more opportunities for control. This sense of the term fits with its earlier usage. From the Greeks on, *hegemony* had meant "a political, or politico-military relationship, not an economic or cultural one" (Wilkinson, 1994:11). For example, a famous document of the Cold War, NSC 68 (1950), described the Soviet Union as an aspirant to hegemony more fanatical than any of its predecessors. Unchecked, the Soviets would turn hegemony into empire. Whenever European powers had sought hegemony, it had taken the other great powers and great wars to rebuff them (NSC 68, in Etzold and Gaddis, 1978:385; cf. Doran, 1971:17–20).

A Field Takes Form

Writing in the shadow of two such wars, E. H. Carr (1939:224) remarked on Britain's earlier, "not too onerous hegemony." Carr had taken an old term, softened its edges, and applied it to a generally peaceful period in Western history. Kindleberger focused on a correlative phenomenon—worldwide prosperity—which he explained by reference to a single, preponderant power whose institutional activities form an intervening variable. Calleo and Rowland also took institutions into account but made them a dependent variable—forms of imposed peace, which bring prosperity in their wake. Intervening variables, such as ideology and history, are needed to explain a hegemonial power's institutional preferences. Kurth made no room for liberal institutions, not to mention peace and prosperity as general phenomena; he offered no theory.

Insofar as scholars could comfortably assume that peace and prosperity form a single variable, Kindleberger's theory had the advantage of simplicity. It also had a normative advantage, at least insofar as its consumers were scholars from the United States embarrassed by talk of imperialism. In the circumstance, Kindleberger's version of the theory prevailed, but not his choice of terms. Many scholars soon began to use the term *hegemony* in place of *leadership* (e.g., Gilpin, 1975; Krasner, 1976; Keohane and Nye, 1977). Kindleberger was always cited as the source of what duly came to be known as the theory of hegemonic stability (Keohane, 1980; Snidal, 1985). The term *stability* refers, rather abstractly, to peace and prosperity; hegemony offers an explanation for long periods of peace and prosperity in the liberal world.

Assured that power still matters, realists were happy to bring hegemony—nineteenth-century British and postwar U.S. hegemony—within the purview of IR. Liberal-institutionalist scholars, whom professionalization had pushed to the field's margins, suddenly found their interests back in fashion. Their status also improved, especially after they adopted the allegedly new language of "regime theory." Even scholars on the left gained a measure of respect for having always insisted on the political importance of the world economy. Robert Gilpin's (1975:26–43; 1976) influential work gave some order to these developments. A realist himself,

Gilpin assigned scholars for whom hegemony mattered to three familiar and complementary traditions: mercantilist-realist, liberal-institutionalist, and Marxist.

Very quickly in the 1970s—indeed, almost inadvertently—Gilpin and a few other scholars staked out IPE as a field of scholarship, complete with an inclusive, standardized ideological spectrum and a history of the field prior to its constitution. Despite a grudging acknowledgment of dependency theory, Gilpin paid the least attention to the diverse scholarly concerns taking their inspiration from Marx. Nevertheless, two such concerns forced themselves into the consciousness of scholars in the United States and became fixtures in IPE.

One concern was sociologist Immanuel Wallerstein's characterization of the modern world system as an alternative to empire; his work burst into view in the mid-1970s (e.g., 1974a:15–16, 229–239; 1974b). The second was Antonio Gramsci's explanation, with Marx's help, of the modern state's success, against Marx's expectations. Although a widely distributed English translation of Gramsci's work appeared in 1971, Robert Cox (1977) was the first IPE scholar to bring Gramsci to the field. Both Wallerstein and Cox made much of hegemony, though they did not use what had already become customary terms.

Initially, Wallerstein mentioned hegemony only in passing (1974b:408, 411–412). Within a few years, however, the term was important enough for him to define it carefully as a recurring condition in the capitalist world economy (1980:38–39; 1984 [1979, 1983]:4–5, 38–43). When one state at the core of the world economy has far greater power than its rivals, it "can largely impose its rules and wishes . . . in the economic, political, military, diplomatic, and even cultural arenas" (Wallerstein, 1984:38).

Hegemonial power is transitory because it depends on a material base itself dependent on the economic efficiency of a capitalist enterprise operating in and from that state. As the world system's most efficient producer, the hegemonial state imposes rules conducive to "global 'liberalism'" (Wallerstein, 1984:41). These rules force rivals to become more efficient and then favor them once they surpass the hegemonial state in efficiency. As power shifts to rivals, the hegemonial moment passes. Wallerstein identified three such moments, adding seventeenth-century Holland to the standard list.

Cox's treatment of hegemony is expressly derived from Gramsci's. Looking back to Machiavelli, Gramsci identified two elements enabling the state to rule successfully: consensus and coercion (Gramsci, 1971:12–13, 169–170; Cox, 1993 [1983]:52). Beyond coercion, Gramsci pointed to the mechanisms by which the state's privileged class could make its interests coterminous with the interests of all classes. These mechanisms operate within the state as an institution so that the state can keep the costs of rule under control. In effect, hegemony, as I have used the term, is an adjunct of hierarchy.

Similar mechanisms operate in the absence of the state as an institution or, as Cox wanted to show (1993:58–62; 1987:105–210), in an institutional setting within which agents function on behalf of states. Cox started with Great Britain and the United States in the middle decades of the nineteenth and twentieth centuries, respectively. As each country reached global dominance, each produced a bourgeois hegemony domestically, very much as Gramsci had conceived it. In both cases, "national hegemony" went world-wide: Institutions, culture, and technology became "patterns for emulation abroad" (1993:61). Cox added ideas—ruling ideas—to "the legal-institutional framework" (1987:149) that powerful states use to dominate rivals, and in the process he made hegemony unconscious, just as Kindleberger suggested leadership might be. In effect, Cox rendered hegemony (in my sense) secondary to and supportive of an informal hierarchy led by a single, powerful state.

The one big "fact" of hegemony reconciled scholarship from across the ideological spectrum by providing a comprehensive explanation for material and social conditions in the liberal world after World War II. What the United States has been to the twentieth century, Great Britain was to the nineteenth, and Holland, perhaps, to the seventeenth. The one big fact of hegemony gives IPE the sweep of history. Its subject is nothing less than the political and economic history of the liberal world.

Events from the mid-1970s on helped to consolidate IPE as a field. The U.S. economy began to lose its dominant position in the world economy. According to the theory of hegemonic stability, the U.S. economic position translated into leadership exercised through liberal institutions. The theory predicts that loss of economic position will lead to the failure of political leadership, breakdown of liberal-institutional arrangements, return of mercantilist policies, rise of conflict, and decline of aggregate wealth. As evidence mounted in the 1980s, many scholars concluded that this prediction was wrong or at least too broadly stated, and they embarked on a revised and extended research program that would do justice to the theory's underlying premise that the world economy has political underpinnings (Lake, 1993).

Rigorous conceptualization and empirical evaluation vouch for the field's professionalization and ensure its status in the world of scholarship. They also wreak havoc with concepts like hegemony and leadership. Increasingly, scholars agree that no one agrees on the meaning of these terms (Rapkin, 1990; Lake, 1993; Chase-Dunn et al., 1994; Wiener, 1995). Everyone still agrees that nineteenth-century Great Britain and the United States after World War II had something in common: They were hegemons, and they were (and still are) liberal. No longer credible as a theory, the theory of hegemonic stability nevertheless remains a point of reference at the very center of the field, its independent variable substantively unchallenged.

HEGEMONY IN THE WORLD OF STATES

Pax Britannica: Hegemony

The theory of hegemonic stability has had many critics. One criticism bears repeating: As the first liberal hegemon, nineteenth-century Great Britain failed to behave as it should have (McKeown, 1983; Stein, 1984). This criticism needs to be extended. The United States behaved much as Great Britain was supposed to in the nineteenth century: It pressed for institutional arrangements that subsequently came to be identified as liberal. Furthermore, the United States resumed this behavior after a brief interruption and, as is widely observed, has yet to behave otherwise.

To put these claims in perspective, we need to review the standard story of nineteenth-century British hegemony. No one has told the story to greater effect than Karl Polanyi (1957). In his telling, hegemony (as we now call it) coincides with a century of peace and prosperity that dates from the end of the Napoleonic era. This is the Pax Britannica.

Under the influence of Smith and Ricardo, Britons came to believe that international free trade maximized prosperity for all. As the world's leading industrial country, Great Britain had the most to gain from free trade. Consequently, Britain acted to its advantage, as well as everyone else's, by giving international markets whatever support they might need to operate smoothly. The most conspicuous evidence of Britain's institutional support was the gold standard, which the country maintained for the duration of the hundred years' peace.

There are two obvious and related problems with this story. First, the hundred years' peace began in 1815, yet Great Britain only slowly gave up protectionism. Not until 1846 did Parliament repeal the Corn Laws, and it waited another three years to repeal the Navigation Acts. How could a free trade Britain be responsible for the long peace when it was not a free trade country? Second, even when Great Britain finally committed itself to free trade, it did so unilaterally. Indeed, Beth Yarbrough and Robert Yarbrough call this an era of "unilateral liberalization" (1992:4). Yet, as Stephen Neff observes, "no other state followed Britain's lead" (1990:45; also see Stein, 1984:366–367). Scott James and David Lake (1989:16–21) argue that Britain dropped agricultural protection in 1846 at least in part to induce the United States to lower its tariff on British industrial goods. The United States did so that same year, which immediately resulted in a significant increase in trade (James and Lake, 1989:9–11). James and Lake (1989:29) conclude that British policy had comparable effects in Europe, though they provide no evidence to support this claim. I have encountered no substantial evidence elsewhere (see, e.g., McKeown, 1983:85–88).

One might argue (with Kindleberger, 1975:50–51) that the diffusion of laissez-faire ideology throughout Europe is a better, more direct explanation for whatever movement there was toward free trade. An ideology that insists that markets emerge spontaneously and regulate themselves would seem on the face of it a poor candidate for institutionalization. Polanyi (1957:139–150) noted that a dramatic increase in the state's administrative powers accompanied liberal ideology's success in Great Britain and elsewhere. The institutionalization of international free trade finally did result from administrative growth within and above states—fully a century later, under the auspices of a different hegemonial power.

In the absence of institutional arrangements conducive to free trade, tariffs rise and fall in response to changing economic conditions, domestic pressures, or shifts in the prevailing ideology. Retaliation confirms the abandonment of free trade; even the threat of retaliation reminds everyone that unilateral policies are just that. In the 1870s, when the United States and Germany passed Great Britain in industrial production and economic depression set in, unilateral protectionist policies found no institutional resistance (Stein, 1984:367–372; Verdier, 1994:69–105). The era of free trade was too short to secure itself institutionally, much less to explain peace in institutional terms.

Polanyi tried to save the story by introducing quite a different institution, not simply British but not international either, to explain the hundred years' peace. That institution was high finance, "a mysterious institution," indeed "one of the most complex institutions the history of man has produced" (Polanyi, 1957:9–11). Because high finance is so elusive, we never learn from Polanyi what it involves, beyond the gold standard. Not fully developed until late in the nineteenth century, the institution of high finance cannot explain the first half of the hundred years' peace. If high finance helps to explain the second half, its "mysterious" character inhibits us from ever knowing how it did so.

Reciprocities: Heteronomy

Polanyi's story of the Pax Britannica makes ideology, institutions, and policies interchangeable. The story never makes clear whether the ideology is national or transnational, the institutions domestic or international, or the policies Great Britain's or many states'. For all the confusion, I believe that Polanyi was nevertheless right to emphasize the importance of institutions. Institutional arrangements that retrospectively seem to be liberal, and therefore a product of British laissez-faire ideology, made nineteenth- and twentieth-century hegemony possible: They are the independent variable, and they constitute the condition of rule I call heteronomy.

When agents stake out their autonomy by making claims about their rights and others' duties, heteronomy results. Scholars in International Relations conventionally date their subject from the Peace of Westphalia in 1648. Only a few years before Westphalia, Hugo Grotius brought the language of rights to the fore (also see Burch, this volume). Nevertheless, it took Europeans another century to appreciate conceptually what they had wrought in practice (Onuf and Onuf, 1993:10–19; Onuf, 1994a). The first person to write about the reciprocal rights and duties of states as we do today was Emmerich de Vattel in 1758, and not, as Neff (1990:24–25) claims, Christian Wolff writing in the 1740s. Emerging from and reinforcing these reciprocities is an institution—we know it today as international law—whose rules writers such as Vattel had compiled and arranged to great effect.

According to these rules, states and their nationals may engage in trade across frontiers with whoever is willing. By the same token, states are free to prevent trade across their frontiers or to regulate and tax it for whatever reason. By formal agreement, two or more states may establish any set of conditions on trade between them as they see fit. Many European states concluded commercial treaties during the eighteenth century, often to relax restrictive policies on one or both sides. In 1713, as part of the Peace of Utrecht, Great Britain and France concluded a commercial treaty, which Parliament rejected because its most-favored-nation clause was inconsistent with the terms of a commercial treaty with Portugal (Nussbaum, 1954:127). Restrictions on trade, unilateral and bilateral, fully comported with the heteronomous conditions of early modern international relations.

Late in the eighteenth century and early in the nineteenth, no country attached greater importance to commercial treaties than the United States did. Given the once conventional view (exemplified by Hartz, 1955) that Lockean liberalism has deep roots in British North America, one might think (as does Neff, 1990:35) that laissez-faire convictions motivated this stance. The best evidence for this view comes early (Onuf and Onuf, 1993:103–108): In 1776 John Adams designed a commercial treaty, liberal for the times and containing a most-favored-nation clause, as a model for negotiations between the U.S. Confederation and European states (Gilbert, 1961:44–54).

Later evidence points to a different conclusion (Crowley, 1993:68–84; Onuf and Onuf, 1993:117–122). The commercial treaty the United States concluded with France in 1778 used most-favored-nation status to support political objectives. As the War of Independence drew to a close, Great Britain decided against a return to prewar trading arrangements that had given a privileged position to the colonies, and erstwhile allies of the Confederation imposed trade restrictions. In response, the United States sought commercial treaties incorporating most-favored-nation provisions but failed in its negotiations with major colonial states.

> This commercial strategy did not anticipate free trade with either the prospective treaty partner or, of course, with nontreaty nations. In fact, the objective of most-favored-nation status in treaties of "amity and commerce" almost contradicted free trade. Such treaties had no point at all if the Confederation opened itself to free trade. . . . The Confederation really sought the privilege of direct trade, with American ships carrying goods to and from treaty partners. (Crowley, 1993:74–75)

British mercantilists understood the advantages of liberalized trade with the United States but would not budge on the long-standing navigation policy confining that trade to British ships. Great Britain's Navigation Laws were the paramount issue to the United States, at least until the issue of neutral rights and the War of 1812 pushed it aside. The shipping conflict turned ostensible liberals in the United States into mercantilists. Smith's *The Wealth of Nations* vindicated both sides because, as John Crowley (1993:93) demonstrates, it was read as both an exposition of liberal theory and as a judicious defense of mercantilist policy.

After Great Britain and the United States returned to peace in 1814, the United States renewed its quest for bilateral trading agreements with European states. At least for the next fifteen years, the issue was still shipping, not markets (Setser, 1937:183; see pp. 182–255 for a detailed account). The United States made a particular effort to gain its merchants access to Britain's West Indian colonies on the same terms applicable to British merchants. With no preferential colonial arrangements to give up in exchange, the United States had no hope of succeeding.

Even though the United States abandoned the effort to negotiate agreements with European states in 1830, its diplomats continued to advocate a reciprocity agreement with Great Britain as late as 1849 (Brauer, 1984:61–65). That same year, Britain abolished its Navigation Laws for practical political reasons, and even then against the wishes of a leading liberal (Semmel, 1970:198–202). In 1854 Great Britain and the United States finally negotiated a reciprocal agreement for trade with Canada, but only because the British thought the treaty would improve Canadian economic conditions. British diplomats thus sought to eliminate pressure in Canada for union with the United States. Conversely, many in the United States favored the treaty "*because* they believed it would lead to annexation" (Brauer, 1984:103–104, his emphasis).

Over a period of decades, the two countries most conspicuous for their liberal heritage, Great Britain and the United States, engaged in a protracted struggle over trade that had no connection to liberal ideology. As a new and embattled country, the United States consistently sought to improve its position through institutionalized reciprocity, an effort Great Britain resisted. Britain's relations with other states show the same pattern of resistance.

In the 1820s and 1830s, Great Britain flirted with reciprocity in negotiations with France, but to no avail (Kindleberger, 1975:34; McKeown, 1983:82–83). At France's initiative, Britain and France finally did conclude in 1860 a commercial treaty calling for most-favored-nation treatment. Specific political concerns and laissez-faire commitments motivated both governments (Dunham, 1930). If, as Arthur Stein (1984:360) has noted, the treaty itself was "mercantilistic," we should remember that commercial treaties had always been so. Although the 1860s saw a burst of enthusiasm for commercial treaties, Great Britain concluded fewer of such treaties than other European states because its officers feared that the give and take of diplomacy would compromise the goal of free trade (Neff, 1990:45; Verdier, 1994:84).

Institutional histories matter (see Ikenberry, 1988:223–226, for a good conceptual summary). The consistency with which the United States pressed for bilateral arrangements suggests that its international position and institutional preferences converged. Great Britain's North American colonies had fought for independence over the issue of rights; formal equality applied equally to individuals, to the states of the Union, and to the Union as a state. Republican theory and sectional concerns mandated the formal division of powers within government and the formal distribution of responsibilities among levels of governance (Onuf and Onuf, 1993:30–91). Having formalized an elaborate arrangement of reciprocities within the country, the Constitution duly became its most important institution.

The United States fostered heteronomous conditions in its relations with other states because it was inclined by history and circumstance to rely on formal institutions to secure heteronomy at home. The United States actively supported international law and favored treaties as diplomatic instruments from the beginning (Corbett, 1959:47–53; Onuf and Onuf, 1993:108–113, 197–211). By contrast, Britons thought their historic rights were protected by history itself. The British Constitution was (and remains) informal. The British government saw international law as a casualty of French lawlessness during revolutionary and Napoleonic times (Onuf and Onuf, 1993:185–190).

The point is not that Great Britain chose to ignore international law during the Pax Britannica; thanks to British power, customary international law largely favored British interests. Britain was also willing to create international legal obligations for itself and others by concluding treaties that served its interests. Among them was a treaty with the United States signed in 1794 that contained, at U.S. insistence, provisions for the arbitration of claims left over from the War of Independence. Arbitration subsequently became a fixture of nineteenth-century liberal international-ism, but the terms of the treaty provoked serious opposition to its ratifica-tion in the United States. British governments took heteronomous condi-tions for granted, saw no particular advantage in institutionalizing these conditions any more than they already had, and selectively exploited the many and varied opportunities for action that these conditions afforded them.

Imperial Ways: Hierarchy

As I have noted, heteronomy is fully compatible with mercantilist policies. It is also compatible with the reciprocal reduction of restrictive policies and indeed with the generalization of such reductions through most-favored-nation clauses in commercial treaties. Institutionalized reciprocities may eventuate in conditions tantamount to the institution of a market, particu-larly if a leading state is committed to institutionalization for its own sake. Polanyi (1957:43–50) failed to recognize this possibility because he drew a needlessly sharp distinction between economies based on the institution of reciprocity and market economies based on generalized exchange.

After World War II, a liberal-minded, institutionally oriented United States orchestrated a complex arrangement of reciprocities that put interna-tional trade on market footing. Multilateral negotiations expedited the process without changing the underlying premise of reciprocity. After 1970, many countries, including the United States, resumed the negotiation of bilateral agreements (Yarbrough and Yarbrough, 1992:68–84). One hundred years earlier, Great Britain had neither instituted international markets nor organized an arrangement of reciprocities that would work like a market. Even if Britain's unilateral free trade policy made little economic sense, staying with it was hardly eccentric. Indeed, a unilateral stance fit the larger context of Britain's global imperial position.

Throughout the nineteenth century, the British glorified their expand-ing empire (Hyam, 1993). Late in the century, high finance may have played a part in this expansion, or so writers on the left have argued ever since. Earlier, Great Britain had practiced "free trade imperialism": It expanded its empire to advance the cause of free trade (Gallagher and Robinson, 1953; Semmel, 1970; cf. Calleo and Rowland, 1973:11, on "lib-eral imperialism"). During the first half of the hundred years' peace, Britain acquired new imperial possessions, consolidated administrative control over others that it had already acquired, and established port facilities wherever the Royal Navy needed them.

Much of this activity involved the threat or use of force. All of it was imposed on colonial peoples without concern for their wishes. British colonial agents systematically replaced, subordinated, or subverted local institutions: Formal imperial rule is manifestly hierarchical. Great Britain adopted the principle of free trade within the empire because the colonies reliably produced agricultural goods and raw materials and had no choice but to consume British manufactures: The terms of imperial trade confirmed the asymmetrical advantages of hierarchical rule.

At the same time, Great Britain informally incorporated the newly independent states of Latin America into its empire. Informal empire employs many of the same means for the imposition of hierarchical rule that formal empire uses, and reaps the same advantages. Instead of direct administrative control, British diplomats offered peremptory advice, subverted and co-opted states' agents, and actively intervened in the affairs of these states when nothing else worked. At first a rival, the United States soon joined Great Britain in administering this informal empire. By minimizing the presence of other European states, Britain and the United States both enjoyed significant advantages in trading with the region.

Later in the nineteenth century, the United States increased its coercive presence in Latin America in order to protect foreign investments, whatever their source. The United States also insisted that Latin American states conclude treaties providing for the arbitration of damage claims. Cumulative arbitration decisions contributed to the development of what the United States soon came to regard as customary international law, which made states responsible for the protection of foreign capital. No country has more assiduously promoted international law for any purpose than the United States has promoted a legal regime for the protection of capital.

Although Great Britain had denied the newly independent United States a privileged position within the old empire, its willingness to make room for the United States in a different, less formal imperial setting undoubtedly contributed to the Pax Britannica. Britain's reluctance to engage in reciprocity with the United States might count as "free trade imperialism," this phrase now meaning that unilateral economic policies served imperial objectives. Some writers on the subject of free trade imperialism (e.g., Kindleberger, 1975:30–34) have suggested that Britain intended its free trade policy to slow down industrialization on the Continent. This policy had no chance for success, because the relative advantages of industrial development were obvious to everyone. It did not succeed in practice.

Nevertheless, Great Britain did have a Continental policy. The other major states of Europe had the same policy orientation, with significant institutional consequences known as the Concert system. The shared goal of these states was to improve heteronomous relations among themselves by replacing the balance of power with, in Paul Schroeder's terms, a "balance of rights" (1992:698; also see Holsti, 1992). Britain wanted more from its Continental policy. A stable and prosperous Europe would serve its global imperial interests.

Nineteenth-century Great Britain did not rule the world. It ruled an empire, formal and informal, in a heteronomously ruled world of states. Quite a few states were committed to making heteronomy more formal. One measure of their success was one hundred years of peace. Other states had empires and spheres of influence. Imperialism, which a number of states engaged in to offset Britain's imperial advantages, was but one factor that brought the peace down.

The Pax Britannica was not Great Britain's alone. Insofar as British power and policy brought peace and prosperity, liberal institutions had little to do with these conditions. British hegemony, such as it was, took the form of imperial control. As Calleo and Rowland (1973:12) pointed out, "Economic imperialism tends to require political imperialism. It is, in fact, difficult to sustain any free trade system without a concomitant political hegemony."

As we have seen, Calleo and Rowland made hegemony, as "overlord-ship," a general phenomenon, and empire a specific institutional form of hegemony. Kurth made empire and hegemony institutionally distinctive realizations of inequality as a general phenomenon. Imperial control is ongoing and direct; colonies result from that control. Hegemonial control is intermittent or indirect, and it results in a sphere of influence. I believe that rule is a general phenomenon. Empire and international hegemony are manifestations of a single form of rule, and they differ only in how formally rule is exercised. This form of rule is *not* hegemony, as most scholars in IPE use the term, but hierarchy.

I am not suggesting that hegemony, as a form of rule, was entirely absent from the Pax Britannica. Empire demands leadership; Great Britain's unilateral commitment to free trade might be construed as leadership by example (Imlah, 1958:12–17; Lake, 1988:40–41). Leading by example is a leading form of hegemonial behavior. Insofar as Britons adopted an imperial ideology accentuating the responsibilities of leadership, the unilateral commitment to free trade was its own reward. When other states ignored Great Britain's example, choosing instead to ride free at its expense, Britons could see themselves as being exploited for their enlightened policies. Thus vindicated, imperialist ideology supported British imperial exploitation. Meanwhile, other states did their best to follow Britain's example by instituting domestic markets and providing them with administrative support and by industrializing rapidly.

If the Pax Britannica exhibited some evidence of hegemonial rule on Great Britain's part, hierarchical rule is far more in evidence. Hierarchy is implicitly coercive; compliance with rules generally obviates the need for coercion. Leadership is an office, whether contested or self-appointed. Leaders appoint lieutenants; self-appointed lieutenants require the leader's tacit approval. During the Pax Britannica, the United States was a self-appointed lieutenant under Britain's leadership. The United States assumed responsibility for keeping other states from interfering with hierarchical arrangements in the Western Hemisphere and for enforcing rules when those at the bottom of the hierarchy failed to comply with them.

After World War II, the United States instituted a somewhat more formalized hierarchy through a system of multilateral alliances, strikingly supported by the hegemonial idea of two worlds, one demonic and threatening, the other free and well defended. The Soviet Union reciprocated by installing a formal hierarchy within its own world. Simultaneously, the United States took the lead in refurbishing heteronomous institutions represented by general international law, the UN, and an ever greater variety of functional regimes, some of them universal and others regional. Liberal ideology has provided many of these regimes and the UN itself with hegemonial support. One consequence of the new heteronomy has been the rapid dismantling of old empires. With the disintegration of Soviet hierarchy, the United States shows signs of reducing the costs of hierarchical leadership. Entwined elements of heteronomy and hegemony are likely to fill the void, but not fully or to everyone's satisfaction.

CONCLUSION

This sketch of the Pax Americana does not imply that hegemonic stability theory tells us nothing. The United States has exercised global leadership more or less commensurate with its material by developing international institutions and putting them to use, unlike Great Britain a century before. Some of these institutions are mainstays of the liberal world economy. Nevertheless, the theory of hegemonic stability does not explain any general phenomenon. It serves as a partial description of conditions in the world of states over the last half century.

By making a place for institutions as an intervening variable, hegemonic stability theory directs attention to rules. As social rules yield social rule, the conditions that hegemonic stability theory describes are conditions of heteronomous rule. Liberals largely take these conditions for granted, but my sketch of the last half century expressly grants these rules their prominence and duly notes the importance of the United States in making them a prominent feature of the contemporary world.

However, on the basis of abundant institutional evidence, my sketch also suggests that U.S. leadership primarily took the form of hierarchical rule. On the evidence of liberal ideology's pervasive presence, one may also infer significant hegemonial support for hierarchical rule under U.S. auspices. The United States sought stability as a primary value; hierarchy served that purpose. With stability ensured, heteronomy brought other benefits, including general economic growth and a diffusion of democratic practices.

In good liberal fashion, hegemonic stability theorists applaud the benign effects of rule, notably, stability itself. I do not wish to disparage these benefits, but I do want to note that rule in whatever form asymmetrically distributes all such benefits *and* the costs of achieving them. Since hegemonic stability theory is descriptively limited to the institutions and benefits of heteronomous rule, it diverts attention from the larger pattern of rule and the full range of its effects. In this respect, the theory performs a double function: It helps make IPE a hegemonially ruled world in its own right, and it complements hierarchical rule in the world of states.

NOTE

I am grateful to Robert Denemark and James Kurth for bringing important materials to my attention and to Kurt Burch, Robert Denemark, Harry Gould, Paul Kowert, and Joseph Ward for critical assistance.

Part 4

Constructing Practices

Mark Rupert 7

Contesting Hegemony: Americanism and Far-Right Ideologies of Globalization

It may be ruled out that immediate economic crises of themselves produce fundamental historical events; they can simply create a terrain more favorable to the dissemination of certain modes of thought, and certain ways of posing and resolving questions involving the entire subsequent development of national [and transnational-MR] life.

—Antonio Gramsci, *Selections from the Prison Notebooks* (1971:184)

Rejecting the mechanical and deterministic interpretations of historical materialism circulating in the international socialist movement in the early decades of the twentieth century, Gramsci insisted that progressive social change would not automatically follow economic development but must instead be produced by historically situated social agents whose actions are enabled and constrained by their social self-understandings (1971:164–165, 326, 375–377, 420). How—indeed whether—such change occurs depends upon struggles to delimit or expand the horizons of these social self-understandings. Thus, for Gramsci, popular "common sense" becomes a critical terrain of political struggle.[1] This chapter is concerned with struggles over the meanings attached to *globalization* in popular common sense in the United States.

As we approach the close of the twentieth century, the "historic bloc" of social forces and ideologies that formed the core of the U.S.-centered hegemonic world order is being reconstructed.[2] Of particular concern for this chapter is the expulsion of U.S. industrial labor from its position as a relatively privileged junior partner in this global power bloc and the corresponding shift in prevailing interpretations of liberal ideology away from a version that endorsed more activist and growth-oriented state policies and legitimized collective bargaining by mass industrial unions. In place of the kinder, gentler liberalism that was hegemonic during the postwar decades—which John Ruggie has called "embedded liberalism"—we now find instead a hard-edged liberalism that strives to focus the violence of market forces directly upon working people through policies that emphasize fiscal retrenchment, containment of inflation, and "flexible labor markets" in a context of rigorous global competition. Historical structures that institutionalized consensual power relations in the nexus between the United States and the global political economy now appear less solid and stable, and out of this more visibly fluid environment may emerge new possibilities for reimagining and reconstructing social relations on a transnational scale.

It is in this context that popular common sense is being more vigorously contested in the United States, and these contests have potentially important implications for the relations linking the United States with the global political economy. A reconstructed corporate liberalism—emphasizing a global economy in which states and corporate capital make the rules with minimal interference from more democratic institutions—is being challenged on at least two fronts. A cosmopolitan democratic response seeks to link communities, unionists, and citizens across national borders and to use these linkages to impose some measure of social responsibility upon transnational economic actors. This vision has brought together elements of organized labor, the environmental movement, and consumer and citizens groups and has steered them toward more active linkages with their counterparts in other countries (Rupert, 1995b). But this is not the only worldview offering itself as an alternative to the dominance of transnational corporate capital. Far-right ideologies of American exceptionalism represent transnational integration as an insidious threat to the divinely inspired constitutional order in the United States, breaching the citadel of God-given rights and liberties, subordinating Americans to a tyrannical "one-world government," and undermining the special identity of America as a (white) Christian nation. In such ways, Americanist ideologies authorize resistance to globalization as well as scapegoating and hostility toward those seen as outside of, different from, or dissenting from their visions of national identity.

The various meanings of globalization in popular common sense carry direct political significance. To the extent that one or another of these visions is able to predominate, it will enable different forms of political action in the nexus of relations linking the United States to the global economy: In the twenty-first century, will these relations be based predominantly upon corporate power, grassroots linkages between democratic communities, or economic/cultural/racial nationalism? As a scholar and sometime activist, I write to clarify the stakes in these debates.[3] My primary purpose here is to point out that populist-oriented opposition to a corporate-dominated transnational political economy is not the exclusive terrain of progressive or democratizing political forces. A counterhegemonic project cannot afford to take this fact for granted or to be insensitive to the differing inflections of common sense that underlie popular opposition to globalization. In a social context that appears increasingly fluid and in which conditions are favorable for reconstructions of popular common sense, it will be important for a progressive political movement to define itself not only in terms of its opposition to the agenda of corporate-dominated globalism but also clearly and explicitly to articulate this opposition with a transnational democratizing vision.

The remainder of this chapter is divided into five parts. In the first section, I sketch the broad contours of the postwar hegemonic order and the post-Fordist political economy that appears now to be supplanting it. I focus in the second section upon public discussion surrounding two major trade agreements, and I suggest that these discussions may be understood not just as debates over specific measures of trade policy but as occasions for public reconsideration of the tensions of liberal democratic capitalism in an era of globalization. By attaching particular meanings to globalization, the various parties to these discussions seek to reshape popular common sense and the horizons of political action in relation to the global political economy. In the third section, I examine in depth the populist critiques of globalization put forth by far-right defenders of American exceptionalism. I briefly discuss some suggestive indications of the global elite's apprehension toward this new populism in the fourth section. Finally, I discuss in the fifth section the tensions and possibilities of post-Fordist common sense and their implications for a politics of global order.

RECONSTRUCTING CAPITALISM
AND COMMON SENSE IN THE UNITED STATES

I argue elsewhere that ideological struggles have played an important role in the construction and reconstruction of U.S. capitalism and the global hegemony based upon it (Rupert, 1995a, 1995b). In the first half of the twentieth century, the social organization of production was being reconstructed in the manufacturing heart of the U.S. economy: Craft-based production was being supplanted by Fordist mass production, and new relations of power were being constructed and contested in the workplace. Fordism entailed increased mechanization of the labor process and the potential for heightened capitalist control over the pace and intensity of work. Emerging from a decades-long process of political struggle, the institutionalization of this system of mass production was associated with a sociopolitical regime that elicited—albeit imperfectly and inconsistently—

the consent of industrial workers to the expanding social powers of capital.

This process entailed bouts of explicit class conflict during which the sociopolitical conditions of liberal capitalism were opened to potential challenge: Contesting liberal capitalism's valorization of individual rights and especially the right of private property, industrial workers counterposed conceptions of "industrial democracy" and collective participation in work life—grounded in the more democratic aspects of popular common sense—in order to legitimate their new and embattled industrial unions. In the postwar context of Cold War fears and access to an unprecedented affluence for unionized industrial workers, such challenges were contained within the bounds of a vision of liberal capitalism as the social system best able to secure—on a global basis, and with the active collaboration of "free trade unions"—individual rights and liberties and a more generalized prosperity. On the basis of union participation in this hegemonic world vision and their acceptance of its implied commitment to the priority of individual rights over collective self-determination, the state and capital accepted industrial unions as junior partners in the postwar project of reconstructing a liberal capitalist world order (Rupert, 1995a:chaps. 4–7).

In the last decade of the twentieth century, this hegemony is transforming itself. With the Soviet Union's disintegration and the official end of the Cold War, anticommunism could no longer serve as a crucial ingredient in the ideological cement that bound together the postwar historic bloc.[4] Further, the postwar prosperity that U.S. industrial labor had enjoyed as a result of its participation in the hegemonic bloc is evaporating. Unions—the central institutions of "industrial democracy" in the United States—are openly attacked by the state and capital, memberships are in long-term decline, and real wages have been effectively reduced even as productivity growth rebounded during the 1980s (Rupert, 1995a: 179). With the mutation of the postwar historic bloc such that transnational financial and industrial capital are increasingly predominant and industrial labor within the United States is no longer a relatively privileged junior partner, sociopolitical relations and popular ideologies that once seemed firmly grounded are now increasingly up for grabs.

Working Americans now increasingly realize that they live in an environment where corporate profits need not correspond to rising standards of living or improving quality of life for workers. Their ability to exercise control over their economic futures is, under current institutional arrangements, quite limited. Mounting evidence of long-term tendencies toward transnational production, corporate "restructuring," subcontracting and outsourcing, plant closings and layoffs, concessionary bargaining and union busting, declining real wages, widening and deepening poverty, intense economic uncertainty, and real fear among average Americans has in recent years been juxtaposed with news of resurgent corporate profits, happy days on Wall Street, and breathtaking inequalities of income and wealth (Mishel and Bernstein, 1993; Anderson, Cavanagh, and Williams, 1995; Baker and Mishel, 1995; Bluestone, 1995; Economic Policy Institute, 1995; Wolff, 1995; *New York Times,* 1996). The liberal vision of a transnational order institutionalizing the values of freedom and prosperity—most firmly embedded in popular common sense during the postwar decades—may begin to seem bitterly ironic to growing numbers of Americans, like a bad joke at their expense. Once solidly hegemonic, the liberal narrative of globalization is now increasingly vulnerable to challenge.

NAFTA/GATT AND COMMON SENSE

The contested meanings of globalization in the United States have surfaced most explicitly in the intense public discussions surrounding recent agreements fostering further international liberalization, especially the North American Free Trade Agreement (NAFTA) and the Uruguay Round of the General Agreement on Tariffs and Trade (GATT), which created the World Trade Organization (WTO). NAFTA and GATT are important not only as agreements to reduce barriers to international trade and investment, but also as occasions for political argument in which latent tensions of liberal democratic capitalism—especially the ambivalence between private property on the one hand and social self-determination on the other—were once again represented in public discourse as open questions, a terrain of active sociopolitical struggle.

A powerful phalanx of social forces has arrayed itself behind the agenda of intensified market-led globalization. Academic economists, major corporations, corporate associations such as the Business Roundtable, and the mainstream press all vigorously supported NAFTA as part of a larger project of continuing global liberalization (Rupert, 1995b:664–669). There were two primary themes that consistently emerged from their pro-NAFTA representations. First, they claimed that NAFTA would encourage greater specialization according to comparative advantage. This specialization, coupled with intensified continental competition and greater economies of scale, would yield significant efficiency gains. Thus, NAFTA would produce lower prices for consumers and, in the long run, more jobs and higher incomes continent-wide (see, e.g., Dornbusch, 1991; Hufbauer and Schott, 1993–1994; Krugman, 1993). Second, editorials in influential newspapers such as the *New York Times* (November 17, 1993) and the *Washington Post* (November 16, 1993) argued that failure to enact the pact would represent not just a lost opportunity but also a potentially catastrophic U.S. abdication of its historic role as promoter of international liberalization, peace, and prosperity. Such abdication represents a giant step backward into the era of isolationism and protectionism. Generally portrayed as promising economic benefits to the American public and serving the national interest by sustaining a more open and liberal world, NAFTA received predominantly favorable press coverage and was editorially endorsed by numerous papers, large and small (Rupert, 1995b:667, 687, n. 11). Sandra Masur, of Eastman Kodak and the Business Roundtable, explained that the U.S. corporate community supported the pact not only because it would present immediate business opportunities but also because it was part of a larger global agenda: "The companies of the Roundtable are seeking across-the-board liberalization of trade in goods, services and investment" (Masur, 1991:102). This perspective was aggressively promoted to the public and to Congress by major corporate supporters and lobbies such as USA*NAFTA (Rupert, 1995b:668–669).

The agenda of increasing liberalization of trade and investment and the global integration of the U.S. economy has not gone unopposed, however. NAFTA in particular prompted vigorous opposition from a constellation of labor unions, consumer groups, environmentalists, and citizen activists, which argued that the trade pact augments the power of multinational capital relative to workers, unions, local communities, and citizens more generally. These groups framed an alternative vision of global political economy based on democratic self-determination and transnational linkages among working people and citizens. Rather than allow unfettered markets and the criterion of private profit to determine social outcomes, they emphasize the common sense value of "democracy" over liberalism's more traditional valuing of private property (Rupert, 1995b).

Left-progressive critics and anti-NAFTA coalitions found common ground not in a strategy of protectionism and closure but in a vision of a more participatory global order and a strategy of "fair trade." They sought to negotiate common labor, health, safety, environmental, and social standards to prevent a race toward the lowest common denominator—"downward harmonization" enforced by intensified market competition (Larudee, 1993). Progressives leveled similar sorts of arguments against the Uruguay Round of GATT, with its World Trade Organization enforcement mechanisms (e.g., Cavanagh, 1992; Nader et al., 1993). Unionists believed that NAFTA would enable corporate employers to use enhanced capital mobility and transcontinental competition ("whipsawing") between countries, plants, and workers to undermine actual or potential solidarity among workers and communities and to intensify exploitation throughout the continent (AFL-CIO, 1991; Moody and McGinn, 1992). In short, fears of a continental, hemispheric, or global political economy dominated by the institutionalized power of corporate capital brought NAFTA's labor critics together with environmental activists, consumer advocates, progressives, and others.

Some progressives framed the basic issue directly and explicitly in terms of democratization. In the words of John Cavanagh (1993:6–7):

> The key to genuine democracy in this decade will be the struggle by communities and citizens' organizations to control their own destinies, to take control of their own lands and natural resources, to collectively make the decisions that affect their futures. The free trade agreements that are currently on the table appropriate these decisions and toss them to the private sector.

Journalist William Greider argues that to achieve meaningful democracy in the United States requires a reorientation of popular thinking in which neither xenophobic nationalism nor a globalism based upon the individualistic ideology of market competition will suffice. Instead, he argues, the future of domestic democracy depends upon an internationalist worldview directly addressing relations of global political-economic inequality and domination:

> For ordinary Americans, traditionally independent and insular, the challenge requires them to think anew their place in the world. The only plausible way that citizens can defend themselves and their nation against the forces of globalization is to link their own interests cooperatively with the interests of other peoples in other nations—that is, with foreigners who are competitors for the jobs and production but who are also victimized by the system. Americans will have to create new democratic alliances across national borders with the less prosperous people caught in the same dilemma. Together, they have to impose new political standards on multinational enterprises and on their own governments. (Greider, 1993:196)

Greider's prescription strikes me as remarkable insofar as it directly addresses popular common sense and calls for the de-reification of conventional boundaries separating politics/economics, state/society, and domestic/international in order to negotiate a more democratic global economy. This vision of a democratizing transnational project resonates strongly with that of other progressives (e.g., Larudee, 1993; Brecher and Costello, 1994).

DEFENDING AMERICAN EXCEPTIONALISM:
FAR-RIGHT CRITIQUES OF GLOBALIZATION

Opposition to NAFTA/GATT was hardly univocal. Some voices of opposition explicitly rejected globalization in favor of nationalism, and interdependence in favor of autonomy. These groups were often dismissively labeled in the mainstream media as "paranoids" and "loonies," as if their perspective on politics and globalization might be explained away by some shared psychological problems. On the contrary, I want to suggest that far-right resistance to globalization is understandable as a response to changing socioeconomic circumstances, a response that draws upon the cognitive resources available in popular common sense to understand a complex and changing world in a way that maintains a stable identity. Far-right antiglobalists tap the most individualistic strains of American common sense, articulated often, but not always, with religious, nativist, and/or racist understandings of "Americanism." They construct an image of American exceptionalism embodying a quasi-religious faith in the divinely inspired wisdom of the original U.S. Constitution and the Founding Fathers as protectors of God-given individual liberties.

This faith leads these self-styled "Patriots" to interpret globalization as an alien tyranny engulfing the United States through a nefarious conspiracy that relentlessly erodes individual rights and liberties. On this view, globalization is profoundly threatening, and acts of resistance ranging from ideological struggle to mass violence may be justified in these terms. When working people and large segments of what used to be called the "middle class" experience chronic socioeconomic degradation unprecedented in postwar experience and formerly hegemonic ideologies appear increasingly threadbare, reconstructions of popular common sense that seem to explain a reality otherwise inscrutable, and that seem to point toward urgent political action, potentially pose far more serious sociopolitical issues than the widespread image of ridiculous dementia suggests.

The Conspiratorial Worldview: A Far-Right Family Resemblance

Although it is misleading to suggest that the far-right shares a single ideology or a unified political program, a conspiratorial worldview underlies various far-right narratives of globalization. Interpreting social life from within the limits of a rigidly individualistic ontology, the organic intellectuals of the far-right suggest that "there are really only two theories of history. Either things happen by accident, neither planned nor caused by anybody, or they happen because they *are* planned and somebody causes them to happen" (Abraham, 1985:9). This kind of reasoning is reflected in the common sense of grassroots Patriots. One member of an Ohio militia group explained to a *New York Times* reporter that he was increasingly inclined to view the world in terms of the conspiratorial belief system he had encountered: "Nothing in government occurs by accident. If it occurs, know that it was planned that way. To be planned . . . there must be planners. If you have planners, you must have a conspiracy" (Janofsky, 1995).

As a consequence of this agent-centered worldview, Patriots are unable to envision, explain, or critique the interrelated structures and processes that left-progressives see at work in the nexus between the United States and the global economy. Conspiratorial authors dismissively equate structural explanations with belief in "mysterious and unexplainable tides of history" (Abraham, 1985:9). The only apparent alternatives, then, are a view of history as essentially random, accidental, a string of implausible coincidences, or a view that looks for "cause and effect" in terms of the purposeful and morally significant actions of individuals and groups. In this way, conspiracy theory and its Manichaean construction of the world elevates itself to the status of scientific analysis of cause and effect (Abraham, 1985:7–16; also North, 1985:x–xi; Perloff, 1988:207–208; Robertson, 1991:8–9).

Far-right ideology generally asserts as axiom that the American system of government is properly understood as a *republic* and not as a democracy: The latter is dangerous and ungodly insofar as it subjects individual rights and liberties to the will of the community. As one subscriber to a Patriot listserv wrote, "Democracy is . . . the foundation of communism" (USA-Forever, June 16, 1995; see also John Birch Society, 1985; and Welch, 1986). The U.S. Founding Fathers designed a republican system of government to protect individual rights and economic liberty. The design of strictly limited government and a "free enterprise" economy is understood to be divinely inspired and the best possible social arrangement (Abraham, 1985:31, 84; McManus, 1995a:91, 99–100; North, 1985:x–xi, 246–249; Robertson, 1991:59, 203–205, 239–247; Jasper, 1992:101–103, 261–269). If something is terribly wrong in America, it cannot be due to flaws intrinsic to this social system; rather, somebody somewhere must be corrupting our political legacy.[5] John F. McManus, president of the John Birch Society (JBS)—long the most influential source of conspiracy doctrine on the far-right (see Mintz, 1985:chap. 7; Diamond, 1995:51–58, 147–152)—points toward "treasonous" and "satanically inspired" forces as the cause of America's ills (1995a:12, 70; see also Perloff, 1988:220–221; Robertson, 1991:9; Jasper, 1992:212–229):

> Most Americans know something is eating away at the foundations of this great nation. Unemployment, national and personal indebtedness, economic slowdown, loss of faith, declining national stature, a vaguely defined "new world order," broken families, and much more have stimulated worries from coast to coast. . . . Sadly, we witness the presence of powerful forces working to destroy the marvelous foundations given us by farseeing and noble men 200 years ago. (McManus, 1995a:ix–x)

The basic conspiracy theory that circulates widely on the far-right holds that cliques of evil individuals have been scheming to subjugate and exploit the world at least since 1776, when Adam Weisshaupt, a Bavarian scholar, formed a secret society known as the Illuminati.[6] Allegedly plotting to "overthrow . . . civil governments, the church, and private property" (Robertson, 1991:67) and to supplant these institutions with their own power and control, the Illuminati infiltrated European Freemasonry in order to insinuate themselves into elite networks of social power. This sect of Illuminated Freemasons, including the fabulously wealthy Rothschild family, is said to have been associated with the French Revolution and the Reign of Terror. Subsequently, the sect reputedly provided the model and funding for the Marxist-Bolshevik conspiracy for global domination. "All Karl Marx really did was to update and codify the very same revolutionary plans and principles set down seventy years earlier by Adam Weisshaupt" (Abraham, 1985:41; also Kah, 1991:24–30, 106–119; Mullins, 1992:3–4, 282–287; Robertson, 1991:67–71, 115, 180–185, 258).

Far-right intellectuals are able to assimilate Marxism into a global elite conspiracy because they do not recognize meaningful distinctions between political ideologies of "left" and "right." Rather, they see the world in terms of a continuum that stretches from complete and anarchic individual liberty on one end to total government domination on the other. The most desirable point on the spectrum is the "Constitutional Republic"—that is, sufficient government to avoid the extremes of anarchy but not enough to destroy individual liberty or to constrain the "free market." Monarchy, socialism, fascism, and elite-dominated and government-supported cartel capitalism are not seen as significantly different but as forms of the same anti-individualistic monopoly of power (Abraham, 1985:32; John Birch Society, 1985; Perloff, 1988:44–46; Robertson, 1991:71, 183).

Thus, it is not inconsistent for far-right intellectuals to claim that international bankers and the superrich are also part of the conspiracy to undermine individual liberties and their republican-free market sanctum. Indeed, the second major tentacle of the conspiracy involves the rise of a clique of international bankers whose almost unfathomable wealth allows them to grant or deny credit to governments, manipulate economies, extract superprofits, and exercise world-historical power. The Rothschilds, Rockefellers, Morgans, and their agents are said to have advanced the conspiratorial design by institutionalizing their financial powers through the creation of a U.S. central bank. They sought to control the money supply, manipulate directly the macroeconomy, facilitate the creation of credit money, and expand private and public debt. They helped establish an income tax through which hardworking citizens could be made to pay for public debt and enrich the megabankers. Patriots also allege that this cabal of the superwealthy bankrolled the Bolshevik revolution, providing an "enemy" against which the governments of the West had to defend themselves, further deepening public debt, expanding the scope of centralized government activity, and laying the basis for comprehensive social control by the financial elite (Abraham, 1985:43–87; Kah, 1991:12–22; Mullins, 1992:6–9, 64–75, 101–109, 214–215; Perloff, 1988:19–48; Robertson, 1991:61, 65, 71–73, 117–143).

The third major tentacle of the conspiracy has involved the fostering of an international "establishment" that would promote a "New World Order," the comprehensive political unification and socialization of the world under the domination of the elite conspirators, "a one-world government that scorns individuality, personality, nationhood, and even private property" (Robertson, 1991:156). In 1891, the Rothschilds and Cecil Rhodes allegedly established the Round Table—"a semi-secret internationalist group headquartered in London" (Perloff, 1988:36)—as a vehicle for promoting their global agenda. The Round Table then spawned both the Royal Institute of International Affairs in Britain and the Council on Foreign Relations (CFR) in the United States. The CFR was putatively dominated by the American members of the Round Table group and associates of the Rothschilds, such as J. P. Morgan and, later on, the Rockefellers. Members of this international establishment have occupied influential posts in government, business, law, journalism, and academia and have quietly but profoundly influenced the policies of the world's most powerful states. In the aftermath of World War II, this shadowy elite promoted the entire institutional infrastructure of the postwar world order: the UN, the Bretton Woods system, the Marshall Plan, and NATO. More recently, the CFR has worked with the Trilateral Commission and the Bilderberg Group toward the globalist agenda (Abraham, 1985:89–108; Kah, 1991:30–56; McManus, 1995a: 1–24, 61–63, 81–82; Mullins, 1992:22–23, 49–53, 163, 192–193, 293; Perloff, 1988:3–38, 71–74, 81–86; Robertson, 1991:33–58, 65–67, 95–115; Jasper, 1992:45–58, 178–181, 241–253; Tucker, 1995).

McManus makes it clear how some Americans may perceive that individual liberty requires resistance to this global agenda and thus how far-right ideology fuses individualism with nationalism:

> The world government sought by the architects of this new world order would mean an end to the nation we inherited, and the destruction of the greatest experiment in human liberty in the history of mankind. World government would also establish socialism in place of the free market system, a certain route to conversion of this nation into another Third World deadend. . . . The stakes are nothing short of a future marked by national independence and personal liberty. (McManus, 1995a:70, 103)

Preserving an individualistic, capitalist, Christian United States in the face of an insidious transnational threat is the necessary condition for avoiding the destruction of individual liberty, limited government, free enterprise, and religious freedom and forestalling their replacement by the unlimited power of global monopoly-socialism and its godless humanism.

This antiglobalist perspective is reproduced in the literature of various grassroots Patriot groups. For example, the Council on Domestic Relations[7] declares that "most, if not all, of the problems that our country is facing are due to the deliberate migration away from the supreme law of our land— the Constitution for the United States [*sic*]. . . . The promoters of this migration are the ultra-rich and ultra-powerful international banking and multinational corporations who seek to increase their power and control by promoting a one-world socialistic government. (Pardon the over-simplification) [*sic*]." Variants of this basic antigovernment, antiglobalist conspiracy narrative—more or less explicitly anti-Semitic or racist—circulate within and among the following (partially overlapping) communities:

1. The John Birch Society, which claims 40,000 to 60,000 members and a readership of more than 50,000 for its magazine, *The New American.*[8]
2. The Liberty Lobby, which has a membership of approximately 20,000 and claims a circulation of 120,000 for its tabloid, *The Spotlight.*[9]
3. The Patriot/militia/gun-rights/antitax/movements, which number approximately 10,000 to 40,000 in armed militia groups. The Militia Task Force of the Southern Poverty Law Center (Klanwatch) identifies 441 armed militias and 809 Patriot groups that are active nationwide.[10]
4. Neo-Nazi and affiliated white supremacy groups (e.g., Aryan Nations, National Alliance), which have attracted some 10,000 to 20,000 hardcore members and perhaps ten times as many sympathizers.[11]
5. Pat Robertson's Christian Coalition, which claims about 1 million members and has 1.8 million adherents on its mailing list. Robertson's publisher claims that approximately 550,000 copies of *New World Order* are now in print.[12]
6. The presidential campaign of Pat Buchanan.[13]

According to Chip Berlet (1995:2–3), the armed militias that have received so much media attention in recent years are an "offshoot of the larger and more diffuse Patriot movement[, which] is bracketed on the moderate side by the John Birch Society and the conspiratorial segment of Pat Robertson's audience, and on the more militant side by the Liberty Lobby and groups promoting themes historically associated with white supremacy and anti-Jewish bigotry."

Estimates of the total number of persons in the United States who are influenced by far-right movements and their conspiratorial antigovernment and antiglobalist ideology vary from a few hundred thousand to several million.[14] Whatever the actual number, it is clear that the worldview of right-wing populism has made inroads into mainstream politics through the influence of Pat Robertson's Christian Coalition (Lind, 1995a), members of the 1994 Republican congressional majority who are sympathetic with far-right ideology (Egan, 1995; Stern, 1996:128, 212–214), and Pat Buchanan's right-populist presidential campaign (J. Bennett, 1995).

Americanism in Peril: NAFTA, GATT, and the New World Order

Viewed from the antiglobalist perspective of the far-right, the significance of trade agreements such as NAFTA and GATT far exceed their economic costs or benefits. As Dan Druck (1993) of the Council on Domestic Relations explained to fellow Patriots in 1993:

> The passage of NAFTA would be a giant step toward a one world socialistic government. With the jelling of the European Economic Community . . . in Europe, NAFTA and GATT in the Americas [*sic*] and the formation of an Asian economic consortium, the three legs of the Tri-Lateralist plan for global unification of commercial and banking interests are rapidly coming to fruition. It is also an overall giant leap toward the New World Order's one-world government. NAFTA impacts far more than our jobs and our economy.

Similar interpretations are easy to find on the Internet. According to the Militia Task Force of the Southern Poverty Law Center, seventy or more World Wide Web pages propagate the worldviews of various far-right sects, from antigovernment Patriots and militias to white supremacists and neo-Nazis (Klanwatch, 1996:16; also Stern, 1996:225–230). Hundreds of computer bulletin boards and news groups do the same. Though variously articulate, the authors of Patriot documents on the Internet express fears that their rights and liberties are under assault by a federal government that is out of control and that their standard of living and identity as Americans are being corroded by processes of global economic and cultural integration driven by the machinations of transnational elites.

Such interpretations echo the ideological leaders of the far-right, such as the John Birch Society and its journal, *The New American*. One JBS writer, William Jasper (1993:19), claims that "the whole NAFTA-APEC-GATT trade waltz has been expertly choreographed by the same globalist Insiders of the Council on Foreign Relations (CFR) and Trilateral Commission (TC) who are also using concerns over supposed 'crises' involving the environment, security, population, poverty, refugees, debt, and nuclear proliferation to empower the United Nations."

Thomas Eddlem (1994:23), another JBS writer, argues that both NAFTA and GATT "call for bigger and more costly government, greater intrusions into the daily affairs of the American people, and a substantial transfer of US sovereignty to a host of new international governmental institutions." These agreements shift the weight of taxation even further away from tariffs, allegedly favored by the Founders, and toward more intrusive and freedom-destroying income taxes. Still more grave, NAFTA and GATT mire the United States in "an artificial state of economic dependency" that, like quicksand, inexorably draws the U.S. economy and political system into a global order dominated by the "Insiders." "The underlying strategy employed by the CFR/Trilateral alliance is that economic power leads to political control, and economic union is a necessary step toward political union" (Eddlem, 1994:27; see also Eddlem, 1992). John McManus assesses economic globalization in stark terms: "The goal is the breakdown of national sovereignty via economics. In the end, unless all of this is stopped, the 'new world order' will emerge and freedom will be a mere memory" (McManus, 1995b:19).

The JBS and the Liberty Lobby are the most important "Americanist" organizations promoting conspiratorial worldviews, but there are significant differences between them. JBS membership tends to be disproportionately well educated, relatively affluent, and professional.[15] Also, the Birch Society shuns explicit racism or anti-Semitism in its well-produced materials. However, the Liberty Lobby and its founder, Willis Carto, regularly participate in pseudo-populist politics promoting (more or less thinly veiled) anti-Semitism, Holocaust revisionism, and racial views of history (Mintz, 1985; L. Campbell, 1992; Diamond, 1995:140–160, 261–265). For the JBS, nationalism protects fundamental values of individualism: The meaning of American exceptionalism involves traditions of strictly limited republican government and free-market, entrepreneurial capitalism. For the Liberty Lobby, however, nationalism becomes intrinsically significant because its vision of Americanism constitutes an ethnic or racial identity. Through its lurid tabloid, *The Spotlight,* Liberty Lobby defends a "populist and nationalist agenda" that expresses "the point of view of the unorganized exploited middle class—the 'producers.'" These hardworking American taxpayers are doubly exploited by social parasites: the wealthy elite of stateless international bankers (read: Jews), who profit from interest payments on national and personal debt, and the welfare recipients (read: blacks and Hispanics), who live off the public dole.[16]

Writers associated with the Liberty Lobby stressed the loss of U.S. sovereignty in their interpretations of NAFTA and GATT, as did writers for the Birch publication. Yet the Lobby's populist pitch more directly addressed the fears of America's working "middle class" in this period of deindustrialization and internationalized production.

> There used to be an unwritten social contract between the middle class
> and the Establishment that went like this: America's capitalist economy
> would provide jobs—good paying jobs in a factory or office—that
> enabled an American worker to support his family on one income. . . . In
> return, the middle class worked hard, paid taxes and raised the next gener-
> ation to follow in their footsteps. . . . But sadly, so much has changed.
> (Hudson, 1993:16)

In the context of a vision of history in which nothing happens unless
some agent causes it to happen, *Spotlight* readers are led to ask: Who killed
the American Dream? In a signed article featured in the special NAFTA
issue of *Spotlight,* Willis Carto (1993:4) explains: "An extremely powerful
political lobby has developed among the community of international
traders. Their loyalty is only to their money, wherever it may be and
derived from whatever source. These capitalists are the greatest advocates
of free trade and are implacable enemies of national sovereignty. They are
far more dangerous to the nation than communists ever were."

Suggesting that the political debate over NAFTA was orchestrated as
part of a globalist conspiracy, *Spotlight* claimed that the corporate moguls
behind powerful and well-funded lobbies such as USA*NAFTA "are internationalists who also have membership in the Council on Foreign
Relations, the Trilateral Commission and the Bilderberg Group" (Arnold,
1993:12).

> Together, the Trilateralists and the Bilderbergers constitute a shadow
> world government, meeting secretly and in concert each spring. David
> Rockefeller dominates the Trilateralists; he shares power with the
> Rothschilds of Europe in the older Bilderberger group. . . . The
> Bilderbergers ordered the secret collection of international financiers,
> political leaders, media personalities, and business leaders to establish an
> "American Union", modeled after the [EC]. (Tucker, 1993:1)

Spotlight has published the commentaries of Eustace Mullins, a notori-
ous anti-Semitic writer,[17] who asserts that the real powers pressing for
globalization are stateless financiers whose only loyalty is to money (again,
read between the lines). "Behind these groups are . . . the super rich. They
are internationalists and have no loyalty to any country. . . . They see governments come and go, but they protect their interests. They are essentially
monopolists" (Mullins 1993:B-14).

Carto spells it out in comic book terms for *Spotlight* readers:

> Today, it is obvious that NAFTA is part of the overall plan for the "New
> World Order." . . . Today, the operating plan is a step-by-step progression
> to the final goal of ownership and control of all natural resources and
> every square inch of land and everything on it by a consortium of interna-
> tional supercapitalists: a gigantic holding company, a super–Bilderberg
> Society of mega-plutocrats. (Carto, 1993:22)

If NAFTA was a step toward the dreaded one-world government, then GATT was a giant leap into "the global plantation," in which "the non-productive global overseers will be siphoning the resources, financial and otherwise, of the world's producers" (Katson, 1994:16). Trisha Katson, Liberty Lobby's point person on GATT, described it as "a world economic government" unencumbered by the constitutional limitations from which the American republic drew its governmental legitimacy. Thus, rather than being viewed as the institutional infrastructure of a globalizing capitalism, GATT was seen as "the very fulfillment of international socialism, the nationless world envisioned by Karl Marx" (Katson, 1994:6, 8; see also Tucker, 1994).

In sum, Liberty Lobby and the JBS emphasize economic policies to support "free enterprise" and a strong "middle class." Both interpret NAFTA/GATT as part of a conspiratorial subversion of American sovereignty by forces dedicated to economic and political globalism, yet the pseudo-populism of Liberty Lobby is more nativist and racist than Birch Society ideology.

The most disturbing narratives of globalization, however, are those explicitly constructed in terms of a white supremacist political project. In these ideologies, the nationalism of the far-right is explicitly incorporated into a view of the world in which environmental differences have—through evolutionary processes—produced biologically unequal races. In its programmatic statement of goals and principles, the neo-Nazi National Alliance (n.d.) declares that "we [white Americans] have an obligation to our race as a collective agent of progress." On this view, "we need an economic system which, in contrast to Marxism, allows individuals to succeed in proportion to their capability and energy, but which, in contrast to capitalism, does not allow them to engage in socially or racially harmful activity, such as stifling competition or importing non white labor." Individual enterprise and initiative are to be encouraged, as long as they occur within a context of racial awareness and responsibility to the racial community. To the extent that they are seen to conflict, then, possibilities for individual gain through free trade may be overridden by racial responsibility.

I encountered these currents of racist antiglobalism at an anti-NAFTA rally primarily organized by and for unionists in the Syracuse, New York, area. Local neo-Nazis circulated through the crowd, distributing audio cassettes of the radio program "American Dissident Voices," produced by the National Alliance and featuring its leader, William Pierce.[18] On the program, Pierce (1992) speaks of the long-term decline of the U.S. economy, which he represents as the result of basic forces "which any high school dropout can understand." According to Pierce, internationalization of production and deindustrialization of the United States are two sides of the same coin and for the past forty-five years have been the deliberate policy of a "power elite." He describes this elite as "New World Order schemers" seeking to "permanently fasten their grip on the power and wealth of the world." There are "men in Washington and New York and London and Tel Aviv who are behind the policies which are exporting American jobs to Mexico and Hong Kong because they want to create a one-world economy in which Mexicans and Chinese and white Americans will have the same living standard." None too cryptically, Pierce refers to members of this hidden power elite as "the eternal outsiders, the eternal parasites whose strength always has been in their ability to manipulate and deceive rather than in their ability to build things." Stealthily, they control the media, public opinion, and the agendas of both major political parties in the United States. They support free trade agreements like NAFTA because they are "hell-bent" on creating "a world without national boundaries or even national distinctions, a world in which every national economy has been submerged in a global economy, a world with a single homogenized labor force and a uniform standard of living."

The inevitable result of global economic integration, Pierce tells his listeners, is racial integration and leveling, the mongrelization of the U.S. workforce and a corresponding loss of racial/national identity among U.S. workers, declining harmony and vigor in the workplace, lowered productivity, and growing social costs for the support of "nonproductive" elements in society. In tones of shock and alarm, his radio cohost characterizes this as "a long-term economic disaster for white American workers." Pierce suggests that the American people blunder into this ultimately self-defeating policy of free trade because "they like being able to buy consumer goods at low prices." These short-term benefits for individual consumers mask the long-term consequences for white American workers, whose standard of living is suppressed to Third World levels and whose national independence and capacity for racial agency is undermined.

To stop their impoverishment and subordination into an interdependent and mongrelized New World Order, Pierce (1992) urges white Americans to educate themselves about their racial identity and interests and to organize accordingly. Thereupon, he chillingly suggests, "You can be sure that we'll have a national cleaning day." Once white Americans regain control of their own destiny, Pierce envisions an economic policy of higher tariffs to protect white America's jobs from nonwhite countries with lower standards of living and thus to end insidious deindustrialization. "We might even justify the elimination of trade barriers between a racially cleansed United States and a selected group of other White countries," provided that these racially similar nations were united under a single political authority that Pierce calls "the Aryan World Order" (Pierce, n.d.).

And what of the rest of the world? To prevent Third World overpopulation from endangering the global ecosystem and thus the racial living spaces of white nations, Pierce explicitly advocates genocide on a global scale. Without equivocation, he calls for "the radical depopulation of the non-White world" using "modern chemical and biological means" (Pierce, n.d.). This horrifying vision of a white supremacist response to globalization—a final solution in the United States followed by global genocide to foster an "Aryan World Order"—illustrates the extremes to which the scapegoating tendencies implicit in conspiratorial narratives so readily lend themselves.

Less explicitly racist or anti-Semitic Patriots may wish to distance themselves from the bile-churning politics of a William Pierce, but identifying scapegoats is implicit in the very structure of a conspiratorial narrative and its central questions: Who is to blame for our problems? How can "they" be stopped? One caller to a Patriot-oriented radio talk show grasped this fundamental logic: "The problem we have right now is who do we shoot . . . ?" (quoted in Stern, 1996:223).

Mainstreaming Far-Right Ideology: Robertson and Buchanan

Conspiratorial ideologies of globalization are hardly the exclusive province of tiny sects of paranoid mountain men or platoons of weekend warriors, as sound-bite stereotypes might suggest. One of the most important conduits channeling far-right conspiratorial ideology toward a more mainstream mass audience is evangelist Pat Robertson, founder of the Christian Broadcasting Network and the politically powerful Christian Coalition (see Durham, 1995; Lind, 1995a; Diamond, 1995:228–256, 289–306, 310–312). In his best-selling book *The New World Order,* Robertson echoes Birch Society rhetoric, claiming that political events "are not the accidents and coincidences we are generally led to believe." Tendencies toward globalization "spring, instead, from the depth of something that is evil" (1991:9). The Establishment (especially the CFR) seeks "to form a world system in which enlightened [i.e., Illuminated-MR] monopolistic capitalism can bring all the diverse currencies, banking systems, credit, manufacturing, and raw materials into one government-supervised whole, policed of course by their own world army" (1991:97). This deeply troubles Robertson because the constitutional order that protects the God-given rights of individual Americans rests in turn upon the foundation of U.S. sovereignty (1991:203–205, 239–247). To undermine that foundation is to imperil God's order, yet this appears to be the precise project of the Establishment's cosmopolitan and godless humanism (1991:95–115, 167–185). Robertson concludes: "The stream of world order flowing from the Illuminati [through the Establishment] is clearly occultic and satanic" (1991:115). Globalization is part and parcel of a diabolical plan to create "a

new order for the human race under the domination of Lucifer and his fol-
lowers" (1991:37).

While readers impressed with Robertson's conjuring of demons might
feel justified in inferring that he would take a dim view of global economic
integration, he expresses instead a quite conventional liberal commitment
to the principle of free trade as a way to increase the total global product
(1991:267; *700 Club:* November 10, 1993; November 28, 1994; November
29, 1994). His positions on specific trade agreements were ambivalent,
however. Robertson reaffirmed his general support for free trade and
endorsed the NAFTA agreement on his television talk show (*700 Club:*
November 10, 1993). But he later described the Uruguay Round of GATT
as "flawed" insofar as the WTO could effectively undermine U.S. sovereignty. He lamented that U.S. trade negotiators and fast-track legislation
had put Americans in a take-it-or-leave-it position where rejecting this
problematic agreement would "blow up world trade." Pondering how we
got into this mess, Robertson explained that "there are a group of people in
America that just cannot stand American sovereignty. They just have to
have a world government that somehow dominates America" (*700 Club:*
November 28, 1994).[19] Clearly, then, Robertson represented GATT as a
step toward the New World Order, a step away from God's design as mani-
fested in the U.S. Constitution, and a victory for the forces of evil.

Another important vehicle for the injection of New World Order ideology into the political mainstream has been the right-populist punditry and
the 1995–1996 presidential campaign of Patrick Buchanan (J. Bennett,
1995, 1996; Sanger, 1995; Frantz and Janofsky, 1996; Gladwell, 1996). In
his columns and speeches, Buchanan focuses attention on the plight of U.S.
workers and describes NAFTA, GATT, and globalization in a narrative of
elite perfidy, the destruction of national identity and individual liberty, and
the creation of a tyrannical New World Order.

Although Buchanan made much of the impoverishment of U.S. workers by globalizing corporations, his primary concern—and that of the conspiratorial far-right—was that NAFTA brought with it "the virus of globalism" (Buchanan, 1993b).

> Though advertised as "free trade", [NAFTA] is anti-freedom, 1,200 pages
> of rules, regulations, laws, fines, commissions . . . setting up no fewer
> than 49 new bureaucracies. . . . It is part of a skeletal structure for world
> government. (Buchanan, 1993a)
>   NAFTA is about America's sovereignty, liberty and destiny. It is
> about whether we hand down to the next generation the same free and
> independent country handed down to us; or whether 21st Century America
> becomes but a subsidiary of the New International Economic Order.
> (Buchanan, 1993b)

In his presidential campaign, Buchanan vigorously denounced globalization and declared: "When I raise my hand to take the oath of office, this whole new world order is coming crashing down" (quoted in Sanger, 1995). Describing what he meant by "new world order," Buchanan explained:

> The UN is its political arm. The so-called International Monetary Fund is going to be the Federal Reserve of the world. The World Bank will provide the income transfers from the United States all over the world. . . . The World Court will prosecute and convict people and their countries, take their citizens and try them in international tribunals. The World Trade Organization . . . will eventually get . . . more and more control of world trade, until one day we wake up like Gulliver, find ourselves tied down . . . with tiny silk strands that by the thousands have been done up during the night, with the strongest nation on earth suddenly immobile. (Buchanan, 1996)

If elected, Buchanan vowed, he would restrict foreign aid, curtail U.S. participation in multilateral institutions and UN peacekeeping missions, withdraw the United States from NAFTA and GATT, and constrict the flow of immigrants into the United States, which he claimed suppressed the wages of U.S. workers (Buchanan, 1995c). He promised to levy selective tariffs upon specific competitor nations that enjoyed a trade surplus with the United States, especially Japan and China. Like some progressives, he also suggested "a social tariff on Third World manufactured goods" to protect U.S. workers from downward pressure on wage, health, safety, and environmental standards (Buchanan, 1995b; Gladwell, 1996). Buchanan called Americans to ride to the sound of the guns in his "second war of American independence, to recapture US sovereignty from faceless global bureaucrats who view our country as but a vast, rich province to be plundered and looted on behalf of their New World Order" (1994).

How is it that the United States, with its extraordinary constitutional system and exceptional power, has "handed off its sovereignty" to global institutions? Who "is pulling the strings"? Buchanan points the finger at "the multinational corporations and the Wall Street financial elite."

> Real power in America belongs to the Manhattan Money Power, the one power to which neither party is any longer able to say "No!" [U.S. Treasury Secretary Robert] Rubin said, "There must be a broad understanding that we really and truly are in a new world where we are dependent on other nations in ways that we never were before." That is the authentic voice of Goldman Sachs, and regrettably, of our own Republican elites. They are saying, all of them, that America's sovereignty, independence and liberty are things of the past. . . . We must all accept our dependency on the New World Order. . . . But we never voted our sovereignty away. If it is gone, they sold us out; they traded it away, without our permission. (Buchanan, 1995a)

When asked by interviewers if his rhetoric included far-right "code words," Buchanan responded directly: "There is nothing code-word about it, I don't need to speak in code. . . . There are embryonic institutions of world government being formed even as we speak" (quoted in J. Bennett, 1996). Buchanan denied charges of anti-Semitism and links to far-right or white supremacist groups, but his campaign was plagued by a series of revelations about unseemly statements by and unsavory connections among members of his staff (Buchanan for President, 1996; Frantz and Janofsky, 1996; Zeskind, 1996). Whether or not Buchanan actually subscribes to the conspiratorial vision of the far-right, he clearly speaks in terms that lend themselves to a conspiratorial interpretation. Far-right antiglobalists can readily situate themselves and find reflections of their xenophobia in his language. Thus, Buchanan's candidacy drew the endorsement of the Liberty Lobby's *Spotlight* and was supported by members of the JBS, various self-described Patriots, and some white supremacists.[20]

In the 1996 presidential primary, Buchanan stunned the Republican Party with his wins in Louisiana and New Hampshire and his strong second-place showings in the rust belt states of Michigan and Wisconsin, but the significance of his campaign cannot be summarized in terms of the number of votes. At a time when the historical structures underlying postwar prosperity are visibly degenerating and ideologies of liberal internationalism appear increasingly dubious to average Americans, Buchanan delivers the ideology of right-populism to their doorstep along with their morning paper. He propels it into areas of public discourse where it might otherwise not have seen the light of day.

FEAR AND LOATHING: THE GLOBAL POWER BLOC RECOGNIZES THE NEW POPULISM

The new populism stoked by Pat Buchanan and company is being taken seriously by the constellation of capitalists, state managers, and intellectuals who have fostered economic globalization as part of a transnational hegemonic project. As Buchanan became a symbol of popular discontent, a flurry of critical commentaries appeared in the mainstream press bashing his policy proposals as atavistic, crude, isolationist, and protectionist (e.g., Friedman, 1996; Hormats, 1996). One such criticism was leveled by James Bacchus, the sole U.S. member of the WTO appeals panel, who characterized Buchananism as a threat to the system of global liberalization painstakingly constructed through postwar decades: "It would be economic suicide to throw it all away now" (quoted in Nordheimer, 1996).

At the 1996 World Economic Forum, an annual meeting of "2,000 or so top businessmen, politicians and academics," the central theme was "sustaining globalization" (*The Economist,* 1996). Forum organizers Klaus

Schwab and Claude Smadja (1996) published an essay in the *International Herald Tribune* suggesting that economic globalization "has entered a critical phase" in which economic and political relationships—both globally and within countries—are being painfully restructured. Schwab and Smadja acknowledge that these changes are devastating large numbers of working people in "the industrial democracies," with heightened mass insecurity resulting in "the rise of a new brand of populist politicians." They fear the absence of effective measures to address the social circumstances of working people and the weakened ideological legitimacy of global capitalism. They warn that the new populism may continue to gain strength, threaten further progress toward the agenda of globalization, and "test the social fabric of the democracies in an unprecedented way."

Ethan Kapstein, director of studies for the Council on Foreign Relations, has suggested that the new populism increasingly evident across the OECD countries represents a backlash against the combination of intensified global competitive pressures and a political climate dominated by the interests of investors. The growth-oriented "embedded liberalism" compromise has been abandoned in favor of anti-inflationary policies that effectively suppresses the real standard of living of working people while maintaining the long-term profitability of investments. Kapstein warns: "If the post-World War II social contract with workers—of full employment and comprehensive social welfare—is to be broken, political support for the burgeoning global economy could easily collapse." In the absence of growth-oriented and internationally coordinated measures to ease the plight of those hardest hit by the new global competition—primarily less skilled workers and middle managers—politics in the industrial countries could well take an ugly turn. "Populists and demogogues of various stripes will find 'solutions' to contemporary economic problems in protectionism and xenophobia" (Kapstein, 1996:16–17). Were that to occur, he suggests, the result would be a loss of the potential aggregate income made available by an extended Smithian division of labor, and the emergence of a zero-sum world in which both peace and prosperity become more difficult to realize.

In these remarkable statements—by representatives of the constellation of social forces whose hegemony gave birth to long-term processes of globalization—the importance of ideological struggle and the potential threat of populism and nationalism to a sustained liberal hegemony are frankly acknowledged. It is hardly clear that this global ruling class is abandoning its consensus policies that magnify the impact of market forces on working people: low inflation and fiscal retrenchment, "flexible labor markets," and free trade (*The Economist*, 1996). However, expressions of popular disaffection are awakening some among this elite to the political fragility of both globalization and their continued global social power.

TENSIONS AND POSSIBILITIES
OF POST-FORDIST COMMON SENSE

We are witnessing the long and painful demise of the Fordist sociopolitical regime through which American industrial workers were incorporated into the hegemonic bloc that constructed the postwar global order (Rupert, 1995a). Like a deceptively stable southern California hillside, the social conditions of life for average Americans are shifting in ways almost unthinkable a relatively short time ago. Finding their economic security and their political identity increasingly problematic, the easy certainties of the Cold War no longer providing fixed ideological reference points, American working people are trying to make sense of a rapidly changing world. It is in this context that alternative narratives of globalization increasingly challenge the blandishments of liberal internationalists. Some of these interpretations emphasize the antidemocratic character of transnational capitalism and the need to construct popular-democratic institutions within the world economy. Others view globalization as a process infused with evil intent, the product of alien treacheries designed to undermine the American Constitutional Republic and its guarantees of individual rights. My claim in this chapter is that these alternative visions of globalization are circulating among various segments of the U.S. population, seeking to embed themselves in popular common sense and thus to define the horizons of political action—and that current sociopolitical conditions create a favorable environment to such counter-hegemonic ideologies.

The worldview of neoliberal internationalism—in which states and corporations create the rules for global economic integration—faces challenges that emphasize different aspects of popular common sense in order to envision alternative possible worlds. Drawing on the democratic strains of popular common sense, what I have called the left-progressive position, would construct a world in which the global economy is explicitly politicized, corporate power is confronted by transnational coalitions of popular forces, and a framework of democratically developed standards provides social accountability for global economic actors. The antiglobalist position of the far-right, on the other hand, envisions a world in which Americans are uniquely privileged inheritors of a divinely inspired sociopolitical order that must at all costs be defended against external intrusions and internal subversion. If I am correct in my belief that the restructuring of the postwar order is creating conditions that are increasingly favorable for reconstructions of popular common sense, then it will be important for a progressive political movement to define itself not only in terms of its opposition to corporate power and neoliberal internationalism—which are themes readily co-opted into the radical right worldview—but also clearly and explicitly to distinguish its democratizing vision from the reactionary nationalism of the populist right.

In these ideological contests, the future shape of transnational political order may be at stake. Although it may be unrealistic to expect the emergence of some simple and homogeneous political identity such as "global proletariat," I contend that transnational production is creating greater overlap in the structural situations of working people in various parts of the world. Even U.S. workers are becoming more sensitive to this tendency, as their formerly privileged position is revoked and they are subjected more directly to global market forces and the power of global capital. The emerging historical structure of transnational capitalism may generate the potential for the construction of political identities and projects that transcend state-centric understandings of politics and facilitate transnational movements to contest the global dominance of capital.

The real danger of the far-right, as I see it, is not so much that they will succeed in constructing a thousand-year Reich in the United States or an "Aryan World Order." Rather, they threaten to submerge the democratic aspects of popular common sense beneath long-standing currents of cultural, racial, or economic nationalism. To the extent that they succeed in doing so, the potential for democratizing transnational political projects will be blocked. U.S. workers will look upon other segments of the global labor pool and will see competitors, rivals, or enemies rather than potential partners in the construction of a new world. They will see themselves and their jobs more closely identified with their employer (and, of course, its profits) than with "foreign" workers, whose alleged willingness to work harder for less will be blamed for the misfortunes of God's chosen people—the American "middle class." Despite its anticorporate banners, far-right ideology not only fails to effectively challenge the power of global capital but actually augments it. Any movement that means to contest that power must also challenge the ideological claims of the nationalist right.

NOTES

Some parts of this chapter have been previously published in "Globalization and the Reconstruction of Popular Common Sense in the US" in S. Gill and J. Mittelman, eds., *Innovation and Transformation in International Studies* (Cambridge University Press, 1997), and are reprinted with the permission of Cambridge University Press.

I am grateful to Kurt Burch for editorial assistance above and beyond the call of duty: This chapter is much the better for his diligence.

1. See Gramsci (1971:323–334, 419–425) for his reflections on popular "common sense." I discuss my appropriation of this concept in Rupert (1997). This chapter participates in an ongoing Gramscian research program in IPE (e.g., Rupert, 1995a, 1995b, 1997). See Gill (1993) for views on the relevance of Gramsci to IPE.

2. "Historic bloc" is a Gramscian concept (e.g., Gramsci, 1971:168, 366, 377). More than a simple coalition of social forces, a *historic bloc* is rooted in material social relations and unites predominant social forces under the umbrella of a

common ideological vision. The formation of a historic bloc is thus a precondition of hegemony.

3. I note for the reader that I have been a participant in these struggles. I make no claims to neutrality. I was active in the Fair Trade Coalition of Central New York, which vigorously opposed NAFTA. My sympathies lie with progressive (as opposed to Americanist) critics of corporate-dominated globalization.

4. By this, I do not mean to say that anticommunist ideology no longer has any significance, but that its significance has changed. In the postwar decades, anti-communism served as a unifying ideology that brought together disparate social forces—such as formerly insurrectionary industrial unions and formerly isolationist conservatives—in the project of reconstructing a liberal capitalist world (see Rupert, 1995a: chaps. 5, 7; Diamond, 1995:29–36). As such, it was a central component in the ideology that enabled a hegemonic project. Its significance today is more negative, disposing popular common sense against political programs that could be labeled "socialist" insofar as they are understood to have been "proven" unworkable by the demise of Stalinism. This situation presents contemporary progressives with the challenges of addressing themes that resonate in popular common sense and articulating their political programs in terms of democratizing an undemocratic transnational political economy.

5. Whereas some variants of this conspiracy narrative are explicitly racist or anti-Semitic, others have attempted to distance themselves from overt anti-Semitism (e.g., Abraham, Robertson, John Birch Society). On Robertson's attempt, see Lind (1995a), and on the ensuing controversy, see Lind (1995b), Heilbrunn (1995), and the *New York Times* (1995: March 2, 4, 5, 9, 20, April 6, 18, 27). On anti-Semitism in the Patriot-militia movement more generally, see Stern (1996:224–227).

6. The Illuminati, existing in Germany between 1776 and 1785, was a briefly popular "rationalistic society" with "affinities" toward Freemasonry (Harris and Levey, 1975:1315). Tales of the "Illuminism conspiracy" have been a part of U.S. nativism since the late eighteenth century (D. Bennett, 1995:22–26).

7. Council on Domestic Relations home page: http://www.logoplex.com/shops/cdr/cdr.html.

8. Interview with John Birch Society officials, October 13, 1995, and phone query to *New American,* May 20, 1996. On JBS more generally, see Mintz (1985:141–162), D. Bennett (1995:315–323, 430–431), and Diamond (1995:51–58, 147–151). The JBS officials with whom I spoke claimed that membership had grown at an increasing rate in recent years, which they attribute to a general sense among U.S. citizens that the federal government is out of control (October 13, 1995). Chip Berlet told me that his estimate of current JBS membership was in the range of 40,000 to 50,000, up from a low of about 20,000 in the 1980s (June 10, 1995). On the broader influence of JBS ideology on the Christian right, see Durham (1995).

9. Telephone query to *Spotlight* circulation department, October 31, 1995. On Liberty Lobby, see Mintz (1985), L. Campbell (1992), Center for Democratic Renewal (1994), D. Bennett (1995:356–357, 430), and Diamond (1995:85, 140–160, 261–265, 295). Material from *Spotlight* is accessible at a number of Patriot movement websites, although Liberty Lobby is controversial among Patriots, some of whom explicitly denounce its anti-Semitic tendencies.

10. Berlet (1995), Klanwatch (1996:5, 58). On the militia/Patriot movement, see also D. Bennett (1995:446–475), Berlet and Lyons (1995), Wills (1995), Dees (1996), and Stern (1996).

11. Based on 1989 estimates compiled by Elinor Langer and reported in Diamond (1995:257). See also D. Bennett (1995:431–445).

12. On Christian Coalition membership, see Lind (1995a:21). *New World Order* copies in print from phone interview with Thomas Nelson Publishers, July 23, 1995. On the influence of JBS ideology within the new Christian right, see Durham (1995). On the rise of the Christian right more generally, see D. Bennett (1995:413–428) and Diamond (1995:228–256).

13. Many useful documents have been available at the official Buchanan for President Campaign web site: http://www.buchanan.org/. More controversial items have appeared at the unofficial Buchanan site: http://www.iac.net:80/~davcam/pat.html.

14. My colleague Michael Barkun is one of the leading students of Christian Identity theology and the racist right (see Barkun, 1994). He believes that the conspiratorial far-right comprises no more than 200,000 people. However, Chip Berlet of Political Research Associates estimates that the so-called Patriot movement— broadly understood as persons or groups under the influence of conspiratorial ideologies—may embrace as many as five million people (Berlet, 1995).

15. Interview with John Birch Society officials, October 31, 1995, who described JBS members as drawn from the ranks of businessmen, doctors, dentists, and police officers. This is generally corroborated by the findings in Kraft (1992), a study based on the 1987 membership mailing list of the JBS obtained by Political Research Associates.

16. The wording I am quoting is from two pamphlets: "Liberty Lobby . . . Looking Forward" and "Why Subscribe to *The Spotlight*?" On producers versus parasites, see L. Campbell (1992) and Berlet (1995). On the Lobby's "populism" more generally, see Diamond (1995:140–152, 261–262).

17. On Mullins's role in the propagation of anti-Semitic conspiracy theories, see Mintz (1985:100) and Heilbrunn (1995). I find it hard to imagine that anyone even dimly aware of the long history of Western anti-Semitism could read Mullins's venomous characterization of cosmopolitan conspirators as biologically predisposed toward parasitism without inferring that the author is talking about Jews and suggesting a final solution (Mullins, 1992:286–297).

18. Pierce has recently gained a measure of national notoriety as the pseudonymous author of *The Turner Diaries,* a fictionalized account of a white supremacist guerrilla war against the federal government that includes a fertilizer bombing of a federal office building. Pierce's book, along with *Spotlight,* were widely reported to be Timothy McVeigh's favorite reading material. On Pierce's career and influence, see Mintz (1985:129), D. Bennett (1995:348–349, 437–438), Dees (1996:135–170, 176–178, 202–203), and Stern (1996:53–55, 192). On the distinct Christian Identity variant of white supremacist ideology, see Barkun (1994).

19. I am grateful to Gene Kapp of the Christian Broadcasting Network for making available to me relevant excerpts of *700 Club* transcripts.

20. For favorable coverage of Buchanan's candidacy in far-right media, see Piper (1995), McManus (1996), and D. Black (n.d.). *The Spotlight* web page features the Buchanan for President campaign logo:http://nethomes.com/Miracle/Spotlight/tws.html. In interviews with officials of the John Birch Society, October 13, 1995, I was told that they viewed Buchanan as being as close as they could probably get to a viable candidate who reflected their perspective. For several months during 1995, I subscribed to a Patriot listserv called USA-Forever: Many subscribers expressed their support for Buchanan, though several hard-core Patriots refused to endorse a candidate unless he or she promised to attack the citadel of financial power by abolishing the Federal Reserve. Others were suspicious of Buchanan's Catholicism. One subscriber denounced him for allegedly swearing an oath of allegiance to the Knights of Malta.

Wayne S. Cox
Claire Turenne Sjolander

8

The Global Village and the Global Ghetto: Realism, Structural Materialism, and Agency in Globalization

When I go to my gas station in Japan, five young men wearing uniforms jump on my car. They not only check the oil but also wash the tires and wash the lights. . . . I pay a lot of money for the gas. . . . Then I come to Washington, and in Washington gas is much cheaper. Nobody washes the tires, nobody does anything for me, but here, too, there are five young men. The five young men who in Japan are employed to wash my car are, here, standing around, unemployed, waiting to rob my car. I still have to pay for them, through my taxes, through imprisonment, through a failed welfare system. I still have to pay for them. But in Japan at least they clean my car.

—Edward Luttwak, quoted in *Harper's* (1996:47)

It is an academic truism in the latter half of the 1990s that the number of studies exploring the meanings and consequences of "globalization" has proliferated. As the world becomes smaller, we are supposed to *think* globally, despite the evident and daunting challenge such thought represents (Barnet and Cavanagh, 1994:13). Globalization appears to be universal and universalizing, intensifying "global" interdependence, compressing space, accelerating time, and increasing the "consciousness of the global whole in the twentieth century" (Robertson, 1992:8; also Mittelman, 1996:3). Globalization scholars assume everyone is subject to the winds of global change and none can escape its dictates.

Despite the homogenizing tendencies of globalization—whether real or merely rhetorical—difference continues to exist. Globalization appears to deny this difference (otherness) and, simultaneously, to bring it more sharply into focus. While globalization's ideological content heralds the borderless and stateless world (Chesnais, 1994:14), local identities and rivalries become all the more apparent. Globalization and its paradoxes make the world both a more *global* and a more *splintered* reality, yet the splintering occurs upon new axes. Thus, the paradoxes of globalization encourage an American to construct "foreign" gas station attendants as "us" (because they have similar values and are nonthreatening and productive despite affiliation to a different ethnic group, state, territory, and class) and to construct some U.S. citizens as "other" (because they have incommensurable values and are threatening and a "drain" on society despite affiliation to the same state and territory).

Identifying "us" and "other" is no longer primarily dependent upon the geopolitical categories of state sovereignty and territory or upon the material categories of capital and labor that oriented the development of International Relations (IR) and International Political Economy (IPE). The categories of "us" and "other" are not simply questions of group identity, ethnicity, or affiliation, for these labels harken the typologies of our traditional paradigms. Globalization transforms "us" and "other" into malleable categories both imposed and chosen by individuals. The traditional paradigms of IR and IPE obscure the (re)creation of difference or "otherness" and thereby obscure the bases of possible political action. In confronting the disciplinary limits of these paradigms, this chapter seeks to pose new questions. Specifically, how does globalization (re)articulate our understanding of the agents of global society? How does it construct agency beyond the traditional paradigmatic categories of state and class? Whom do these new agencies empower and whom do they exploit?

Although tensions between constructions of "sameness" and "otherness" are not new, globalization may now manifest them more pervasively than in the past. Yet the fields of IR and IPE have not confronted these tensions. We believe that this inability results from the fields' traditional theoretical tools. We illustrate this argument by briefly examining realism and structural materialism, two of the central and evolving paradigms in the study of IR/IPE. Each of these approaches enables us to see different "parts" of the globalization processes, but in vastly different and partial ways. Realist analyses of the changing global order leave us with a need to externalize and territorialize conceptions of otherness. Structural materialists focus on the universalizing elements of globalization to an extent that it makes it difficult to conceive "otherness." The main theoretical perspectives of IR/IPE enable us to see either *political* territorial constructions of "us" and "other" or the universalizing *economic* processes of global capital. Pairing these perspectives informs globalization as a process of both integration and fragmentation, but it does not illuminate how these processes are intimately linked to the *social* realities of human experience.

Precisely because globalization cannot be limited to geopolitical or material categories, it becomes important to broaden our inquiry. Constructivist methods do not answer all the challenges posed by the processes of globalization, but they allow us to see and frame the issues. Peoples' experiences with globalization and reactions to it depend intrinsically upon how globalization redefines agency. Such redefinitions inherently affect political action at the close of the twentieth century. In short, the question of how IR/IPE constructs globalization is not merely an academic exercise, but an exercise in the construction of globalization itself. What our theoretical constructs permit us to see and what they hide from view are critical to the global complexities we help to decipher—and to shape.

INTERNATIONAL RELATIONS, REALISM, AND "OTHERNESS"

Dualist categories of "us" and "them" are not new to IR/IPE. In particular, the realist paradigm constructs these dualisms as fundamental to its theoretical understanding of global politics. Realism assumes that the state and the subsumed national interest represent a collective "us." Competing states represent the collective "other." That is, realists tie "us" and "other" to the nation-state and to the idea of territory. Realists territorialize "sameness" and "otherness" as matters of political sovereignty. Then, guided by the premise of global anarchy, realism finds structure in balances of power between "us" and "other."

When confronted by the contradictions of globalization, realists hold to "core" concepts: the sovereign state, (state) power, anarchy, and national (thereby global) security. Realists "territorialize" new "transnational" or "globalized" challenges to state authority and primacy.

> The 1990s . . . demand a redefinition of what constitutes *national* security. In the 1970s the concept was expanded to include international economics as it became clear that the U.S. economy was no longer the independent force it had once been, but was powerfully affected by economic policies in dozens of other countries. Global developments now suggest the need for another, analogous, broadening of the definition of *national* security to include resource, environmental, and demographic issues. (Mathews, 1994:274, italics added)

The dualist categories of "us" and "other" were easily constructed and maintained by the Cold War system. Each side in a balance-of-power system constructs itself as "us" and imposes "otherness" upon adversaries in crude yet politically effective ways. Indeed, Cold War practices enshrined the conceptual construction of the geopolitical/territorial "us" and "other." Yet with the collapse of the Cold War, "us" versus "them" dualisms persist.

For realists, the demise of the Cold War has not ended the anarchic global environment or limited states' use of "power" to pursue national interests. Although an East-West balance of power is largely past, what remains are realism's basic assumptions about the central actors in global politics, prevailing conditions, and the requirements for achieving stability in the context of global anarchy. Realists understand the new challenges to (state) security through theoretical frameworks that compartmentalize those challenges. One may reasonably ask, Have new "global" challenges significantly altered the theoretical constructs of realism? Mearsheimer (1990), for example, does not think so. He argues that global processes may have eroded the Cold War system, and he mourns its absence.

Gray (1996:248) re-emphasizes the seeming permanence of territorial geopolitics: "Today, notwithstanding the reality and exaggeration of transnational phenomena, world politics is still keyed to territorially based and defined states." Sovereignty and state power continue to be "pervasive in world politics" (Gray, 1996:248). Power relations among states result in power systems that are, for realists, relatively stable and therefore relatively peaceful. The task of identifying "good/us" and "bad/other" states becomes fairly easy. During most of the twentieth century, the important "others" were those who attempted to challenge the stability of an international system of state-based power relationships. "Good" states do not challenge the status quo; "bad" states challenge the territory and therefore the sovereignty of existing states.

This Western, realist logic easily constructed the Soviet Union as an expansive, aggressive, land-grabbing, evil empire that was intrinsically "other." Of course, Cold War constructions were reciprocal. Soviet leaders cast the United States as an expansionist capitalist empire, an "other." Both the United States and the Soviet Union shared an interest in maintaining the international system and dominating a bloc. However, each constructed the other as an adversary that violated the international rules of territorially based conduct. Further, realism constructs adversaries among other states (high politics) and nonstate destabilizing forces that challenge the legitimacy of existing sovereign units. In this sense, realism constructed two levels of adversary, the most important of which was elevated to the level of high politics.

In the wake of the collapse of the Cold War system, Saddam Hussein's greatest transgression was not his genocidal treatment of domestic populations, but his violation of the "basic rules of conduct" governing the behavior of states in the international system. He posed a threat to (state) sovereignty. His other transgressions were fodder for the construction of an image of the Iraqi state and citizenry (under the individualized label of "Saddam") as evil, despotic, anti-Western, and antiprogressive. In short, Saddam Hussein became the personification of "otherness" regardless of the political and social context from which his and the Iraqi state's actions emerged (W. Cox, 1994:77). The use of such dualisms, fundamental to realism, did not end with the Cold War. They remain central to realism's theoretical construction of the post–Cold War (globalizing) world.

Although states may be central in constructing the dualisms associated with war, they are less able to construct or constrain other globalizing phenomena. Consider the frustrated efforts of realists to "territorialize" cyberspace by attempting to (re)establish the primacy of sovereign state boundaries. Sovereign states are to use cyberspace *in order to advance state power* and therefore to ensure geopolitical stability through the exercise of hegemonic control:

> In some ways, extended information dominance is a version of traditional arms shipments. But supplying bitstreams has several advantages over supplying arms. First, bitstreams do not leave the kind of fingerprints that arms do. Secondly, bitstreams multiply forces while arms add to them. Thirdly, bitstreams are easier to deliver and easier to turn off. . . . Fourthly, once a bitstream is generated, making a second copy is cheap, while a tank sent abroad is a tank one no longer has. Lastly, offering allies specific illuminated vision of the battlespace does far more to lend one's own perspective on conflict than the mere provision of material can. (Libicki, 1996:267)

Territorialization of that which has so far largely defied territory is not only necessary to preserve state control, but also it is the only possible "solution" that can be proposed to the anarchy of the Internet by a perspective that continues to privilege the state.

Although the information revolution often associated with the processes of globalization is not easily (territorially) compartmentalized, realist tools are deployed to understand it. Cyberspace, currently a potential "other," can be "tamed" (and made "us") through the creation of an information monopoly that deliberately imposes a hegemonic order. In this reading, control over the emerging information highway holds the potential to replace the coercive tools of military force predominant throughout most of the twentieth century.

> Information can make [such] intervention easier and reduce the still immense geographical impediments to conventional military assistance. If warfare evolves to hide-and-seek, and seeking systems can be unplugged from the forces they serve, the United States may be able to help almost as much as it does now with conventional arms and personnel, but more frequently and for far longer with indirect rather than direct assistance. By extending information dominance to its allies, Washington can itself remain concealed while multiplying its allies' power—in some respects, by ten—or a hundred-fold. (Libicki, 1996:266)

Libicki (1996:271) also suggests that globalized information may promote international political stability by promoting "transparency of action," making effectively impossible the manipulation of destabilizing events and political protest movements: "From a broader perspective, a global watch on the global village may actually be conducive to the kind of world the United States seeks. . . . With the United States' global military dominance essentially assumed, every other power operates at a disadvantage. It must challenge the status quo in order to achieve equality." Without a hegemonic monopoly on the diffusion of information and information technologies, "others" (developing countries and "renegade" states) may cause havoc through their attempts to control or interrupt cyberspace.

Libicki's comments illustrate realist appropriations of globalization themes. Mearsheimer, Gray, and Libicki draw the traditional realist conclusion that states the need to reassert "control" over transnational conditions and dynamics in order to maintain stability. Ironically, it is only by imposing territorial and dualist categories that state-centered actors may apprehend and gain control over global phenomena. Efforts to address environmental decay, narcotics distribution, profound demographic shifts, and cyberspace must be understood territorially, or they cannot be managed at all. Global processes that question the centrality of the state themselves become threatening "others" and must be territorialized. Thus, the construction of "us" and "other" continues to depend, much as it did during the Cold War, upon the existence of state sovereignty and territory.

Of course, globalization splinters civil society as it simultaneously universalizes economy, politics, culture, and ideology. By these dynamics, "others" become increasingly evident within the territorially defined "us." Here, too, realists try to externalize "the enemy within" by assuming a link between the end of the Cold War and the emergence of domestic instability in industrialized societies (Desch, 1996:260). For example, the conventionally dichotomous categories of "us" and "other" typically render threats as external and territorial: Mexico in NAFTA draws jobs out of the United States, the "Arabs" bomb the World Trade Center and, as initially reported, may have been responsible for the Oklahoma City bombing, Colombia is responsible for the U.S. drug problem, and Japan is responsible for the performance of the U.S. economy. Simultaneously, the press, public, and politicians construct domestic "others": The Michigan Militia becomes "foreign" because it possesses incommensurable values and threatens basic norms. It cannot be part of "us."

Thus, realists understand the splintering effects of globalization as a consequence of geopolitics and the end of the Cold War. They extend "us/other" dualism to externalize these effects.

INTERNATIONAL POLITICAL ECONOMY, STRUCTURAL MATERIALISM, AND THE "UNIVERSAL GLOBAL"

Whereas realist discussions of globalization construct and externalize territorial "others," theorists inspired by the structural materialist tradition emphasize the universalizing aspects of new global realities. Such universalizing marginalizes the territorial "us" and "others" heralded by realists, obscuring aspects of their construction. As Ross and Trachte (1990:2, italics added) argue, "A new system of power has been erected on a world scale, and its agents are *able to obtain their will around the world*. . . . The New Leviathan is not the state. . . . It is the system of global capitalism itself, not any of its powerful parts." By this view, global capitalism penetrates all regions of the world, particularly since the collapse of the Berlin Wall, and subjects both citizens and states to a universal market logic.

Unsurprisingly, scholars first applied neo-Marxist tools to understand the global political economy in studies of imperialism. The fundamental characteristic of capital was to be found in its need to expand on a worldwide scale. For Marxists, imperialism promoted a vision of eventual worldwide capitalist development, whereas neo-Marxists of the dependency and later the world-systems school anticipate chronic underdevelopment. Each perspective assumes a potentially universalizing dynamic of capitalism. In that respect, descriptions of globalization as the further extension of capital hold nothing particularly new for structural theorists. As R. Cox (1996:21) suggests, "Capitalism has always been global, . . . in vocation if not in geographic extent."

Although capital exists as a totalizing or universalizing condition of the modern era, actors construct capitalism in different forms. The global economy comprises constructed regions—centers and peripheries, the rich and the poor—that lay claim to a greater or lesser versatility as conditioned by the capacities of their states. This relationship entails an inherent dialectic by which center and periphery construct each other.

In contrast, neo-Gramscians address the processes not as the inevitable expansion of global capitalism, but as a less deterministic, more multifaceted dynamic. Elements include the internationalization of production (economics), the increasing role of global finance, the internationalization of the state (politics), the emergence of a new international division of labor with consequences for global poverty migrations, the fragmentation of civil society (social processes), and the delegitimation of Keynesianism causing the reification of monetarist discourses (ideology). Thus, neo-Gramscian scholars strive to overcome the deterministic and material biases of structural materialist theorists by trying to explain the universalism of capitalist expansion (despite its differential worldwide consequences) *and* the differences that arise from nonmaterial processes. By this view, economic engines drive globalization. Indeed, "the chain of causality runs from the spatial reorganization of production to international trade and to the integration of financial markets" (Mittelman, 1996:3).

The "internationalization of production" evokes immediate conceptions of world (re)organization, with severe consequences for states. R. Cox (1991:342–344) regards the hyperliberal state—most clearly evident in Thatcher's Great Britain and Reagan's United States—as the most likely political consequence of globalization. However, the neo-Gramscian view is less explicit about how states structure these global processes. For R. Cox, production constrains the state as much as the state confines production, yet discussions of globalization marginalize this dialectical relationship. While states fostered the structures of global production, the focus of globalization is on the variety of subsequent effects on states and state forms. States and state forms become a consequence of globalization understood as the internationalization of production. While as a consequence they act to facilitate such globalization, they are primarily *responsive* players in this process.

Ling (1996:2) seriously critiques neo-Gramscian analyses. "By presenting internationalization as an exclusively externalizing, modernizing, and Westernizing process, liberals and Gramscians alike render all internationalizing states as mute, passive, plastic Western states-in-training." Given the structural prevalence of the globalizing economy, states become more marginal, functionally similar, and essentially indistinguishable actors.

This conception of the global order provokes questions. For R. Cox, the emergence of a new international division of labor—born of increased automation and the advent of post-Fordist production—signals a new global order. The contemporary global division of labor fragments labor within core states and the periphery. Global labor and production relations increase migration pressures from South to North, which exaggerates such fragmentation. "The internationalizing of production, as it penetrates into the peripheries of the world economy, benefits some social groups as it disadvantages others . . . creating a migratory pressure directed, first, towards the nearby urban areas, and then outward towards other countries wherever access, legal or (more usually) illegal, is possible" (R. Cox, 1991:339). Although global production introduces a universal character to some global relations, it also rends societies. Thus, the new global order brings a "widespread but uneven tendency toward [the] decomposition of civil society . . . , [a tendency that is] accompanied by a resurgent affirmation of identities" (R. Cox, 1996:27).

R. Cox decries such social fragmentation and marginalization as he ponders the prospects of a counterhegemony to confront globalization. To

advance such prospects, marginalized peoples need first to become conscious of their marginalization *as a consequence of* structural changes in
the processes of globalized production. The difficulty here is that R. Cox
(1996:26) himself defines the marginalized primarily in terms of their relationship to production. They are marginalized because globalization as a
material force has marginalized them, and their counterhegemonic actions
would stem from this self-definition as marginalized *economic* actors. "Cox
fails adequately to incorporate into his analyses the ways in which social
subjects understand *themselves* and their relations to social structures,
structures which are in turn constituted in and by social practices informed
by intersubjective understandings" (Laffey, 1992:1). Whitworth (1994:126)
supplements this critique and suggests, with respect to gender, that "without a more thorough analysis of ideas and ideology, the notion of gender
. . . cannot be incorporated within existing work in IPE because gender
does not simply exist at the material level but at the level of ideas and institutions as well."

Understanding globalization as an economic process before all others
limits our ability to understand globalization as a process that has roots in
ethnic, national, or gender identity and the construction of some forms of
"otherness." Despite attempts to assess globalization with subtlety, many
neo-Gramscian analyses return to the primacy of materialism. They understand global changes by presuming homogenous identities defined in relation to production rather than as matters of "difference."

"DIFFERENCE," "OTHERNESS," AND "US" UNDER GLOBALIZATION

Realist analyses conceive "others" in a territorial fashion. Structural materialist analyses emphasize the universalizing elements of globalization
rather than the multiple fragmentations of civil society linked to globalization, making "otherness" difficult to construct. From these two strands,
however, we craft a more complete *structural* picture of the universalizing
and splintering processes inherent in the new global order. It becomes
important to investigate globalization in terms of these universalizing and
splintering processes because globalization is not reducible to geopolitical
or material categories. To complement analyses of the structural character
of globalization, scholars in IR and IPE should examine more closely how
globalization transforms agency and political action in the new global village. As global technoculture promotes myths that reinforce and empower
social and economic elites and disguise, marginalize, and oppress the
world's dispossessed, attention to globalization's consequences for political
action may illuminate dimensions and directions of social change.

Globalization constructs "other" not in one's own image, but as "not us." There is a profound distinction between the concepts of "difference" and "otherness." Difference is to be celebrated and permits a construction of globalization as "global." The key to "difference" lies in the aesthetic (physical difference), and the values underlying the celebration of difference can be found in the equality of individuals regardless of their difference. Differences in gender, race, language, or religion are to be included in the category of sameness (or "us"). The obvious physical differences of these groups (to the traditionally empowered) are to be overlooked, provided they are the "same" in terms of their belief in the mythology of the equality of all individuals. Within the increasingly universal popular culture, an emphasis upon the exotic difference (beautiful Asian or black women in the traditionally Western commercial image—slim, fashionably dressed, cosmopolitan, etc.) is exploited and propagated as the reality that "they" are a part of "us," and that "us" is global.

The commercial and political construction and exploitation of this aesthetic imagery is the pop(ular) face of globalization. "They" are a part of "us" because they look so good in our clothes, live in our cities, mouth similar notions of individual difference, eat the same food, like the same movies, and read the same books. "They" are the universalized "us," who accept the rules, values, myths, and truths of a singular transnational modern individual. The "us" and "other" dualisms of realist literature are transformed by globalization into an increasingly homogenized modern cosmopolitan identity that integrates difference into "us" and constructs a new "other." The new "others" at the end of the twentieth century are those who challenge the emerging social and economic hegemony built upon the notions of individual values, modernization, the celebration of difference, free markets at the global and national levels, secularism, and so forth. Such "others" comprise at least two groups. First, some "others" might once have been "us": America's "poor white trash," vigilantes like the Michigan Militia or the Unabomber, the politically correct, blacks who cling to the ideas of collective racial oppression, or women who do the same. Second, other "others" reject either the notion of modernizing globalization altogether—such as "Islamic fundamentalists," Christian fundamentalists, communists, and many indigenous peoples—or those who live in areas marginalized by the supposedly "global" nature of globalization, as in sub-Saharan Africa, parts of Asia, the Middle East, and Central and South America (Davis, 1990:83).

The incorporation of "difference" into the identity of "us" within popular culture excludes the possibility that all "others" are systematically exploited because of their race, gender, language, or religion. The image of physically attractive, successful, exotic, refined, and cultured women of color equally at home in New York, Bangkok, Paris, or Hong Kong suggests that anyone can be "us." It undermines the possibility of systematic exploitation based upon any of the attributes traditionally associated with subordination. Such cultural incorporation also suggests that those very traits may be transformed into assets if individuals can simply think of themselves as "modern women," "progressive citizens," or the like. In this view, a "modern woman" becomes "one of us" because she acts and thinks like us. The incorporation of difference into the category of "us" has been made possible by an emerging global culture in which communications, markets and marketing, capital, labor, and information move with dramatic speed (Barnet and Cavanagh, 1994:15). Within this imagery of globalization, the old "progressive" politics of the past, which were built upon the empowerment of the disempowered, are not progressive at all. They are antimodern, promote difference and hate, and ignore the paramountcy of individual rights (Berman, 1982:128).

Such cultural incorporation also makes twentieth-century conceptual dualisms seem simplistic and potentially dangerous (Said, 1978:291, 320). More significantly, globalization's redefinition of the dualist categories "us" and "other" redefines social and economic power relations. Since globalization presents fluid and complex social categories, resulting power relations become similarly more complex and difficult to see.

In addition to redefining and obviating traditional social categories, globalization requires and constructs broader and homogenizing categories. In this process, globalization reconstructs social categories by necessitating difference as part of their definition. Thus, globalization reconstitutes new power relationships that are as exclusive and subordinating as the ones it destroys, though the consequent hegemonic social orders are less visible, less stable, and therefore potentially more destructive. The popular notion of a pluralist class of "modern individuals," aesthetically and culturally mixed, whose interests are efficient, modern, and progressive is *not* an inclusive category. It celebrates difference as it aspires to global representation; however, the popular "myth" of the modern global individual is not in any way indicative of the way the vast majority of people experience globalization.

Theoretical efforts to deconstruct the processes of globalization risk constructing their own orthodoxies and power structures that are oblivious to the rapidly transforming world around them. They perceive part, but not all, of the puzzle. Berman (1982:5) defines modernism as

> any attempt by modern men and women to become subjects as well as objects of modernization, to get a grip on the modern world and make themselves at home in it. . . . It implies an open and expansive way of understanding culture; very different from the curatorial approach that breaks up human activity into fragments and locks fragments into separate cases, labelled by time, place, language, genre and academic discipline.

However, contemporary modernization makes the possibilities for "getting a grip on the modern world and making ourselves at home in it" almost impossible. The mythology of the "modern individual" is the seductive side of a process that makes it increasingly difficult for those who aspire to be "us" to achieve it. Globalization increases the disparity of wealth at a phenomenal rate, further subjugates the world's dispossessed, and increases the size and space of the privileged (Davis, 1990:195–196; Barnet and Cavanagh, 1994:427). The popular myth of a wealthy, well-educated, beautiful woman of color in the cosmopolitan world is a lie propagated by the few who want "them," the "others," to believe that such a myth is true and attainable. For every wealthy person, hundreds nationally—indeed millions globally—are poor. For every wealthy person of color, vast numbers live enslaved in poverty and ghettos. For every well-educated person, hundreds are undereducated and must endure decreasing access to education (Barnet and Cavanagh, 1994:427).

The aesthetic popular image of beauty is an unrealistic construction of advertising executives and multinational corporations (Wolf, 1990:278). Those who live privileged lives in the elite wealthy cosmopolitan centers of the First and Third Worlds compose but a fraction of the modern world's citizens. Yet such an image of the "difference" in "us" is imposed upon the world's increasingly growing and dispossessed population. It looms and entices as the "reality" of the age of globalization. Worse still, many believe it.

CONCLUSIONS

The modern, contemporary technoculture depicts consumers worldwide quenching their thirst with Coca-Colas, happily devouring Big Macs, or sharing the wonders of their newest IBM computers. Universal commercial jingles break down traditional language barriers to suggest, for at least a moment, that all of the diverse peoples of the world can stand as one and "sing in perfect harmony." That moment occurs when we each buy a Coke (Pendergrast, 1993:306). Beyond the ubiquitous corporate trademarks, logos, and advertising campaigns, "modern times" provide other global images and idols. Michael Jackson sells as many CDs in South America as he does in the United States; Bart Simpson represents the neighborhood brat in as many languages and cultures as translators can find; moviegoers in Japan, Thailand, Taiwan, and South Korea flock to see Arnold Schwarzenegger's latest action film (Barnet and Cavanagh, 1994:153–160). Beyond the universalization of (U.S.) culture, the late twentieth century also witnesses Mexican separatist movements in Chiapas coordinate themselves over the Internet (Vincent, 1996:A1, A8) or learns that Saddam

Hussein barricaded himself and aides to watch CNN for updates on the Gulf War.

The seeming homogenization or universalization of global culture is, in true dialectical fashion, impregnated with its opposite. The aesthetic and cultural myths of globalization offer individuals the basis for a multilevel social consciousness. While the global aspirations of the modern condition create a myth of the modern individual that celebrates difference in the construction of "us," social groups based on real difference persist in the modern world and continue to be central agents in the international political economy. As the myth of the modern individual propagated by global technoculture often inadequately represents the individual's life, the prospects for alienation are immense. At the same time, the extensive technical and information explosion accompanying globalization may politicize and socialize subordinate social groups. The "modern world" offers one the opportunity to be amused by Hollywood's latest epic. The "modern world" similarly offers guerrillas on the Kurdish front the opportunity to use the Internet to discover recent moves by the Turkish government against Kurdish villages in eastern Anatolia. Globalization precipitates its own particular paradox: "Perhaps one of the most critical consequences of the process of globalization is the shattering of the homogeneous, standardized cultures in an international order whose main political actors were the nation-states. Globalization paradoxically led to the emergence of local identities" (Kadioglü, 1996:189–190).

Realism and structural materialism allow us to make certain observations about the construction of "other" within a universalizing process of globalization. Each reveals a part of the impact of globalization upon the social. Deterministic and materialist explanations that are essential to the central paradigms of IR/IPE examined here limit our understanding of the construction of "us" and "others." At the same time, explanations based upon the externalization of "others" do not allow us to understand how difference—and indeed "otherness"—can be part of the construction of "us." Ling (1996:2) argues that "internationalization promotes, rather than eliminates, hybridity." Although universalizing tendencies are real, they increase some material choices as they foreclose others. These choices are not merely aesthetic; they fundamentally define who we are and how we are constructed socially within the processes of globalization. The difficulty for existing theoretical traditions in IR/IPE is that those constructions are no longer congruent with territorial conceptions or realities. Some features of globalization are indeed universalizing, if not universal. Although marginalization is often based on relationships to production, difference is not found only between rich and poor. We need to move beyond the "us/other" dualism, but not so far as to argue that the "other" *is* a universalized "us." Rather, the universalizing processes of globalization permit the construction of a multiple "us," each of which contains within it its own "other." In the recognition of these "others" within "us," political strategies can be found that escape the simplistic dualism, determinism, or nihilism of scholarly traditions on globalization.

It seems that the constructive approach discussed in this chapter at least offers IR/IPE the possibility of identifying the appropriation of "difference" in the definition of "us." This is a crucial advantage given the limits of agency imposed through the lenses of realism and structural materialism. As the world shrinks and the "global village" beckons, for many the world appears more as a "global ghetto" in which traditional identities are obscured by a discourse that celebrates and propagates the universal village (life) erected by globalization. However, it comes as no surprise to those in the global ghetto that political movements based upon nation, region, race, class, gender, religion, and other affiliations persist. After all, globalization both erodes and reconstructs these social categories.

NOTE

A previous version of this chapter was presented at the sixty-eighth annual meeting of the Canadian Political Science Association, June 2–4, 1996, Brock University, St. Catharines, Ontario, Canada. The authors would like to thank Miguel de Larrinaga and Nadine May for able research assistance. We are particularly grateful to Eleanor MacDonald, Charles Pentland, Kathleen Rühland, Kurt Burch, and Bob Denemark for helpful comments on an earlier draft of this chapter.

Part **5**

Constructing
Alternative Approaches

James C. Roberts 9

The Rational Constitution of Agents and Structures

Scholars have recently engaged in a debate on the ontological nature of the international political economy: Do international agents, including nation-states, individuals, organizations, and corporations, form through their interactions social structures that then constrain their behavior, or is there a relationship between structure and agent in which they are simultaneously and mutually constituted?

Agents and structures cannot be examined separately in the international political economy. Agents create structures that constitute agents. Indeed, the use of the word *international* to describe the species of study implies an entire web of agent-structure relations that cannot be unwoven without losing essential characteristics. The recent debates about the position of agents and structures in the constitution of the international political economy have been primarily descriptive and fail to provide adequate causal explanations. This chapter presents a critique of the ontological basis of those debates and proposes a conception of agents and structures that accounts for their mutual generation. I begin by examining the constitution of agents and structures in the wholly anarchic context of a ship on the open seas.

RULES OF THE ROAD AND SHIPS AT SEA

When two vessels approach each other in open water, each captain must know what the other captain intends. Thus, international rules for avoiding collisions set forth rights-of-way for vessels that encounter each other in nearly every circumstance. For instance, a sailing vessel on a port tack must give way to a vessel on a starboard tack if the vessels are on a collision course. If both vessels are on the same tack, the vessel to windward must keep free of the vessel to leeward. The rules of the road generate certainty in an uncertain environment. When steam or power vessels approach each other head-on, each should alter its course to starboard so that it can pass on the port side. There is no functional reason two steam vessels should pass on the port side of each other; there is nothing special about the port side of a ship. The virtue of the rule is its ability to provide a ship's captain with an expectation of what the other ship is likely to do. Guides to seamanship emphasize rules and intentions. For example: "All changes of course in the presence of another vessel should be so pronounced and definite that they will be noticed and properly evaluated by the other boat's skipper. Slight changes in course may fail to make your intentions clear" (Chapman, 1983:93, caption, fig. 503).

The rules of the road have existed in one form or another since the earliest days of maritime transport. Indeed, Babylonian law, codified by Hammurabi about 2200 B.C., included rules regarding marine collisions (Gold, 1981:5).

> The mariners of all waters had common lives, fears, and experiences, guided by the sun by day and the stars at night and regulated by the common custom of sea merchants—the ancient sea law. This formed a system by itself, which centuries later would be absorbed in the various territorial laws of nation-states. However, for almost 5,000 years it lived its own separate existence—not a sovereign formulation, but one that although only slowly and gradually codified, was obeyed by all—at times even by the outlaw of the sea, the pirate. (Gold, 1981:4)

The rules of the road at sea, passed from one generation of mariner to the next, classified agents' actions into those that followed the rules and those that did not. The utility of these instruction rules is found in the desire to avoid a collision. If a captain breaks the rule, he or his company is liable for the damage. "Ask the insurer or owner of a ship at fault in a collision at sea whether the International Rules are enforceable. His answer will be an emphatic yes!" (Brittin, 1986: 110).

The dramatic growth of oceanic shipping in the eighteenth and nineteenth centuries sparked a direct regulatory interest in preventing collisions and determining fault when a collision occurred. In turn, governments developed legal interests in international efforts to codify a set of "rules of the road" for ocean vessels. Thus, a movement toward assessing civil damages generated a ruler of the waves during the last half of the nineteenth century.

Great Britain's Parliament enacted the first comprehensive rules of the road in 1862, but the rules affected only British ships or ships within British jurisdictions. The insurer, Lloyds of London, sponsored an international conference of private shipowners, shippers, and underwriters in 1864 to draw up rules of the road and insurance processing (McFee, 1950:283). British representatives urged other nations to accept British laws as standards for their ships and sailing conduct. For the same purpose the United States (1890) sponsored an international conference in 1889. British agents drafted the shipping rules considered at the conference, which produced not a treaty but an agreement that formed the basis for many national laws on the rules of the road. Subsequent changes in the rules introduced by Great Britain were often copied by other maritime powers. If Britannia did not rule the waves, it did at least rule the rules of the waves.

In the formation of the navigation rules, practices developed among autonomous actors pursuing their own interests without the aid of an overarching government or coordinating institutions. Instruction rules constituted these practices that involved avoiding collisions, determining liabilities, calling conferences, and the like. Great Britain, the nation most vested in the rules because of its enormous fleet (McFee, 1950:279), actively argued to other nations that following the rules would lead to higher utility for each participant. In short, Britain attempted to make the rules regulative. Simultaneously, insurers strenuously pressured national governments to codify international rules to better enable the insurance carriers to resolve claim disputes. Thus, by making and following rules, international actors structured their relations, yet simultaneously, the actors were constituted by the relations and practices. A lone ship at sea is not constituted as an actor in the practice of the international rules. Only when the ship encounters another is it then constituted as an actor by those rules, for only then can it act vis-à-vis the structure of the system.

This simple example illustrates many themes that are important for understanding the agent-structure relationship. In the international political economy, an actor is known by its actions. These actions are reducible to the actor's preferences and cognitions. In this way, an actor *is* its preferences. That is, rational choice theorists distinguish an actor solely in terms of the actor's preferences, yet those preferences are neither static nor innate. Rather, preferences arise as actors reflexively monitor the outcomes of their actions over a long history of social and cultural interaction. Rules, learned or decreed throughout that history, mold preferences. Thus, it is important to International Political Economy (IPE) to understand how preferences constitute agents and how agents form rules that then mold those preferences.

This chapter examines the agent-structure problem in IPE and the international political economy, and it provides strategies for resolving the problem. The first section discusses the roots of the agent-structure problem and proposes that rational choice theory provides a causal explanation of the difficulty. The second section examines the rational choice construction of the agent as a set of preferences. The third section explores how agents form rules and practices that mold preferences and thus constitute agents. In the fourth and final section, I propose that a progressive view of rational choice explains the agent-structure problem and provides a progressive, emancipatory understanding of how the international political economy is constituted.

THE CURRENT DEBATE AND ITS ONTOLOGIES

Kenneth Waltz's (1979) restatement of realist theory sparked the agent-structure debate in International Relations (IR) and IPE (see Ashley, 1981, 1984; Ruggie, 1983; Wendt, 1987; Dessler, 1989; Klink, 1993, 1994; Mercer, 1995). Neorealism—also called technical realism (Ashley, 1981), structural realism (Keohane, 1983), and political realism (Gilpin, 1984)—describes how structures of autonomy create anarchy that constrains and guides the actions of agents. The structures responsible for providing this constraint and guidance are generated in the interactions of autonomous units, much like a market results from the coaction of individual sellers and buyers (Waltz, 1979:91). Neorealism describes how the international system derives from the "deep structure" (Ruggie, 1983:135) of the ordering principle of anarchy, which compels states to conduct their affairs "in the brooding shadow of violence" (Waltz, 1979: 101). Anarchy limits cooperation by forcing states to consider relative gains vis-à-vis other states rather than absolute gains of power and resources. Anarchy forces states to subordinate economic gain to political interest (Waltz, 1979:107).

Dessler (1989) provides an excellent review of the ontology of neorealism, which can be little improved here. Dessler (1989:449, fig. 1) characterizes the neorealist ontology as a two-level positional model whereby interactions create the arrangement of the units at the level of the system. This arrangement of units produces the uniform outcomes that Waltz sees in the international system, despite varying inputs from the units (Waltz, 1979:73). In short, the interaction of units constitutes the ordering principle of the system and thus the system itself: "Ontologically speaking, it is the interaction of the units that creates the structure" (Dessler, 1989:449).

As anarchy yields system structure, autonomy yields anarchy, but realism does not derive autonomy. Waltz condemns as reductionist any attempts to understand autonomy. However, failure to recognize the social construction of the autonomy of the state means failure to recognize the social construction of the international system. The state is reified as an actor in a way that "ahistorically projects an image of the present back into the past" (Tickner, 1992a:ix).

Neorealism does not describe how system structures constitute states as autonomous actors, a critique that has sparked the agent-structure debates. "The causal powers of the state to maintain control over territory etc., are conferred upon it by the domestic and international social structures in virtue of which it is a state in the first place" (Wendt, 1987:360). That is, sovereignty, which was constituted by autonomy, constitutes autonomy. Wendt's (1987) article on the agent-structure problem addresses this mutual constitution of agent and structure in the context of structuration theory. "Structuration theory conceptualizes agents and structures as mutually constitutive yet ontologically distinct entities. Each is in some sense an effect of the other—they are co-determined" (Wendt, 1987:360). Wendt's analysis draws heavily on the work of Giddens (1979, 1984) and Thrift (1983). Giddens (1979:66) defines *structure* as "rules and resources organized as properties of social systems"; he defines *system* as "reproduced relations between actors or collectivities, organized as regular social practices"; and *structuration* comprises "conditions governing the continuity or transformation of structures, and therefore the reproduction of systems."

Social practice provides the ontological basis of structuration theory. Thrift (1983:29) states that practices constitute social structures, yet those structures provide the "medium of this constitution." Practices result from purposeful human activities. Indeed, as Giddens (1984:3) declares, "to be human is to be a purposive agent, who both has reasons for his or her activities and is able, if asked, to elaborate discursively upon those reasons (including lying about them)." From these practices arise the structures that recursively affect the conditions for action. Yet structuration provides no endogenous theory of the agent that explains motivations. Thus, structuration theory fails to critique neorealism's lack of a causal theory of agent and structure and cannot provide a causal theory of its own.

Onuf (1989) has conceived the theory of constructivism as an approach to the agent-structure problem, naming it thus "to indicate . . . that individuals and society continuously constitute each other through the medium of rules" (1994b:4). That is to say, constructivism describes rules as proximate causes of agents and structures (cf. Wendt, 1992:393). Rules *constitute* practices in two ways: by defining which actions are (not) performed in accordance with the practice and by guiding agents who desire to achieve an outcome through a practice. At the same time, rules *regulate* practices by providing implicit or explicit sanctions for those agents who do not follow the rules of the practice.[1]

Rules derived from language are the ontological primitives in the constructivist approach. Agents are "permitted" or "allowed" to exist by virtue of the constitutive function of rules and are constituted by those rules. Structures are constituted by rules that form the "standardized, relatively unchanging practices" (Dessler, 1989:456) of the international political economy. Rules themselves are constituted by language. For Onuf, rules are constructed in speech acts (see Searle, 1969), which "do something" without reference to physical action. Assertive speech acts, such as "I state that . . . ," convey instructional rules. Directive speech acts, such as "I request that . . . ," indicate directive rules that invoke sanctions if the rules are not followed. Commissive speech acts, such as "I promise that . . . ," communicate commitment rules, which, like contracts, grant rights and responsibilities and establish authorities (Onuf, 1994b:10–13; also Onuf 1989 and in Chapter 1 of this volume).

Through the reliance on practice and conduct, rules must derive from motivations. Constructivism describes *that* rules constitute agents and structures but fails to provide an adequate explanation of *how* rules constitute agents and structures. Similarly, constructivism describes *what* constitutes rules (language, speech acts, inferences, instantiations, etc.) but fails to offer an adequate explanation of *how* and *why* rules are constituted. Thus, constructivism offers a proximal cause of the agent-structure relationship—found in rules—but does not provide a distal cause of the agents and structures themselves.

To find cause is to find irreducible generative mechanisms that are able to account for the simultaneous generation of agents and structures. This statement expresses an explicitly scientific realist epistemology (see Wendt, 1987; Dessler, 1989). Scientific realism premises that theories provide knowledge about the unobservable through "inference to the best explanation" (O'Hear, 1989:111). A theory provides the best explanation if it explains data better than any other theory. The explanatory power of a theory is derived from its ontology, specifically from its ability "to show how apparently unconnected phenomena are actually products of a common ontology" (Dessler, 1989:446). Bhaskar (1975:47) characterizes the ontological objects of a theory as generative mechanisms that "combine to generate the flux of phenomena that constitute the actual states and happenings of the world."

What, then, is needed in a generative theory of the mutual constitution of agent and structure? Giddens (1979:49) demands "a theory of the human agent, or of the subject; an account of the conditions and consequences of action; and an interpretation of structure as somehow embroiled in both conditions and consequences." He proposes a "stratification model" of human action based on reflexive monitoring of conduct, the intentional or purposive character of human behavior, and the rationalization of action (Giddens, 1979:56). Individuals rationalize their behaviors by explaining "why they act . . . by giving reasons for their conduct" (p. 57). Indeed, many of us judge others' behavior by the reasons they give.

The search for the generative mechanisms of the constitution of agents and structures is more than a casual philosophical exercise. Agents use structures to account for conduct that affects both the objective and the subjective bases of the international political economy. The objective base is affected beneficially or malevolently in exchange relations and detrimentally in structural violence. The subjective base is affected in the social construction of actors—individual, national, and international—and in the reification of race, gender, class, and ethnicity in international practices.

Rational choice theory builds from ontological roots that promote explanations of the agent-structure problem. In rational choice theory, preferences and cognitions constitute agents; the practices formed by rules constitute structures. Perceptions about utilities form rules, which create agents by defining sets of preferences.

THE AGENT IN RATIONAL CHOICE THEORY

As Dryzek (1995:111) notes, "Rational choice has been the most visible and successful interdisciplinary research program in the last decade or two of Western social science, which makes it all the more important for critical theory to try to make sense of it." Yet critical objections to rational choice theory are legion. The primary target of these objections is rational choice's sacrosanct assumption of a rational, self-interested actor who performs like an automaton actions based on simple ahistorical, acultural criteria with little regard for context. Taylor (1985:103) lambastes rational choice explanations of political behavior because they "always end up either laughable, or begging the major question, or both." He accepts that rational choice informs economic knowledge and understandings, because the cultural conditions of economics have evolved to a state where a "certain form of rationality is a (if not the) dominant value" (Taylor 1985:103). Even so, Taylor notes that economic reasoning provides for the ordinary agent an imprecise guide that is useless when applied outside economics. "Economic behavior can be predictable . . . because the goals sought and the criteria for attainment are closely circumscribed in a given domain. But for that very reason, a theory of this kind could never help explain our motivated action in general" (Taylor 1985:103).

Although Taylor's critique is, unfortunately, well founded owing to the short-sighted analyses that have so often appeared in the literature, it nonetheless ignores the potential contributions that rational choice theory can make. Rational choice is too often used only as an instrumental theory that predicts the actions of wholly formed, highly circumscribed models of actors that frequently do not represent their real world counterparts. Rational choice *can* inform a critical evaluation of human action by stepping backward from its predictive outcomes to examine what it means to be rational and to explore the conditions in which rationality is an appropriate criterion for choice and action. To examine rationality critically can rescue rational choice "from several impasses, and also make its political program less unsavory" (Dryzek 1995:112).

Elster (1986:1-2) discusses both a descriptive and a normative approach to rational choice theory. Elster's descriptive approach characterizes rational choice theory as positivist, behavioral, and instrumental in those cases when the rational agent's actions fit expected patterns and may be described and predicted wholly in terms of rational choice assumptions. As a normative theory, rational choice attempts to explain what it is to be rational; this explanation provides insight into human and institutional theories of motivation and action. Normatively oriented rational choice theory explores the circumstances conditioning rational behavior and asks how that rationality can be interpreted and given meaning in a social context. Since the conditions can but often do not include the full range of human, cultural, historical, and institutional qualities, such a normative theory of rational choice may provide a deep interpretive basis for understanding social interactions. Morgenstern understood this when he stated that game theory "does not assume rational behavior, rather it attempts to determine what 'rational' can mean when an individual is confronted with the problem of optimal behavior in games and equivalent situations" (Morgenstern, 1968:62).

The two approaches to rational choice theory differ in their cognitive interests as well.[2] The descriptive approach provides technical knowledge that can be used to control strategic interactions. The normative approach offers practical knowledge by extending intersubjective understanding of rational and irrational actions. Despite the differences, the two approaches share common components. Rational choice theory, in its most elemental form, consists of two statements: (1) Intentions cause actions, and (2) the agent is an organism that perceives the world, interprets it, evaluates it, and makes choices that affect it (Riker, 1990:172; Burns, 1994:202). The first statement axiomatically declares the causes of actions; the second describes the nature of the agent. Recent scholarship on the philosophy of rational choice bases the first statement on the work of Davidson (1963, 1980), whose purpose was "to defend the ancient—and commonsense—position that rationalization is a species of ordinary causal explanation" (1963:685). One rationalizes when citing a belief and an intention as the reason for acting. Davidson (1963:686) claims that an actor's behavior depends upon "desires, wantings, urges, promptings, and a great variety of moral views, aesthetic principles, economics prejudices, social conventions and public and private goals and values insofar as these can be interpreted as attitudes of an agent directed towards actions." Further, Elster (1985b, 1986) sees rational choice as a subspecies of intentional explanation. He adds the restrictions that beliefs and desires, which cause actions, must be internally consistent and grounded in the available evidence (1986:13).

The agent is defined in terms of its ability to perform. "To explain a piece of behaviour is to show that it derives from an intention of the individual exhibiting it. A successful intentional explanation establishes the behaviour as an *action* and the performer as an *agent*" (Elster, 1985b:60, emphasis in original). However, the constitution of the agent in rational choice theory is deeper than a mere empirical observation. The agent is constituted as a set of processes embedded in preferences and cognitions. "To consider an organism an agent is an expression of our willingness to consider it a rational psychological system, that is, to describe its behavior in terms appropriate for assessment in accordance with canons of rationality, and make sense of its decisions and actions as issuing in appropriate ways from its preferences and cognitions" (Kim, 1985:376–377).

Critics of rational choice theory scrutinize the qualities attributed to agents. Since few authors tackle the question of how preferences and cognitions are formed, one is left to presume the nature of the agent. Most rational choice analysts, especially those who take the descriptive approach, assume that the agent is constructed as a set of consistent, stable, complete, and transitive preferences. When authors construct such an agent a priori, they deny the social, historical, cultural, and economic context of the formation of preferences. Yet this asocial agent is not a necessary construct of rational choice theory. Preferences can (and do) derive from the environment. Satz and Ferejohn (1995:72) argue that the individualist conception of the agent as free from social context denies the explanatory power of nonpsychological variables such as class and social position that determine preferences. Referring to Przeworski (1986), they maintain that Marxists explain political outcomes in terms of workers' resources and institutional constraints. Marxist explanations attribute interests to workers not by their individual preferences, but as deduced from the environment.

Conventional rational choice theories presume that all agents evaluate their options by similar principles, and these theories emphasize a decision's *outcome* rather than a decisionmaking *process*. Rational choice theorists often construct agents with full strategic knowledge, including decision options, outcomes, strategies, payoffs, opponent's payoffs, and other aspects of "complete information." However, constructed in these terms, agents possess virtually no cultural or institutional knowledge (Burns, 1994:207). More important, theorists often construct these agents without knowledge of how they can transform the context of their interaction.

Rational choice theorists can address many of these criticisms if they turn to the question of how preferences are socially constructed. Examining this issue requires an understanding of what Elster calls "supra-intentional causality" (Elster, 1985a:22). In this situation, "individuals, acting for some goal of their own, bring about something that was no part of their intention." Such unintended consequences may help explain the behavior that caused them, thereby opening the door for the mutual and simultaneous constitution of agents and structures. For instance, markets, though unintended by individual agents, result from the cultural rules related to market optimization that define the preferences for outcomes and strategies on the part of the agent (Warren, 1995:248). In this way the cultural context defines the preferred behavior (market optimization) that defines the structure (market) that defines the cultural context. In rational choice theory, wherein the agent is constituted as its preferences and cognitions, agents constitute structures that constitute agents.[3]

Theorists can avoid much of the universalism that plagues rational choice theory by recognizing that agents face multiple socially and culturally defined rationalities. Agents play different roles and therefore face different social rules of interaction regarding strategic behavior. Burns notes, for example, that to maximize relative gain as imposed by the rules of the market would be an inappropriate standard to apply to family interaction. Rationality, he states, "is a function of the rules rather than rules being a simple expression of rationality" (Burns, 1994:200). Burns proposes a "social game theory" that recognizes the "social embeddedness" of games. Social game theory redirects analyses away from the choice process and toward finding normative rules that guide agents' behavior.

AGENTS, RULES, PRACTICES, AND STRUCTURES

Max Black (1958, 1962) analyzes rules as linguistic formations. He argues that rules define a class of actions and indicate whether the acts are required, permitted, or forbidden (Black, 1962:108). Thus, for Black, rules classify actions and actors into two groups: rule-following and rule-violating. Wittgenstein (1958:39) calls rules "signposts" that indicate the direction to be followed in a given circumstance. He states that "we look to the rule for instruction and *do something,* without appealing to anything else for guidance" (Wittgenstein, 1958:86, emphasis in original). Thus, for Wittgenstein, not only do rules classify actions and actors, but rules also indicate which class of action should be performed. For example, the sailor on a port tack approaching another on a starboard tack knows to alter course without appeal to anything other than Rule 17 of the International Rules. Ryle (1949:121–122) calls rules "inference tickets" that license actors to "provide explanations of given facts to bring about desired states of affairs" (see also Gottlieb, 1968:33–34). Rules are more general than commands; indeed, they "must be distinguished from particular commands addressed *ad hominem.* This [distinction] underlines one of the basic functions of rules: to guide reasoning to like conclusions in like situations" (Gottlieb, 1968:42, emphasis in original).

Similarly, Ganz (1971:19–23) describes a rule as a general statement when it applies to a general class of either actors or circumstances.

Kratochwil (1989:10) discusses rules as "guidance devices which are designed to simplify choices and impart 'rationality' to situations by delineating the factors that a decision-maker has to take into account." Rules "assist their users in drawing inferences as to how they should act" (Onuf, 1989:79). Raz (1975) and Schauer (1991) connect rules to motivation. They maintain that from the agent's point of view, rules provide reasons to act. In rational choice terms, guidance for action and reasons for actions are both inferred from expected utility.

Thus, I define a rule generally: a statement that defines classes of actions from which rational actors draw inferences about which class of actions may lead to higher utility and should thereby be performed. In short, rules communicate actions through linguistic entities, utterances, or inscriptions. Rules aid actors by defining a binary choice between actions that follow a rule and those that break a rule. As rules identify choices, rational actors assign utilities to the choices. Yet if a rule is to provide Wittgenstein's "signposts" to an actor, it must also imply which class of actions will benefit the actor's utility. This part of the definition defines a rule in terms of the calculus of rational choice.

How do rules affect an actor's utility? Black distinguishes three types of rules relevant to this chapter. First, Black identifies rules that regulate. Identifiable authors enact and may also enforce regulation rules. One enforces regulatory rules by placing a utility price on the performance of the specified actions. The enforcer affects the subject's utility by direct transfer of a positive payment or a negative sanction or punishment.

Second, Black identifies instruction rules. Examples include statements such as "In solving quadratic equations, first eliminate the cubic term" and "Do not plant tomatoes until after the last frost" (Black, 1962:110). Instruction rules cannot be enforced, rescinded, or reinstated. They have uncertain or obscured authors and histories. Nonetheless, instruction rules provide signals about a subject's (expected) utility. Assuming that a captain wishes to avoid a collision, the International Rules, if followed, specify actions that presumably benefit the captain and others.

Third, Black identifies rules that are moral precepts or prudential maxims. Precept rules are not as neutral as instruction rules, and they convey two types of information about the believed effect of a proposed action on one's utility. Initially, these rules identify means for "achieving certain specified purposes" that members of a common culture believe provide utility (Black 1962:111). Concomitantly, these rules signal the implied utility cost of violating culturally approved behaviors or norms. That is, rule breaking is costly, though the costs clearly range in severity from merely informal disapproval to explicitly ceremonial sanctions such as banishment or death.

A rule does not specify actions that definitely will, when performed, benefit the utility of the subjects. Rather, a rule merely implies that by following the rule, one reasonably expects improved utility. The rule identifies the alternatives (rule breaking or rule following) and imparts information about the expected utility of the alternatives. A social practice exists when the behavior of a group of actors conforms to a set of relevant rules. Rules defining constraints on utility-maximizing behavior constitute such practices. Although rules do not predict exactly what agents will do in any given situation, they promote consistent action by (de)limiting behaviors.

Practices form because acting on a case-by-case basis causes confusion (Rawls, 1955:24). Rawls views practices as new forms of activity that permit coordinated behavior. Social practices necessarily require that autonomous actors forego the full sovereignty to act on the utilitarian principle applied to individual cases. Social practices form when actions converge around rules that are recognized by participants. No participant in the present can rationally change the rules. Rules of a *social* practice emerge from strategic interaction. Individuals can and do create *private* practices when they establish sets of rules that guide their behavior in certain contingencies.

Practices empower actors to act according to the rules that establish the practice. In doing so, practices constitute the individual actor by defining sets of preferred actions in given social situations. The practice of sovereignty emerges from an individual actor's desire to maintain autonomy. Sovereignty, then, defines the preferred actions that constitute the actor.

In the sets of preferences held by individual agents, one finds the ontological objects of the agent-structure problem. Rules of practice condition those preferences, and through the rules agents gain identity. Agents form rules through their reflexive monitoring of the utility gained (or lost) by their action. Thus, such rules form generalized guides for action. Since such rules form and mold actors' preferred actions in given contingencies, they define or constitute active agents.

THE PROGRESSIVE RATIONAL AGENT

A theory of agent and structure in the international political economy that starts with preferences and rules as its ontology can ground the agent-structure problem in history, culture, and practice. By constructing the agent as a set of malleable preferences and cognitions that are molded by rules established in social practice, the question of understanding international events becomes one of tracing the formation of these preferences through time rather than analyzing individual cases constrained by static a priori structures. This interpretation recognizes the social construction of the agent and the practices within which the agent is engaged and defined as an actor.

A research program is progressive by Lakatos's standards if it produces theory that has "excess empirical content over its predecessor, that is, if it predicts some novel, hitherto unexpected fact" (Lakatos, 1978:33). The rational choice conception of agents, rules, and structures presented in this chapter provides a foundation for progressive theory by providing a theory of motivation that neorealism, structuration, and constructivism lack. Although I explicitly derive the approach I outline here from rational choice theory, its arguments are logically prior to the actual choice process. I have discussed how preferences form in the interactions of agents; I have not discussed individual choices based on those preferences.

By examining the formation of preferences in the practices of international political economy, this approach rejects the practical and technical cognitive interests previously associated with the analysis of realism and instead promotes emancipatory interests. Ashley (1984) discusses classical realism as an attempt to promote intersubjective understanding through its dialectic between idealism and realpolitik. He criticizes neorealism for turning this interpretive exercise into an endeavor to exert control over the environment of international relations and losing the interpretive qualities of classical realism. The rational choice approach to understanding agents and structures reconstructs the relationship between intentional agents and the world that creates them (Johnson, 1991). It can uncover meanings hidden in the reified and instantiated structures of the international political economy by laying bare the dynamic and socially constructed rules that constitute the structures and preferences that constitute the agents.

NOTES

For help with this chapter, I owe many thanks to Nicholas Onuf, Frank Klink, Reneé Marlin-Bennett, Elaine Vaurio, Kurt Burch, and Robert Denemark. A faculty research grant from Towson State University helped make this research possible.

1. Theorists in the literature widely discuss the functional distinction between the constitutive and the regulative function of rules (e.g., Rawls, 1955). Searle (1969:33) notes that "regulative rules regulate antecedently or independently existing forms of behavior," whereas constitutive rules "create or define new forms of behavior." Dessler's (1989:455–458) discussion of the agent-structure problem maintains this distinction. However, Onuf (1994b:7), Giddens (1979:66), and I reject this classification of rules, noting instead that all rules have both constitutive and regulative qualities.

2. Habermas (1971) discusses *knowledge-constitutive cognitive interests*. Ashley (1981) discusses three types of cognitive interests applied to realism. *Practical cognitive interest* is knowledge for the purpose of furthering intersubjective understanding. *Technical interest* is knowledge for the purpose of controlling

the environment. *Emancipatory cognitive interest* is knowledge that attempts to achieve human autonomy by discovering the determinants of the human self-formative process.

3. To make a similar point, Warren (1995:233) writes that "when, for example, Marx criticizes structural concepts (like the English political economists' concept of a market), his aim is to show how they depend on individual activities under specific circumstances, as well as on the ways individuals have been formed by these same structural outcomes and circumstances."

Ralph Pettman # 10

The Limits to a Rationalist Understanding of IPE

The first thing I did was make a mistake. I thought I had understood capitalism, but what I had done was assume an attitude—melancholy sadness—toward it. This attitude is not correct. Fortunately your let-ter came, at that instant. "Dear Rupert, I love you every day. You are the world, which is life. I love you I adore you I am crazy about you. Love, Marta." Reading between the lines, I understood your critique of my attitude toward capitalism. Always mindful that the critic must "studiare da un punto di vista formalistico semiologico il rapporto fra lingua di un testo e codificazione di un—"*But here a big thumb smudges the text—the thumb of capitalism, which we are all under. Darkness falls. My neighbour continues to commit suicide, once a fortnight. I have his suicides geared into my schedule because my role is to save him; once I was late and he spent two days uncon-scious on the floor. But now that I have understood that I have not understood capitalism, perhaps a less equivocal position toward it can be "hammered out". My daughter demands more Mr. Bubble for her bath. The shrimp boats lower their nets. A book called* Humorists of the 18th Century *is published.*[1]

oOo

The contemporary study of world affairs, which includes the study of International Political Economy (IPE), is overwhelmingly rationalistic. Most of those who study this subject place great importance upon the ratio-nal way in which it can be done. They privilege "reason," the intellect, the functioning forebrain. They repress "emotion," the affect, the limbic sys-tem. They assume that thinking and feeling are discrete mental activities, and they see reason as more important than emotion for understanding IPE.

Radical rationalists say that people ought to employ reason alone. It is the "light of the mind," they believe, that shows us what is most real. It is by the exercise of this capacity, "independently of experience," that we learn "important and substantive truths" (Cottingham, 1984:7). The scholarly canon is seen as a vast tribute to what we can do as intellectual beings.

The intellect is valued not only because it allows people to play with their own brains, however; it is valued also because of the way it can be used systematically—that is, in self-conscious accord with rules of logic. When used like this, the intellect is an amazingly fertile source of novel and dependable knowledge. Indeed, rationalists value what they acquire from the systematic use of reason more highly than any other knowledge (Cottingham, 1984:3).

What about evidence and empirical knowledge? What roles do they play? Radical empiricists say that the senses alone provide us with knowledge of what is true. It is by attending to sense facts and not intellectual fancies, they argue, that we know what is real. Not all who privilege the senses would go this far, however. Few would believe that using our experiential capacities alone is all we need to do to approximate truths. Most would say that how we use our senses is just as important—whether we use them in a structured way or not. Most would also add that important sources of human knowledge include the intellectual assumptions that make sense of our senses and the intellectual capacity for reflection.

Moderate forms of empiricism and moderate forms of rationalism clearly converge. While impressed by our capacity "not based on experience" to generate hypotheses about "what in general the world might possibly be like" (Nagel, 1986:83), moderate rationalists admit that what we learn by using that capacity has to be checked against what we learn by experiential means. This makes for a rationalism that tempers a priori cogitation with sense experience. Moderate empiricists, though obviously impressed by our diverse powers of observation, admit that what we learn by using those powers owes much to and is extended by what we find out using the intellect. This makes for an empiricism that tempers experiential outlooks with analytic insights.

Moderate empiricism and moderate rationalism both advocate the use of the mind's thinking and sensing skills. Although the ancient Greeks were the first, in the European tradition, to discriminate in a sustained way between the systematic and the unsystematic use of human reason, Anglo-European Enlightenment thinkers were the first to make a sustained case for discriminating between the systematic and the unsystematic use of the human senses.

The convergence of moderate empiricism and moderate rationalism has been used to make a "rationalism" of extraordinary significance. The Anglo-European Enlighteners first realized the full potential of combining the controlled use of the senses with logically coherent thinking in the specific form called *experiment.* Called in due course *science,* it was a combination that produced extraordinary amounts of new and reliable knowledge. This approach made it possible to approximate the real world with a degree of technical accuracy and public veracity theretofore unparalleled. Systematic and integrated sensing and thinking seemed to focus the faculties of the mind like the beam of a torch, and we as a species began to "see" further into the night of the unknown than we had ever done before.

Brought to bear on world affairs, this hypothetico-deductive, "scientific" approach became known as *behavioralism*. Hedley Bull attacked the behavioralist turn in the discipline as trivializing, but even Bull felt obliged to argue that the "theory of international relations should . . . attempt to be scientific in the sense of . . . being consistent with the philosophical foundations of modern science" (Bull, 1966:375). Bull was and still is far from alone. Take, for example, a scholar as contemporary as David Campbell, who understands only too well "how our understanding of politics is heavily indebted to . . . reason [and] rationality . . . [which] are licensed as superior to unreason [and] irrationality" (Campbell, 1992:10). We might expect such a scholar to write less rationalistically, but like Bull, he does not.

In the light of "scientific" rationalism, both extreme empiricists and radical rationalists would be considered irrational. The unstructured use of the intellect allows for the free play of the imagination. The unstructured use of the senses allows for the free play of the feelings. In terms of scientific rationalism, however, these activities are antirational, in that the knowledge they provide is not systematic. This does not mean that the unbridled imagination and the undisciplined use of the senses have no value or that reasons cannot be given for using and valuing them. It simply means that from the perspective of scientific rationalism, they are not activities that contribute to our knowledge of what might be true. It might be good or beautiful or delicious or honorable or spiritually uplifting to use the mind in these ways. Yet unless these activities analytically engage the intellectual part of the mind, and allow experiment, they cannot provide us with anything true by the standards of scientific rationalism.

If we reject the truth-claims of extreme rationalism and extreme empiricism, moderates say, we would nonetheless do well to retain some semblance of them in a tempered form. Let us not throw out the baby with the bathwater. We need moderate rationality because to reject rationality "is not, and cannot be, to pave the way for the development of a 'higher' or 'deeper' truth; instead it is simply to opt out of the whole business of making truth-claims" (Cottingham, 1984:5). A moderate empiricist would also see any outright rejection of sense experience as an attempt to opt out of the truth-making business. The trick is to have each entail the other in a falsifiable/experimental way.

Is this true, however? Is it possible, despite the reservations of moderate rationalists and empiricists, to use the intellect or the senses in less highly structured and therefore nonrational ways? Is it possible to attain knowledge that is true? To see far we have learned to focus our faculties in ways earlier discussed. Might we not want to see wide as well? Might we want to avert our gaze to encompass other aspects of reality to which the bright beam of the mind makes us blind?

It is certainly difficult to think of any way of knowing what is true without using the intellect at all, since thinking of any way of knowing is an intellectual activity in itself. To think of a way of knowing is to have already used the intellect. Not to think of a way of knowing is not to use the intellect, and that is, to most of us, literally unthinkable. Similarly, knowing what is true without using the senses at all would seem to entail such an extraordinary intellectual feat that few dare admit the possibility. As a consequence, moderate rationalists and moderate empiricists usually let the whole matter rest there.

Because what rationalism means today is mostly what moderate rationalists and moderate empiricists say it means, and because the success of using their definition is so clearly evident in terms of new and reliable knowledge, it is no surprise to find so little interest in exploring the limits of this conception of rationalism. Radical rationalists and extreme empiricists may get marginalized in the process, but scientific rationalists see this as a small price to pay for the cumulative progress in knowledge that their mixed and more moderate approach provides.

I am unsure this neglect is as warranted as scientific rationalists assume. The power of the scientific attitude relies on the disciplined and combined use of both our intellectual and sensual capacities. Although I have the utmost respect for what this combination has allowed us to do— indeed, I'm using a similar combination of logic and evidence at this very moment—I suspect that truths may also be gleaned from the less disciplined realms that lie beyond the limits set by analysis and experiment. The existence of such truths would not matter if we could say with confidence that they are unlikely to contribute anything relevant to our understanding of reality in general and of international political economy in particular. I'm not so sure we can say that, however, and this chapter is a tentative exploration of that lack of surety.

I start secure in the knowledge that some of the most notable advances in contemporary "science" have been made by bold flights of ill-disciplined imagination and/or intuition. Such flight occurs in the physical sciences, where it accounts, as Nagel points out, "for the extremely high ratio of rational [that is, intellectual] to empirical grounds for great theoretical advances like Newton's theory of gravitation or the special and general theories of relativity" (Nagel, 1986:84). This also occurs in IPE and the other social sciences. A short story like the one told throughout this chapter, for example, provides information and insights arguably as "true" as any textbook treatment of its putative subject, the "rise of capitalism." Indeed, it arguably contains information and insights not at all available in a scientifically rationalistic way.

oOo

Capitalism places every man in competition with his fellows for a share of the available wealth. A few people accumulate big piles, but most do not. The sense of community falls victim to this struggle. Increased abundance and prosperity are tied to growing "productivity". A hierarchy of functionaries interposes itself between the people and the leadership. The good of the private corporation is seen as prior to the public good. The world market system tightens control in the capitalist countries and terrorizes the Third World. All things are manipulated to these ends. The King of Jordan sits at his ham radio, inviting strangers to the palace. I visit my assistant mistress, 'Well, Azalea,' I say, sitting in the best chair, 'what has happened to you since my last visit?' Azalea tells me what has happened to her. She has covered a sofa, and written a novel. Jack has behaved badly. Roger has lost his job (replaced by an electric eye). Gigi's children are in the hospital being detoxified, all three. Azalea herself is dying of love. I stroke her buttocks, which are perfection, if you can have perfection, under the capitalistic system. "It is better to marry than to burn," St. Paul says, but St. Paul is largely discredited now, for the toughness of his views does not accord with the experience of advanced industrial societies. I smoke a cigar, to disoblige the cat.

oOo

Not only is the study of world affairs highly rationalistic in the scientific sense, but those who practice most of the world's affairs, including its politico-economic ones, also privilege scientific rationalism. Although the purpose and tone of a Greenpeace executive meeting in Tokyo will differ from a meeting of IBM executives in New York, both sets of executives will use the language of scientific rationalism. Like the automatic weapon, the U.S. dollar, the business suit, and the English language, scientific rationalism is now a global tool.

Subsistence villagers in the Solomon Islands do not speak the language of scientific rationalism, though their state makers must be able to do so in the conduct of their country's diplomatic, strategic, commercial, and cultural global affairs. Although self-evidently "in" the world, these subsistence villagers are equally clearly not yet "of" the state-made, capitalist, modernist structures rapidly being assembled around them.

Relatively more Euro-Americans than Solomon Island villagers master the mores of scientific rationalism, but it is a Euro-American invention anyway, made global by European and American (neo)imperialists. Nonetheless, large numbers of Euro-Americans fail to learn it well or never get the chance to do so, because they grow up in education systems that fail to foster a sufficiently vigorous spirit of scientific inquiry and the appropriate forms of mental speech.

I do not underestimate the mental breakthrough that scientific rationalism represents. I have already noted my own sincere admiration for it and my own commitment to it. In the computer jargon of the day, one might say that we, as a species, have had for more than 100,000 years the physiological hardware to generate ever more expansive amounts of new and reliable knowledge. This hardware seems to have been necessary but not sufficient. To realize our physiological potential, we also needed the requisite software. We acquired this software only 300 years ago but have been exploring its full potential for only the last 100 years.

Any critique of such a breakthrough would seem distinctly retrograde. Indeed, European thinkers demeaned such criticism when they first articulated scientific rationalism as such. Nonetheless, I hold profound doubts: Can our species survive this narrow, though highly efficient and effective, use of the mind? Optimists remain sanguine, pointing to the extraordinary power of scientific rationalism to solve problems, any problems, even those engendered by the use of scientific rationalism itself. Pessimists are notably less sure that humans ably cope with our current uses of rationalism, let alone what we might do with it in the future.

Although I freely acknowledge the benefits of scientific rationalism and readily grant the astounding success of the approach in generating new and reliable knowledge, as a pessimist I am concerned with its limits and its costs. How applicable is scientific rationalism to IPE? What limits does it set? What might the costs of those limits be?

oOo

Meanwhile Marta is getting angry. "Rupert", she says, "you are no better than a damn dawg! A plain dawg has more sensibility than you, when it comes to a woman's heart!" I try to explain that it is not my fault but capitalism's. She will have none of it. "I stand behind the capitalistic system", Marta says. "It has given us everything we have—the streets, the parks, the great avenues and boulevards, the promenades and malls—and other things, too, that I can't think of right now." But what has the market been doing? I scan the list of the fifteen Most Loved Stocks:

Occident Pet	*983,100 20 5/8 +*	*3 3/4*
Natomas	*912,300 58 3/8 + 18 1/2*	

What chagrin! Why wasn't I into Natomas, as into a fine garment, that will win you social credit when you wear it to the ball? I am not rich again this morning! I put my head between Azalea's breasts, to hide my shame.

oOo

Scientific rationalism is, most notably, thinking and feeling that is abstract and objectified; that is, rationalistic thinking and feeling is "objectifying" thinking and feeling. It means standing back to take a look, both emotionally and intellectually. It means getting "outside of ourselves" to view the world "from nowhere" as it were (Nagel, 1986:67). As Heidegger (1987a) points out, we do not achieve this view just by "picturing" the world; we must also think of and feel about the world-as-a-picture with ourselves apart from that picture. This way of thinking and feeling sharpens our focus not only on the world-as-a-picture but also on ourselves as apart from that picture. That is, this conception or picture of the world identifies us as discrete beings, as "individuals."

Heidegger considers this objectifying, picturing, individuating process the most characteristic feature of the modern age. He argues that this kind of seeing is unique to this era. Humans did not simply evolve or move from a medieval world-picture to a modern world-picture; rather, what distinguishes our age from all others, Heidegger says, is our making of the whole world into a picture. For example, the Greek philosophers were rationalistic, but they placed themselves in the picture and saw themselves as taking precedence over whatever else was there. Descartes, however, placed the world in front of us in a completely figurative fashion. It gets fixed there by the doing of "research" (Heidegger, 1987a:118–128).

This view is problematic from the start, since it involves a sleight-of-the-mind, albeit a very productive one. As I step back mentally and emotionally to look at "the world" and at "myself" in that world, I create a schizophrenic self somewhere in my mind. If I detach myself too successfully in this way, I will go mad. Moreover, "however often we may try to step outside of ourselves, something will have to stay behind the lens, something in us will determine the resulting picture, and this will give grounds for doubt that we are really getting any closer to reality." Thus, "the idea of objectivity . . . seems to undermine itself" (Nagel, 1986:68).

Heidegger claims to identify here an absolute limit to what scientific rationalism can do. When we represent the world scientifically, he says, we cannot tell whether the world is revealed to us in all its fullness. All scientific theories are circumscribed by the decision to make reality into objects and make ourselves into objectified subjects (Heidegger, 1987b:174). This decision applies not only to quantum physics or biology but also to IPE. We can never tell, in other words, if what we seek to know is being revealed or concealed. We cannot know whether there are other kinds of reality, because we do not know if objectifying/subjectifying is the most appropriate way to proceed, despite Descartes's conviction to the contrary. Hence the "strange restlessness" that Heidegger discerns throughout the natural and social sciences. Hence the sense that the scientific project floats in midair, with no foundations other than those we have made for it.

Although this argument does not inhibit in the least those scientific rationalists who go on giving us pharmaceuticals, astrophysics, industrial production, and advertising statistics, it can make us more alert to signs—"evidences," as Heidegger calls them—of a time when we might come to know more than scientific rationalism can say about what is essentially real or true. Unfortunately, Heidegger does not tell us what these "evidences" are or what "essentially" might mean in this context. He does remind us, however, to stay alert to what scientific rationalism does not and arguably cannot say. This prompts us in turn to ask whether scientific rationalism is able to say anything "essential" about IPE at all.

oOo

Honoré de Balzac went to the movies. He was watching his favourite flick, The Rise of Capitalism, *with Simone Simon and Raymond Radiguet. When he had finished viewing the film, he went out and bought a printing plant, for fifty thousand francs. "Henceforth", he said, "I will publish myself, in handsome expensive de-luxe editions, cheap editions, and foreign editions, duodecimo, sextodecimo, octodecimo. I will also publish atlases, stamp albums, collected sermons, volumes of sex education, remarks, memoirs, diaries, railroad timetables, daily newspapers, telephone books, racing forms, manifestos, libretti, abecedaries, works on acupuncture, and cookbooks." And then Honoré went out and got drunk, and visited his girl friend's house, and, roaring and stomping on the stairs, frightened her husband to death. And the husband was buried, and everyone stood silently around the grave, thinking of where they had been and where they were going, and the last handfuls of wet earth were cast upon the grave, and Honoré was sorry.*

oOo

An overwhelming sense of personal and immediate continuity with the universe does not and indeed cannot sustain an objectifying worldview. It provides no ontological basis for that way of using the mind that "sees" the self so objectively. An objectifying "self," however, is able to posit an objective reality other than the self. The knowing observer perceives, both intellectually and emotionally, phenomena "out there" (such as trading nations) even when the events being observed are self-evidently ones that are "in here" (like brain states). This sense is learned. Although we are all born genetically unique and are in this respect individual, the cultural decision to exacerbate or mitigate this fact—that is, the choice of whether and how far to individuate us as we grow up—is made by the society into which we are born.

The societies that exacerbate the sense of self are those that, not coincidentally, privilege the objectifying mind-self and scientific rationalism. The choice is built into the languages these societies use. In detaching their young mentally from "reality," so that they might better look back or down upon it, those who promote the culture upon which such societies are based are making a choice, whether they know it or not. The language they use represents this choice, since objectified language is language devoid of magic meaning, made up of mere sounds that signify signs that signify things.

The objectifying mind-set and scientific rationalism also exacerbate what could be called "linearity." The logics that characterize systematic thinking and the kind of experiences that characterize scientific experiments are linear; they foster a linear sense of time. Cause-and-effect experimental sequences and the logic of analytic consistency and falsifiability are before-and-after practices. They presage open-ended progress, like trickle-down development or "laws" of history that predict the catastrophic collapse of capitalism. They specifically dispel myths of eternal return.

Linearity also makes it difficult to consider wholes in terms of their parts. Consider world trade. In the attempt to understand world trading practices, objectifying rationalists concentrate upon what they see as cause-and-effect sequences and the relationships between component particulars. They view the forest in terms of its trees. They talk about "the General Agreement on Tariffs and Trade," "protection versus free trade," and hundreds of other issue areas in analytically linear ways. Analysts then combine their conclusions in the expectation that an assemblage of cause-and-effect accounts of particular aspects of world trade will make the whole subject of world trade more readily understood. The problem is that the attempt to assemble a forest from analytically clear-cut sections of it makes for analytically clear-cut forests, too. It does not make for a nuanced understanding of the unlogged whole. Attempts to weave together linear accounts of aspects of world trade may confuse as much as they clarify our under-standing of it. They may make it harder, not easier, to appreciate the emer-gent properties of "world trade" as a whole.

By contrast, radical rationalists would approach world trade with *intel-lects* as unconfined as possible. They would note the "capacity of experts to store in memory tens of thousands of typical situations and rapidly and effortlessly to see the present situation as similar to one of these" (Dreyfus and Dreyfus, 1987:341). They would suggest that the brain does not work like a "heuristically programmed digital computer applying rules to bits of information [i.e., linearly]"; rather, the brain works "holographically, super-imposing the records of whole situations and measuring their similarity" (Dreyfus and Dreyfus, 1987:341). Radical rationalists would privilege this capacity and seek in its exercise information and insights about world trade that logical and falsifiable hypothesizing does not and arguably cannot provide.

By contrast, extreme empiricists would approach world trade with all their *senses* as unconfined as possible. They would manifest an active con-cern not for the systematic search and the intellectual assessment of the "facts," but for the feel of the facts as well. They would try to experience world trade in nonscientific ways and would expect to learn significant amounts about what world trade involves by doing so.

oOo

The Achievements of Capitalism:
 (a) The curtain wall
 (b) Artificial rain
 (c) Rockefeller Center
 (d) Casals
 (e) Mystification

oOo

Some of the limits set by objectifying thinking and feeling are readily reconciled with an objectifying mind-move. Linearity can be put in the context of concepts like "emergent outcomes," for example, or compen-sated for in terms of theories of "complexity," "chaos," or "probability." Scientific rationalists do, after all, admit that because we are finite beings, our knowledge of the world must of necessity be "fragmentary," obsolesc-ing, and incomplete (Nagel, 1986:86). This is especially true if the universe is not only stranger than we imagine but stranger than we can imagine.

Some limits, such as the heightened sense of alienation that objectify-ing can bring, are harder to overcome. Nagel calls this sense "excessive impersonality." He notes the "split in self" that objectifying creates, the fact that as this split "gradually widens, the problems of integration . . . become severe, particularly in regard to ethics and personal life." Thus we are obliged to view the world "both from nowhere and from here, and to live accordingly," cultivating a kind of "double vision" (Nagel, 1986:86). Of course, rather than Nagel's binocularity, alienation can prompt either a romantic retreat into extreme empiricism or an earnest forward march in the hope that an ever more radical rationalism will restore our sense of purpose and meaning—but this sense of restoration may turn out to be no more than a kind of nihilistic indifference, a watching of the play of light on the water, as it were.

oOo

"Capitalism sure is sunny!" cried the unemployed Laredo toolmaker, as I was out walking, in the streets of Laredo. "None of that noxious Central European miserabilism for us!" And indeed, everything I see about me seems to support his position. Laredo is doing very well now, thanks to application of the brilliant principles of the "new capitalism". Its Gross Laredo Product is up, and its internal contradictions are down. Catfish-farming, a new initiative in the agri-business sector, has worked wonders. The dram-house and the card-house are each nineteen stories high. "No matter," Azalea says. "You are still a damn dawg, even if you have 'unveiled existence.'" At the Laredo Country Club, men and women are discussing the cathedrals of France, where all of them have just been. Some liked Tours, some Lyon, some Clermont. "A pious fear of God makes itself felt in this spot."

oOo

Limits are also set by what Nagel (1986:87) calls false objectification:

The success of a particular form of objectivity in expanding our grasp of some aspects of reality may tempt us to apply the same methods in areas where they will not work, either because those areas require a new kind of objectivity or because they are in some respect irreducibly subjective. The failure to recognize these limits produces various kinds of objective obstinacy—most notably reductive analyses of one type of thing in terms that are taken from the objective understanding of another.

IPE is arguably one such issue-area of "irreducible" subjectivity. Trying to summarize its subjectivities in objectifying ways assumes either that IPE possesses no subjective significance worth describing and explaining or that logical and experimental means successfully capture its subjective contents. However, given the constraints that objectivizing sets, it is unclear that either obtains. If so, then those who insist on objectivizing will misconstrue the subject.

Scientific rationalists dispute the significance of such irreducibility and the extent of the failure it portends. They do not think the failure is significant compared to the new and reliable knowledge that scientific rationalism makes possible. They are wont to argue, therefore, in terms of how one sets one's face. The grail of objective knowledge may lie forever beyond our grasp, they say, but that does not mean we should stop reaching toward it. Although describing and explaining the realities of IPE can never be done completely objectively, scientific rationalists see this as no reason to shun such an approach.

oOo

Capitalism arose and took off its pyjamas. Another day, another dollar. Each man is valued at what he will bring in the marketplace. Meaning has been drained from work and assigned instead to remuneration. Unemployment obliterates the world of the unemployed individual. Cultural underdevelopment of the workers, as a technique of domination, is found everywhere under late capitalism. Authentic self-determination by individuals is thwarted. The false consciousness created and catered to by mass culture perpetuates ignorance and powerlessness. Strands of raven hair floating on the surface of the Ganges . . . Why can't they clean up the Ganges? If the wealthy capitalists who operate the Ganges wig factories could be forced to install sieves at the mouths of their plants . . . And now the sacred Ganges is choked with hair, and the river no longer knows where to put its flow, and the moonlight on the Ganges is swallowed by the hair, and the water darkens. By Vishnu! This is an intolerable situation! Shouldn't something be done about it?

oOo

The most intractable limit set by objectifying is intrinsic to the act of objectifying itself. Such mind-moves both conceal and reveal. In standing back to look at the world, using logic and experiment, we create models of the world that we manipulate in our minds and test empirically to determine how well these models seem to fit the world. This is the scientifically rationalistic way to objectify, and scientific rationalists say we can learn a lot by this method. But what do we fail to learn from this way? What does objectifying obscure?

Both the objectifying mind-gaze and the scientific rationalism it fosters take the "complex, ambiguous, and heterogeneous matrix of existence" that comprises IPE and reduces it to a "simplistic, universalized image of the 'real' world." Objectifying rationalism detaches IPE "fundamentally" from the "everyday experience" of the world (George, 1994:11). It marginalizes whatever does not fit its focus, rendering the "other" invisible and mute. It treats values, in its passion for dispassion, as "noncognitive emotional responses or private . . . preferences" (Bernstein, 1983:46–47).

Those who decry the limitations set by this reductionism, marginalizing, and passion for dispassion recommend taking an interpretive turn. Interpretive social science sees IPE as an "on-going process of self-interpretation and self-definition by [the] human collectivities" taking part in it (Neufeld, 1993a:57). It uses a "broader and more subtle conception of reason . . . than that which underlies . . . the positivist tenet of 'truth as correspondence'" (Neufeld, 1993b:60). Interpretive social science deliberately pushes out into non–logically falsifiable and nonexperimental realms. It establishes a distinction between what Habermas calls the "empirical-analytic" sciences and the "historical-hermeneutic" ones. Interpretive knowledge fosters not only "technical control over objectified processes" but also a "practical cognitive interest" in the "understanding of meaning, not observation" (Habermas, 1978:308–309).

To quote Charles Taylor (1987:67–68):

> In a hermeneutical science a certain measure of insight is indispensable, and this insight cannot be communicated by the gathering of brute data, or initiation in modes of formal reasoning or some combination of these. It is unformalizable. But this is a scandalous result according to the authoritative conception of science. . . . it means that this is not a study in which anyone can engage, regardless of their level of insight.

Indeed, it means that IPE is a study in which some differences will be "nonarbitrable by further evidence." A lack of understanding may require one to develop one's "intuitions" or, more radically, to change one's self. This means that "we can speak here not only of error, but of illusion" (Taylor, 1987:67–68).

The international political economy (ipe) is not "there" in the world the same way as a physical or chemical or biological entity is "there." It is real enough, to be sure. If we decide to default on a debt or dishonor a contract or if we try to sell our labor-time to people who do not want to buy it, we quickly find out how tangible ipe can be. The reality of IPE is constituted, though. It is made as well as found, thus introducing a degree of voluntarism into the knowing process that the physical world largely lacks, Heisenberg notwithstanding. Imagine, for example, if everyone decided at the same moment to repudiate the concept of contract. Capitalism would cease to work at once. However, a similar collective decision to disobey the law of gravity—to levitate, for example—would have no appreciable effect. Objectifying, scientific rationalism obscures the constituted quality of IPE. It obscures how "at every stage of the process by which we come to know the world, we are engaged with it, to the extent that the facts of the world . . . are always bound up with the way we give meaning to them and accord them their 'real' status" (George, 1994:22).

Deciding to take the interpretative turn—to stand close and listen—rather than to take the objectifying turn—to stand back and look—does not, of course, provide any guarantees that what we hear will be true. The speakers may lie, for example; they may be misled or deluded. The listeners may be misled or deluded, too, or they may be lying to themselves. Hermeneutics, in other words, raises problems of its own, the most intractable of which concerns relativism. If we find that there is no essential, universal, and timeless Truth against which to measure the content of what we hear, what establishes the point of doing so in the first place? The strength of our convictions? Yet that means argument by advocacy, not analysis, and invites yet more false consciousness. Hence, we encounter the ongoing need for critical theories that try to determine what might distort what we see and hear and that seek to understand how we look at and listen to ourselves. This in turn sends us standing back once more to make some analytic distance, fruitless though this step appears to be in interpretive terms. And so it goes.

We stand back to get a better perspective, but we find that the costs of doing so are insupportable in terms of a subject like IPE. We surrender that perspective for one more cognizant of the constituted nature of all human knowledge and therefore of IPE. We stand close to listen. When this mind-move proves incapable of discriminating between false and less false forms of consciousness, we look for ways to be more critical. We rediscover in the process the strengths of scientific rationalism, and we stand back to get some perspective again. And so it goes. The only alternative is madness or the radical disavowal of the desire to "know" anything at all. There is a third option—cosmic consciousness—but that seems to be given to very few (Bucke, 1947).

oOo

Friends for dinner! The crudites are prepared, green and fresh . . .
The good paper napkins are laid out . . . Everyone is talking about
capitalism (although some people are talking about the psychology of
aging, and some about the human use of human beings, and some
about the politics of experience). "How can you say that?" Azalea
shouts, and Marta shouts, "What about the air?" As the flower moves

toward the florist, women move toward men who are not good for
them. Self-actualization is not to be achieved in terms of another per-
son, but you don't know that, when you begin. The negation of the
negation is based on a correct reading of the wrong books. The immi-
nent heat-death of the universe is not a bad thing, because it is a long
way off. Chaos is a position, but a weak one, related to that "unfo-
cusedness" about which I have forgotten to speak. And now the saints
come marching in, saint upon saint, to deliver their message! Here
are St. Albert (who taught Thomas Aquinas), and St. Almachius (mar-
tyred trying to put an end to gladiatorial contests), and St. Amadour
(the hermit), and St. Andrew of Crete (whose "Great Kanon" runs to
two hundred and fifty strophes), and St. Anthony of the Caves, and St.
Athanasius the Anthonite, and St. Aubry of the Pillar, and many oth-
ers. "Listen!" the saints say. "He who desires true rest and happiness
must raise his hope from things that perish and pass away and place
it in the Word of God, so that, cleaving to that which abides forever,
he may also together with it abide forever." Alas! It is the same old
message. "Rupert," Marta says, "the embourgeoisment of all classes
of men has reached a disgusting nadir in your case. A damn dawg has
more sense than you. At least a damn dawg doesn't go in for the 'bul-
let wrapped in sugar,' as the Chinese say." She is right.

oOo

The search for truths about IPE that are arguably unavailable to scientific rationalists—not accessible, that is, to their objectifying methods of
logic and experiment—dates from the beginnings of the discipline. In
its modern form, though, it has only just begun. Where, for example, is
the disciplinary recognition of the narratives of those people who are
"women"? Why do those who express a serious concern for "East Asian
values"—as articulated, for example, by East Asian models of "development"—not get a more sympathetic disciplinary hearing? Where are the
writings that render IPE intelligible in ways that scientific rationalism does
not? Why can so many IPE scholars direct novice readers to detached and
rationalistic accounts of wage labor, for example, but so few can direct
readers to graphic accounts of the same phenomenon? David Lodge (1980),
for example, conveys wage-laboring concisely, comprehensively, coher-
ently, and in a compellingly interpretive manner. Does one learn nothing
from Lodge? Indeed, the conspicuous absence of hermeneutic accounts of
IPE in the professional literature points to a deep defense of the objectifying mind-move and of scientific rationalism.

One alternative to complying with or colluding in the defense of scientific rationalism is to seek out and to feature as prominently as possible

nonrationalist accounts of IPE. Though they exist in profusion (Pettman, 1996), they may seem at first glance too anecdotal, too impressionistic, or too insubstantial to merit scholarly attention. Many accounts are undeniably all these things and more, but many others are not. Many address directly the "'non-rational' nature of [our] changing subjectivity" and the ways in which we "sustain certain identities and act in the world," yet in so doing they place "pressure" upon "abstraction" by conveying the "deep human experience of . . . social organisations . . . connecting us to the human agency and opportunity within such patterns" (Amaturo, 1995:19). This is a necessary connection if we are ever to be able to understand the "full range of human experience and conviction" (Amaturo, 1995:24–25).

Regrettably, most IPE scholars ignore informative and engaging work that fails to meet the standards of scientific rationalism. They do so as if this were natural and therefore right. Even those who are aware of the limits of rationalism—those who talk about the need to allow for "thinking spaces" and to listen to the voices of the marginalized and invisibilized in IPE—do little actual listening in their published works. They do much less than seems warranted by the interpretive turn to create venues to air such voices (Walker, 1988; George, 1994).

Another alternative to the defense of scientific rationalism is to undertake some nonrationalist research oneself. The most active form of such research is "participant observation" (Spradley, 1980; Burawoy, 1991:291–300). In this alternative, one sets out to experience what one would like to understand, with the express purpose of garnering new and reliable, albeit nonrational, knowledge. Sometimes this happens unintentionally. For example, the astronaut Edgar Mitchell was so moved by his extraterrestrial travels that he concluded that "instead of an intellectual search" there is also a "nonrational way of understanding," a way that goes "beyond . . . previous experience."[2] "We went to the moon as technicians" he said, but "we returned as humanitarians" (Kelley, 1988:137–138). Yet without traveling to the moon to conduct nonrationalist research, we can garner information and insights by becoming more aware of our own experiences as socially determined beings and those of others (Sampson, 1973).

By becoming more introspective and alert, it is possible to learn a good deal about how and why IPE works the way it does. "Introspection may not seem 'objective', but it is a tool all of us use to understand new situations and to gain skill at following cultural rules" (Spradley, 1980:57). It is a tool anyone can use to study the beliefs they have learned and the practices these beliefs predispose. These beliefs include, for example, work, property, self-aggrandizement, and social responsibility, and they are fundamental to the contemporary global political economy. What cultural rules apply to IPE? How do we embody them ourselves?

The temptation is to report the fruits of such introspection in scientifically rationalistic terms. One may do so as a ploy to be heard by those who would not otherwise listen. However, unless such rationalistic talk is ironic, it will be hypocritical. To try to transcend rationalistically the limits of rationalism is a contradiction in terms. One way to resist this temptation is to remind ourselves of the kind of human being that is fostered by scientific rationalism and a scientifically rationalistic world political economy. The objectifying, alienated person is a property-owning, consuming, wage-earning individual. Ideal as denizens of industrial capitalism, people like this have certainly not fulfilled all human potential. Nor is it clear that such human beings are morally desirable or sustainable in the longer term.

oOo

Smoke, rain, abulia. What can the concerned citizen do to fight the rise of capitalism, in his own community? Study of the tides of conflict and power in a system in which there is a structural inequality is an important task. A knowledge of European intellectual history since 1789 provides a useful background. Information theory offers interesting new possibilities. Passion is helpful, especially those types of passion which are non-licit. Doubt is a necessary precondition to meaningful action. Fear is the great mover, in the end.

oOo

The use of nonrationalist representations of IPE allows us to explore not only alternative ways of knowing but also alternative modes of being human. This may, in turn, be one way to reconstitute IPE in more humane terms.

NOTES

1. This is the first paragraph of a short story by Donald Barthelme (1972). The story is written as a series of episodes, each reproduced here in turn.
2. Oleg Makarov, a cosmonaut and a rationalist, says that "within seconds of attaining Earth orbit, every cosmonaut, without exception . . . uttered the same sort of confused expression of delight and wonder." "Curious," he says, "I analyzed the initial conversations for a variety of missions and discovered an interesting pattern. . . . no one has been able to restrain his heartfelt wonder at the sight of the enthralling panorama of the Earth. The emotional outburst lasted forty-two seconds average" (Kelley, 1988:preface). Can it be a coincidence that Douglas Adams hits upon the same number as his explanation for the whole universe (Adams, 1979)?

Part 6

Commentaries

Joshua S. Goldstein **11**

Taking Off the
Gender Blinders in IPE

This volume, consciously devoted to exploring the "construction" of the field of International Political Economy (IPE), gives surprisingly little attention to the role of gender in that construction. With the exception of Runyan's intriguing chapter and a few passing references elsewhere—and presumably Peterson's chapter, which I have not seen—the discussion presumes that IPE scholarship can be analyzed as though gender did not matter. Gender themes appear in many of the chapters, but in invisible ink, so to speak. I cannot fill the gap or fully explore gender's role in the construction of IPE. Rather, I point to some relevant directions for interested scholars.

"Interested scholars" should include those who, like myself, inhabit male bodies. Gender does not equal "women"; obviously, males also have gender. If, as many feminist scholars have argued, scholarship in fields like IPE is influenced by gendered views of the subject, those gendered views are more often masculine than feminine, since more IPE scholars and policymakers are male than female. It is disturbing, after decades of these arguments, to find an overwhelming absence of men in the ranks of International Relations (IR) scholars who take gender seriously—even after Keohane (1989) put the stamp of legitimacy on the subject for the benefit of his insecure colleagues. To be sure, some scholars, male and female, are wedded to frames of reference that exclude gender—whether realist, behavioralist, or whatever. Yet for those who deliberately call into question the basic assumptions of traditional scholarship—as in this volume—gender blinders are harder to condone.

Gender shapes IPE scholarship on three levels. First, and most superficially, traditional studies of IPE have tended to ignore the role of women in the international economy. For example, "globalization" entails shifts in the participation of women and men in labor forces in both rich and poor countries. (I recall, for example, a photo of Muslim women on an Indonesian assembly line producing Barbie dolls [Goldstein, 1996:379].)

Cox and Sjolander's chapter in this volume, which views globalization in terms of identity ("us" and "them") rather than production, raises but barely addresses questions of changing gender identities as central to that process. A different aspect of women's participation in IPE constitutes the "women in development" subfield. This approach, the most developed area of feminist scholarship in IPE, touches such subjects as World Bank loans, national account statistics, International Monetary Fund conditionality, and women's cooperatives and banks. Yet another aspect of the women's-participation issue is the insight that women participate differently from men in reproduction, production, and exchange processes. From this insight flows a critique of contemporary economic liberalism, which is preoccupied with the market (exchange) while downplaying production and ignoring reproduction (Runyan, this volume).

On a second, deeper level, gendered concepts can be identified throughout theories of IPE, which are disguised as genderless constructs. I find this level, which Runyan's chapter in this volume begins to elaborate, the most interesting. Critiques of traditional theoretical constructs as masculine in nature have generated a growing literature in international *security* affairs in the past decade but are just now moving with equal vigor into IPE. Many of these critiques connect gender to the split in political theory between public (political and, by extension, international) and private (domestic, in both senses) spaces.

Object relations theory, as noted by Runyan (Chapter 5), is a common starting point for these discussions. Although Runyan (after Chodorow) emphasizes the Freudian roots of this theory, centering on the infant's sense of frustration, she does not give adequate attention to the subsequent differentiation of gender identity in boys and girls. (I may, however, have missed some nuances, since I read the paragraph about "fathers who are typically distant caretakers" with a squirming two-year-old boy in my lap.)

The basic idea here has been developed theoretically and empirically in developmental psychology, notably in Gilligan's (1982) very accessible *In a Different Voice*. Since almost all young children have female caretakers, girls develop gender identity based on similarity with the caretaker (and, by extension, the social environment). Boys develop gender identity based on separation and differentiation from the caretaker and environment. From these roots grow the highly gendered concepts of autonomy versus connection.

To oversimplify somewhat, psychologists find that males tend to value independence and fear entanglement, whereas females tend to value intimacy and fear abandonment. Thus, the traditional focus of realism generally and IPE specifically—on the interactions of separate and autonomous states—reflects a masculine construction of the subject. This is nowhere truer than in mainstream IPE scholarship, which clings stubbornly to the notion of state sovereignty in the face of cross-cutting economic processes. Even neoliberal studies of international reciprocity and regimes seldom break out of the framework of autonomous, self-interested states, which nonetheless can achieve cooperation despite their autonomy under international "anarchy."

Studies of children at play show marked gender differences in interaction styles (Maccoby, 1990). Boys tend to play in larger groups, in larger and more public spaces, play more competitive and rougher games, and form or break friendships easily based on mutual interests in activities. Girls tend to form closer, more intimate, and longer-lasting friendships, play in more private spaces, and react more emotionally to the breakup of friendships. Boys, much more often than girls, learn to play with enemies and compete with friends according to the rules of a game. They use legal debates to resolve disputes, whereas girls might simply break off the game if a dispute threatened friendships. Boys' speech (notably interrupting, threatening, commanding, boasting) promotes dominance and individuality, whereas girls' speech (notably expressing agreement with a previous speaker or pausing to let another speaker in) promotes social connection.

These gender differences in children's play map easily onto central constructs and practices in IR and IPE. In realism, the equivalence of friends and enemies and the fluidity of alliances reflect a masculine worldview. In IPE, the obsession with the market as a public, competitive, individualistic activity governed by shared rules similarly reflects masculine values (Tickner, 1992b:73).

Again, neoliberals as well as realists construct theoretical frameworks with masculine building blocks. For example, the concept of international regimes—sets of rules, norms, and procedures that govern the participation of self-interested and autonomous actors—reflects the play style of boys, not girls. And hegemonic stability theory emphasizes the importance of well-defined dominance relations in managing the conflicts arising from individual self-interest. A feminist framework of analysis for IPE—presumably reflecting the importance of empathy and stable connections in a web of highly interdependent political-economic relationships—barely exists today.

The third and deepest level of gender influence on IPE concerns feminist epistemology—the idea that gender shapes our notions about the nature and validity of knowledge. This idea developed as a critique in natural sciences and then found applications in social sciences, including IR. For example, Keller (1985:158–176) analyzes geneticist Barbara McClintock's methods, which sought a "feeling for the organism" in all its complexity instead of looking for a central dogma based on abstract rules and detachment from the subject. Feminist scholarship—to oversimplify again!—is more likely than traditional scholarship to value engagement with (rather than detachment from) its subjects, to look at context and detail rather than cover many cases with a few abstract rules and formulas, and to care more about effects and outcomes of scholarship rather than profess value neutrality.

By these standards, not only traditional IPE but also the present volume seem to have been little affected by feminist epistemology. Onuf's preoccupation with rules (Chapters 1 and 6) seems to reflect boys' style of play. Even the categories of "speech acts" he refers to (from Searle)—assertive, directive, and commissive—seem abstract and instrumental; Leaper's (1991) speech-act categories in developmental psychology include both "collaborative" and "controlling" acts, reflecting the affiliation versus distancing found in girls' and boys' discourses, respectively. Roberts's chapter also makes extensive use of "rules," including rules in international regimes, without reflecting on the gendered assumptions behind the concept: "practices developed among *autonomous* actors pursuing their own *interests*"(p. 157, emphasis added).

Pettman's chapter makes no explicit gender arguments yet includes paragraphs that seem to counterpose capitalism against various images of female bodies and mistresses. Rosow's chapter notes that the construction of the Adam Smith story omits women—but he does not follow up the point. I suspect that in Rupert's interesting discussion of right-wing ideologies of globalization (Chapter 7) there is an omitted element regarding the gender aspects of the Patriot groups he describes; these aspects may in fact play an important role in the construction of those groups' views on economic globalization. In each of these chapters, gender doors open briefly, then abruptly close again.

Space does not permit a review of the relevant feminist literatures here. Interested scholars—and I mean especially my fellow "fellas"—can explore some of these authors, among others: in international relations, Cynthia Enloe, Rebecca Grant, Kathleen Newland, V. Spike Peterson, Betty Reardon, Judith Stiehm, Christine Sylvester, J. Ann Tickner, and Sandra Whitworth; in political theory, Nancy Chodorow, Jean Elshtain, Nancy Hartsock, Nancy Hirschmann, and Sara Ruddick; in feminist epistemology, Sandra Harding, Donna Haraway, and Evelyn Fox Keller; and in developmental psychology, Carol Gilligan, Janet Lever, and Eleanor Maccoby. (If you are short on time, just read the male authors on that list.) I try to situate feminist scholarship in relation to the field of IR in Goldstein (1996:108–125).

The study of IR has proven surprisingly resistant to feminist scholarship, despite (or perhaps because of) the fact that its core concepts such as sovereignty, power, and war are deeply gender laden. As feminists have followed the most logical routes of entry—critiques of realism and the war system—IPE has received less attention. Now, as basic concepts and assumptions of IPE (and neoliberal institutionalism in particular) are being re-examined and criticized, political scientists have an excellent opportunity to bring the role of gender to the forefront. Since such an approach promises new insights and potential theoretical advances, it can benefit both male and female scholars. Actually, we (especially we men) have used gender in the construction of IPE for a long time; the question is whether we are mature and secure enough to think reflectively about those uses.

James K. Oliver　12

Constituting, Deconstructing, and Reconstituting IPE

Constituting International Political Economy proceeds from Wendt's (1987) and Onuf's (1989) reconstruction of the agent-structure problematique: Structures and agents are understood to be reciprocally and continuously co-constitutive of one another. The upshot is a complexly interdependent and interpenetrated social construction in which "we (as people, scholars) make the world and the world makes us" (Onuf, "Manifesto," p. 7). Likewise, ontology constrains policy prescriptions and practices, even as policy choices and their outcomes constrain and reconstitute ontology. To constitute International Political Economy is to co-constitute policy that in turn (re)shapes IPE. IPE is a world that makes us but is also a world to be made.

Insofar as the premises and perspectives of IPE are co-constitutive of policy, then a no less critical policy analysis would seem an option— indeed, a necessity. The opportunities for agency unlocked by the constructivist move invite the purposive generation of alternative premises, policies, and practices. In this volume there is abundant critical analysis and deconstruction of the premises and philosophical underpinnings of the prevailing liberal IPE, but little reconstituting of IPE, its political principles, or practices. I examine each in turn. All quotations, unless noted, come from this volume.

Burch deconstructs IPE to the seventeenth-century European "bifurcation" in property rights that established a "foundational ontological grid" encompassing sovereignty and the politics/economics split upon which the edifice of IPE takes shape. But this IPE is understood to be "less a discipline or subject than an ideological architecture" deficient in "theories of the state, capitalism, and the global system [and a]lso typically lacking . . . history, interpretation, socially contingent behavior, and attention to the emergence of historical structures" (p. 37). Rosow insists that the consequence of this construction of "liberal ideology" has been an insipid neoliberal "politics of reassurance" in which political liberalism's traditional concern for equality and justice are now diminished (p. 50).

Inayatullah and Blaney no less forcefully critique both the reigning curator of liberal neorealism, Gilpin, and his critic, Ashley, for reifying and thus detaching the economy from its co-constitutive social and political settings. Gilpin constructs the economy as a dangerously "homogenizing" force that threatens international relations. Accordingly, Gilpin's neorealism becomes an apologia for hegemonic domination: The economic juggernaut can be contained only by an overbearing hegemonic counterforce. Ashley is similarly anxious that "the economy freezes the entire social order [and] . . . destroys political life" (p. 62), but his reified asocial view of the economy is played against "politics" understood as a "logic" concerned with social relations. In this construction economy is a cold and inhumane preoccupation with power and domination, and politics is concerned with human value, liberation, and change (pp. 67–68).

Neither position can be generative of the "dialectical social theory and criticism" (p. 60) deemed necessary for establishing a reconstructed IPE. Rather, Inayatullah and Blaney call for a return to earlier dialectical and critical social theory. They prefer Polanyi's insistence upon the "social embeddedness" of the economy, for it allows political economy to be constituted as social practice. So constituted, "IPE theorists conduct intrinsically ethical inquiries that [may] affirm or challenge our most basic commitments and taken-for-granted social practices" (pp. 75–76).

Not the least of these practices, Runyan insists, is "the most often told story of IPE," a story of men, states, and markets (p. 79). This story is built upon interlocking inversions, repressions, bifurcations, and denials: the discounting of social welfare needs; privileging the "market" (exchange) over the meeting of basic needs undertaken by women (care); public production over private, domestic reproductive work; the separation of the economic, political, and the social (family); and "invisibilizing" relations of reciprocity. Runyan is skeptical of IPE's organizational forms, including international regimes (p. 88), and concludes that "mutual respect, care, and welfare can only arise through struggles for nonhierarchical gender relations" (p. 89).

If, however, this point is a *precondition* of reconstituting IPE, then the goal recedes beyond the conceptual horizon. Nonetheless, Runyan plants her marker, as do few others in this volume. One can infer from these critical analyses *approaches* to alternative IPEs. Thus, Onuf begins with his constructivist manifesto from which he opens the opportunity for generating new worlds. However, in Chapter 6, Onuf urges us to understand and liberate ourselves from the constrictive implications of IPE's preoccupation with its (mis)construction of "hegemony" as a form of rule. Roberts offers rational choice as an approach that will best realize a reconstituted IPE, but

Pettman smothers the incipient project in skepticism concerning the "rationalist understanding":

> We stand back to get a better perspective, but we find that the costs of doing so are insupportable in terms of a subject like IPE. We surrender that perspective for one more cognizant of the constituted nature of all human knowledge and therefore of IPE. We stand close to listen. When this mind-move proves incapable of discriminating between false and less false forms of consciousness, we look for ways to be more critical. We rediscover in the process the strengths of scientific rationalism, and we stand back to get some perspective again. And so it goes. (p. 182)

Indeed. But where? Should we "attend to the contradictory structures of purpose and meaning constituting political economy" and move "into deliberations on the merits of political economy as a global mode of social life" (Inayatullah and Blaney, p. 76)? What might this entail? An "ongoing process of making sense of the meanings and purposes of" relationships among key normative concepts is clearly necessary (p. 74), but if "IPE is thereby necessarily an exploration of who we might be and how we might live differently," then "theoretical inquiry needs to own up to its status as political and social intervention" (Inayatullah and Blaney, p. 75). But are we to understand this political and social intervention as entailing something beyond "a deliberation"?

Rupert thinks so. He affirms the urgent necessity of venturing beyond theory and into the domain of policy principles and practices because working people everywhere are dangerously alienated by neoliberal internationalist economic integration. The antiglobalist populist right may, therefore, capture "popular common sense" from which "democratizing transnational political projects" might otherwise be launched.

"Left-progressives" must construct an "explicitly politicized" global economy activated by "transnational coalitions of popular forces" that will confront and constrain "corporate power" with "a framework of democratically developed standards" enforcing "social accountability for global economic actors" (Rupert, p. 135). In this way, the populist right's reactionary appeals to nationalism, individualism, and racism can be preempted, the high ground of common sense seized, and the left-progressive IPE constructed. If the project fails, then U.S. workers will see themselves as struggling alone against foreign armies of low-wage workers: enemies, not potential allies in global coalitions arrayed against global capital. Indeed, they may turn to global capital for illusory surcease.

It is, one suspects, later in the day than this projection suggests. The object of this political struggle is larger and more diverse than might be inferred from the analysis. Rupert is rightly dubious that U.S. labor will identify with a "global proletariat"; how much less likely are such allegiances among downsized middle managers and high technology industry technicians? Indeed, how likely are the latter to identify with *U.S.* workers?

How then are critical and/or constructivist theorists to respond to Onuf's manifesto or Rupert's analysis? This volume demonstrates the *critical,* deconstructive capacity of constructivist IPE: exposition of the constructed and essentially ideological quality of IPE and the tentative identification of alternative, albeit contested, approaches to a reconstituted IPE. But there is the opportunity—indeed the necessity—for more. If, as Rupert asserts, there is nothing less under way here than a struggle "to define the horizons of political action," then constructivist IPE must move beyond "deliberations," conversations, and discoveries that the regnant IPE is the ideological embodiment of transnational capitalism and U.S. foreign policy and that this hegemony extends to the very heart of the scholarly enterprise.

Constructivist theorists should recall that an earlier generation of "critical" International Relations (IR) theorists drew similar connections between the dominant theoretical and policy constructs of their era. Like liberal IPE today, "the strategy of conflict" dominated academic IR discourse from the late 1950s through the early 1980s. Schelling (1960) wrote the "hegemonic" or "paradigmatic" statement, but Kahn, Kisssinger, and Wohlstetter penned thematic variations. This tradition defined the boundaries of "important" research and provided opportunities for career-making publications and entrée into policy circles. However, by the onset of "Cold War II" and the arrival of the Reagan administration, the defining "paradigm" became manifest in Waltz's (1979) "theory of international politics." Central to this theory was not only the neorealist construct but also the claim that the most stable (best?) of worlds was that spanned by a bipolar balance of power (Waltz, 1979:170–193). The apotheosis of IR theory constituted, therefore, a congratulatory affirmation of U.S. foreign policy. That this hegemonic construct had been deconstructed brilliantly in the mid-1960s by Green (1966) was not sufficient, however, to reconstruct IR theory and practice.

Deconstructions are necessary but not sufficient—not even to so reformist a task as confronting transnational capital with standards of global social accountability. Moreover, even this modest goal begs fundamental questions concerning the substantive content of the standards, procedures for development, and enforcement. Insofar as political practices are addressed in these analyses, they are allusions to "democratically developed standards" (Rupert, p. 135), "knowledgeable practice" in which "actors know and negotiate the rules, forces, and tensions of modern economic life" (Inayatullah and Blaney, p. 75), and "diffuse reciprocity" (Runyan, p. 88, after Keohane).

This is, however, the language of the scorned "neo-institutionalists and regime theorists [who] promote functionalist management and cooperation"

(Rosow, p. 51). This is an ironic, if inadvertent, move for theorists who are implicitly or explicitly dismissive of "managerial liberalism." Finally, it is but a minor additional move to constitute these constructivist principles as political action to "control and steer" the system purposefully "without presuming the presence of hierarchy" (Rosenau, 1995:14) or to "govern without sovereign authority, relationships that transcend national frontiers" (Finklestein, 1995:369).

This is, of course, to put regime theory and "global governance" words into the mouths of constructivist IPE theorists. Until, however, these theorists construct their own IPE and a co-constituted course of political action (thereby fulfilling the promise of their critical perspective), it is not an implausible construction.

V. Spike Peterson 13
Commenting on *Constituting IPE*

This volume makes a welcome contribution to IPE scholarship by clarifying constructivist theory and research.[1] It is also a pleasure to read: clear, tight prose in the service of well-organized, thoughtful, and often creative essays. I enjoyed the volume immensely, though I share here only some of the reasons. I also pose questions and concerns prompted by my ongoing interests and fueled by points raised in the text. First, as matters of metatheory, I consider the notions of exploitation and rationality expressed or implied by the authors in this volume. I then turn to old and new problems raised by theorizations of agency.

Onuf's manifesto (Chapter 1) sets the tone for the book by clearly and concisely rendering constructivism's fundamentals: Rules bridge agents and structures; they "foster rational choice"; they enable agency and "stable arrangements"; "rules yield rule," and "rule, as such, always involves some manner and degree of domination and exploitation." Roberts (Chapter 9) also addresses metatheoretical issues. His wonderfully accessible chapter offers a theory of motivation—"how and why rules are constituted"— which he argues (and I agree) that constructivism otherwise lacks. Drawing on rational choice theory, Roberts generates an explanatory (causal) theory by focusing on preference *formation* ("the interactive practice of agents") rather than the actual choice situation.

From a different angle on methods and metatheory, Pettman creatively augments his indictment of scientific rationalism by interspersing paragraphs from nonobjectifying fiction. The incongruity of these excerpts brings his argument "to life" and (though I would have preferred a less heterosexist short story) illustrates the tremendous distance between "objective" and "subjective" accounts, suggesting, if only briefly, how much our rationalist inclinations exclude.

In regard to metatheoretical issues, I am most concerned here with how domination and rationality are cast in service to constructivism. For example, I do not understand why rules *necessarily* yield exploitative rule, as Burch (Chapter 2) and Onuf (Chapter 6) state. Taking language as analogous, I accept that linguistic rules constrain what I can intelligibly say/

communicate and in that sense "rule" my speaking actions. Yet language does so in ways that may *or may not* constitute domination. Further, although power relations differentially locate speakers—thereby structuring who gets to say what, when, where, and with what effects—such power relations constitute *varyingly* exploitative dynamics. (I find a Foucauldian perspective more appropriate for characterizing how we speak and act: Rules and power are ubiquitous conditions that simultaneously constrain and enable—regulate and constitute—speech and action.) In sum, I accept that rules are a way of describing how social life is constituted/made possible/rendered intelligible and that rules *may and frequently do* constitute exploitative relations. But insisting that all rules *necessarily* yield exploitative rule seems to entail one of the following.

First, the constructivist claim implies that there are no nonexploitative actions. In this case, *exploitation* is a nondiscriminating term that either tells us nothing (by precluding "useful" distinctions) or specifically/intentionally tells us that all human interaction is exploitative. In the latter case, constructivist premises are complicit in reproducing exploitation, by virtue of excluding all alternative characterizations of human interaction. (If exploitation is cast as ubiquitous, we are left without any tools for discriminating among forms of exploitative and transformative possibilities.)

A second implication holds that nonexploitative actions are not rule-governed. If so, then constructivism is not a theory of social relations but a theory of exploitative relations. Third, perhaps I misunderstand how constructivists are deploying the terms *exploitation* and *domination,* in which case I am probably not the only reader to do so! As constructivists, in particular, know, language matters. In short, my objection here is to the political (immobilizing, nondiscerning, and perhaps misleading) effects of the linguistic framing that constructivists adopt.

In regard to rationality, it is difficult to be brief yet sufficiently clear in articulating my concerns. Constructivists are critical of dualistic framing, yet they appear to reproduce the (hierarchical and profoundly gendered) dichotomy of rationality-irrationality. How and where do constructivists address the power (and ruling effects) of ambiguity, emotion, contradiction, desire, and attachment? Constructivists emphasize social context, yet their privileging of "rules" and rationality tends toward the abstract, generating disembedded and disembodied accounts. Where are real people with variously conflicting and crosscutting agendas, identities, and practical consciousness? How do constructivists address not only conflicting objectives but different time frames, different moods, and different common senses? In short, how is constructivist rationality adequate to its contextual tasks?

My concerns here reflect long-standing skepticism regarding conventional privileging of rationality, as exemplified in rational choice theory. They also reflect long-standing feminist skepticism regarding disembedded and disembodied theory (Peterson, 1992, 1997). I am *not* arguing "against reason/rationality"; that would be a nonsensical claim outside of binary thought. I am suggesting that "rationality" as typically posited cannot bear the weight we assign it. We deploy it as if its meaning was clear and stable, yet how rationality is constituted remains a core problematique—of epistemology and politics. That is, rethinking rationality is not coincidental but key to moving beyond positivist and liberal binaries. The latter are (among other limitations) simply and profoundly too monological and reductionist to serve as adequate framing devices for understanding social relations/reality; they deny and therefore cannot address the complexity that specifically constitutes social relations/reality. Instead, conventional "rationality" presupposes a metaphysics of identity in which either-or constructions dominate and through which simplicity is imposed on inherently complex and ambiguous phenomena. Hence, by acritically adopting "rationality," constructivism remains within and reproduces positivist and liberal "givens"—even as its theorists disavow those boundaries. Moreover, *it prevents us from taking alternative formulations (e.g., coherence) seriously* (not to abandon reason, but to recast it).

Other chapters less directly engage metatheory, though they build on constructivist principles. At a minimum, each chapter presupposes the interaction of societal dimensions and the importance of *embedding agents in social structures*. This is all to the good! I especially appreciated Chapter 2, in which Burch (re)tells the co-constituting story of liberalism that naturalizes "our modern sense of domestic and international politics, a separate system of economic relations, and the centrality of reason and certainty as the measures of human practice (p. 38)." This descriptive account, like Roberts's story of sea rules (Chapter 9) and Onuf's rewriting of hegemony (Chapter 6), demonstrates admirably *how* co-constitution works, how it *makes* or constructs "reality." Such accounts open up—even as they "fill in"—our understanding of reified themes and hence their political effects.

Rosow (Chapter 3) renders a different but overlapping story that describes how economic liberalism displaces political liberalism such that "commercial society" appears to be a "natural" progression of human endeavor and, hence, to be celebrated. Again, economics eclipses politics. Inayatullah and Blaney (Chapter 4) seek to de-reify the economy and embed it in social relations. Telling a story of anxiety in regard to the economy (by reference to Gilpin's economic "laws" and Ashley's [alleged] "asocial economics"), they urge IPE to begin from a hermeneutic perspective.

These three chapters interrogate both the *making* of "separate spheres" and, especially, the *consequences* for accountable (liberal) politics. Runyan (Chapter 5) shifts the angle of vision to analyze IPE as a tale of "men, states, and markets" that needs retelling. At issue is not only the neoclassical separation of politics from economics (a theme in most chapters) but also the ideological separation of production from reproduction and the family/household from both politics and economics. Runyan notes, as do others, that the market comes to dominate the political. But she goes further to analyze how the reproductive sphere—*the primary site of "making"*—is rendered invisible by the preoccupation with politics and economics.

Feminist scholarship relentlessly documents how variations of the public/private split eclipse women's lives and socially necessary reproductive activities and how they are foundational to the construction of masculinist theory/practice. In spite of this extensive scholarship (e.g., Pateman, 1988, 1989), conventional and even constructivist authors continue to deploy and critique liberalism as if it were a gender-neutral ideology/practice and as if feminist critiques were irrelevant to the very issues at hand.

Feminists, on the contrary and with considerable evidence to support their case, insist that the private sphere of family/household (*made* invisible and ostensibly irrelevant by privileging only the public/private of politics/economics) is not peripheral but *constitutive* of political and economic "man." This private sphere is an ineluctable site of social relations; it is where agents, identities, cognitive maps, ideologies, and institutions are first inculcated and systemically reproduced. If we are interested in social *construction,* this site is key. Analysts cannot "embed" actors and relations "in the social" if they ignore this context. Rather than elaborate these themes here, I draw readers' attention to feminist scholarship most relevant to IPE.[2]

Addressing political construction and consequences, Rupert (Chapter 7) argues that globalization fosters counterhegemonic ideologies and complicates ensuring that their implications are progressive. At stake are people's constructions of "common sense" about globalization and how these constructions fuel both left-progressive and right-reactionary political action. The threat is both short-term complicity in extremist projects and long-term subversion of "the democratic aspects of popular common sense."

Cox and Sjolander (Chapter 8) also consider refigured agency and complicated consciousness. They argue that traditional identities based on state-centric, territorial, and class relations are no longer primary. In increasingly globalized popular culture, "othering" takes new and more mystified forms. "Difference" is now celebrated but only when co-opted for depoliticizing, universalizing, and commercializing purposes. The new (universalized) "us" are those who accept and identify with neoliberal modernity. New "others" include diverse critics of modernity and the culturally and economically marginalized—in short, all those who don't get with the neoliberal, modernist program. Thus, the actual exploitation and cultural trivialization of the planet's majority gets erased as conventional vectors of domination become discredited. As Cox and Sjolander declare, profound implications follow: We must rethink social categories and "false consciousness" as we never have before.

These two chapters starkly illuminate the *new* complexities we confront. They further complicate our understanding of "common sense," "practical consciousness," rules, and (once again) rationality. It is both an old (never adequately dealt with) and new question: What do we, as social/political theorists, *make* of "false consciousness"? It remains a problem not only for politicos/activists—now "othered" as hopelessly out of step—but for all theorists, though positivism sweeps it aside. If we care at all about progressive politics, these chapters are key. They illustrate both the difficult challenges we face and the costs of our "ignore-ance." They illuminate our refusal to see, our failure to grasp how much is at stake, and our need to recognize the importance of thinking not only clearly but politically.

NOTES

1. As a former student of Onuf, I have long admired the extraordinary breadth and depth of his intellect. I consider him one of the finest theorists in our field and am deeply gratified to see his scholarship honored in this and other recent publications.

2. On feminist economics generally, see the journal *Feminist Economics,* Waring (1988), England (1993), Ferber and Nelson (1993), Landry and MacLean (1993), and Peterson and Brown (1994). On women and economics in general, see Einhorn (1993), Funk and Mueller (1993), and Moghadam (1994). On feminist IPE, restructuring, and "women/gender and development," see the extensive literature featuring Mies (1986), Joekes (1987), Mies et al. (1988), Elson (1991), Vickers (1991), Beneria and Feldman (1992), Bakker (1994), Rowbotham and Mitter (1994), and Peterson (1996). On women and restructuring, see Commonwealth Secretariat (1989), Ward (1990), *Economic Development Quarterly* (1994), and *World Development* (1995).

Roger Tooze # 14

Constructive Criticism: Threats, Imperatives, and Opportunities of a Constitutive IPE

The chapters in this volume are a significant development in and for the theory and practice of International Political Economy (IPE). They are an important intervention in a challenging, burgeoning, but often deeply frustrating professional field of inquiry. Frustration arises because the limitations and implications of current mainstream work in IPE seem all too obvious to many of us at a time when the domestic political economies of states in the Organization of Economic Cooperation and Development have never been more unequal, when the world political economy is creating ever greater storms of change and suffering, and when the contemporary triumph of capital over other social forces and movements is all too apparent. The limitations of mainstream IPE are additionally frustrating because achieving change in ideas, theory, practices, and concrete structures in the face of an embedded orthodoxy is difficult and takes much effort and time.

The arguments in this volume themselves constitute a powerful and forward-looking critique of existing thinking in IPE, a critique I support and encourage as a part of the necessary and overdue theoretical opening of this Anglo-Saxon but U.S.-dominated practice. The "success" of these arguments will be, of course, neither easy to assess in the short term nor (crucially) dependent upon the inherent quality of their ideas and/or the substantive content of their analyses. Resistance to the versions of IPE that move beyond the empiricism of scientific rationalism, such as those discussed in the chapter by Ralph Pettman, will be strong. Such versions, including the constructivism of this volume, challenge the basis of the existing orthodoxy in IPE and the benign picture of contemporary world political economy currently constructed by and through neoliberal globalization (Mittelman, 1996). The key move for a constitutive IPE is to reveal that claims to legitimate knowledge based upon positivist methodology and empiricist epistemology (Smith, 1996) are socially constructed. This critique is just as applicable to, say, the contention over the North American Free Trade Agreement or a common European currency as it is to the theoretical contestation within IPE. By revealing the previously hidden elements of power and interest in the production of knowledge and social practice, a constitutive IPE has the clear potential to delegitimize existing practices and their institutions.

Within the terms of a more formal theoretical discourse, constructivism offers a "constitutive" move away from the positivist basis of mainstream theory toward an epistemology that allows for shared intersubjective meanings to constitute and co-constitute objective reality. This move modifies the criteria for legitimate knowledge and "good" theory; hence, it also modifies the social basis for the reception and evaluation of theory. For example, positivists or neopositivists emphasize an empirically validated, objective external reality, which they perhaps interpret or understand through socially constructed "paradigms" that claim to give objective and empirically verifiable scientific knowledge. In contrast, a constitutive IPE posits a reality that is itself socially constructed and validated by shared meanings and institutions. Hence, a "constitutive" epistemology enables—indeed, it requires—knowledge *of a form of reality not accessible via positivist methodology and empiricist epistemology.*

This is an important and specific claim that cannot be articulated at any length in this short commentary. However, the claim is based upon a critique of the limitations of the empiricist practices that International Relations and IPE inherited from social science. This inheritance has produced, according to Stephen Krasner (1996:109), an IPE "deeply embedded in the standard epistemological methodology of the social sciences which . . . simply means stating a proposition and testing it against external evidence." Such a methodology relies on a form of empiricism that effectively makes invisible many of the structures of everyday life and many of the inhabitants of the world (Tooze and Murphy, 1996). This empirical methodology is predicated on a specific and partial view of human beings and human rationality that has been increasingly challenged (Augelli and Murphy, 1997).

In the (different) reality of a constitutive IPE, power is about the contestation of knowledge, ideas, and claims to truth in both a more overt and epistemologically necessary way. If knowledge is socially constituted, then that which is good knowledge and that which is legitimate knowledge are also socially constituted. Hence, the success of constructivist theoretical intervention is, on its own epistemological terms, a matter of politics—that is, the small "p" politics of the construction of everyday life and death, including the politics of constructing IPE as formal academic knowledge. This politics is just as important as the big "P" Politics of elections and heads of government. Indeed, it is necessary to Politics as conventionally constructed.

The challenge of a "constitutive" IPE confronts conventional IPE at all levels and carries with it threats, imperatives, and opportunities.

THREATS

By treating the production of academic knowledge as constituted by the social processes of academic life, rather than as an objective/neutral process of knowledge discovery, a constitutive IPE is a potential threat to those who define and defend the "orthodox" empiricism in the academic practice of IPE and those whose position depends on them being able to do so. A constitutive IPE enables us to see the academic practice of IPE as something different from an unvarnished seeking of "the scientific truth." That is not to say that those who practice conventional academic IPE are not seeking "truth." Rather, it means that the deep structures of their practice produce a specific and limited version of that "truth." Because of the rules embodied in this practice regarding the nature and function of theory, IPE scholars are often unaware of this consequence.

By underscoring the central role of epistemological considerations in IPE, this observation emphasizes the magnitude of the constructivist challenge to conventional IPE. In this context, "epistemology matters because it determines of what we can have knowledge" (Smith, 1996:18). Moreover, because "of what we can have knowledge" becomes institutionalized and taken for granted, it forms the basis of common sense (the "doxa") that serves to construct the limits to action: "Defining common sense is therefore the ultimate act of political power" (Smith, 1996:13; see also Gramsci, 1971; Bourdieu, 1977). What is at stake here is nothing less than the definition of the common sense of the world political economy by those who practice academic IPE.

As already discussed, a constitutive IPE may revise many of the long held analyses and conclusions regarding the nature and structure of the world political economy. The potential delegitimization this revision may entail always threatens conventional descriptions of the commonsense version of the world political economy and conventional power holders in it. Scholars will surely resist threats to conventional versions by claiming that the constitutive version is "biased" and "nonscientific" and that it does not understanding the reality of political economy. This resistance demonstrates that those who define the common sense of the world political economy have no doubt that they themselves operate within and through a constitutive political economy—that is, they continually and instrumentally use this reality to achieve and maintain control and power and to capture markets (e.g., Cox and Sjolander's chapter, this volume). This fact makes the denial of such a reality by academic IPE all the more perplexing and perhaps all the more political.

IMPERATIVES

The move to a constitutive IPE, however, also imposes certain imperatives on those who practice academic IPE. These imperatives come principally from the epistemological logic of a constitutive IPE, and they partly focus on the consequences of challenging the established empiricism.

A constitutive IPE is not only more explicitly concerned with the metatheoretical basis of its own theory—and hence concerned with methodology, epistemology, and ontology—but it also has to be fully reflexive if it is to avoid embodying epistemological contradiction. This means that a constitutive IPE needs to account for its own production within the overall structures of world political economy. To do this necessarily entails historicizing concepts and theory by looking at the practices that construct particular concepts at particular conjunctures of time and space. However, reflexivity is sometimes a harsh imperative.

In this volume, Onuf (Chapter 6) presents just such a thoughtful, reflexive account of IPE. However, although this account is in accord with the imperative of reflexivity, it seems to fall prey to one of the dangers of constitutive theory—that is, to its potential ethnocentrism. Onuf's account of the emergence of IPE is purely American; it certainly does not fit with my own (admittedly also ethnocentric) experience of being involved in the development of IPE since 1972. Nor, I suspect, would many outside the United States construct a similar account. Indeed, Onuf's account of IPE is almost an example of the "hegemony" that the author criticizes. The imperative here is to ask the question "*whose* construction?" By implication, we need to look again at the epistemological rules for legitimate knowledge.

The imperative to historicize is difficult to translate in practice. With even the best intentions, the result is often the reification of key entities and concepts. Inayatullah and Blaney (Chapter 4) illustrate this difficulty in Richard Ashley's work. However, Roberts's chapter illustrates many of the same difficulties and problems. Roberts clearly presents an innovative and intriguing argument, but the logic of his argument ultimately depends upon a particular and historical *construction* of "rationality," as does all contemporary rational choice analysis. Theorists often derive from Vilfredo Pareto a construction of rationality as "simple" rationality and posit a pattern of "individualistic, rationalistic judgement of the relative desirability of things apprehended by the immediate senses" (Augelli and Murphy, 1997). Yet critics challenge the Paretian construction of human psychology as too narrow, because it leaves out important attributes of human behavior. Thus, this construction produces a specific and distorted sense of human interaction that is inappropriate to collectivities of human beings. So, rather than treat "rationality" as a universal concept against which other concepts can be measured or identified, a constitutive IPE should historicize rationality; otherwise that concept, too, will be reified or misappropriated.

OPPORTUNITIES

This volume demonstrates or brings to the foreground some of the opportunities that a constitutive IPE presents. Four are significant:

- The benefits of a reflexive understanding of academic IPE that neither places theory outside or above the reality it purports to describe nor promotes reification
- The opportunity to develop a historical understanding of IPE that could lead to an adequate theory of historical change in the world political economy
- The analysis of the practices by which the core dichotomies of economics/politics, public/private, and domestic/international are maintained and reproduced
- The "thicker" and more complete descriptions of world political economy that are both desirable and possible—in contrast to the imposed parsimony of rational empiricism—which may lead to the identification and analysis of previously hidden or fuzzy modes of control and sources of power

Some of these opportunities are created by any of several versions of IPE that reject the simple empiricist epistemology associated with the conventional IPE described by Krasner (1996). Yet a constitutive IPE—whatever its specific content or theoretical emphases—stresses the processes whereby power is defined and wielded by and through social construction. There are, of course, a host of theoretical and philosophical problems that need to be resolved. Not the least is the foundational status of constitutive IPE and its relationship to concrete material forces. However, what is important in this book is the attempt to offer analyses that provide a version of IPE different from that purveyed by the mainstream. Progress in understanding and explaining the world political economy can come from the contestation of different versions of IPE, not just from different results using the same methodology. The key distinction in constitutive IPE is the epistemology used by its theorists. This epistemology can enable us to have knowledge of a different reality of the world political economy and hence

construct a different IPE and a different "common sense." Only by changing the way that IPE defines "common sense" will a constitutive IPE
achieve real change.

Bibliography

Numbers in brackets indicate the
chapters in this book where the reference is cited.

ABRAHAM, Larry, ed. (1985) *Call It Conspiracy*. Wauna, WA: Double A Publications. [7]

ADAMS, Douglas. (1979) *The Hitchhiker's Guide to the Galaxy*. London: Pan Press. [10]

AFL-CIO. (1991) *Exploiting Both Sides: U.S.-Mexico Free Trade*. Washington, DC: AFL-CIO. [7]

AGNEW, John A. (1994) "Timeless Space and State-Centrism: The Geographical Assumptions of International Relations Theory." In S. Rosow et al., eds., *The Global Economy as Political Space*, 87–106. Boulder, CO: Lynne Rienner. [2]

AMATURO, Winifred. (1995) "Literature and International Relations: The Question of Culture in the Production of International Power." *Millennium: Journal of International Studies* 24 (1) Spring: 1–25. [10]

ANDERSON, Perry. (1974) *Lineages of the Absolutist State*. London: New Left Books. [3]

ANDERSON, Sarah, John CAVANAGH, and Jonathan WILLIAMS. (1995) "Workers Lose, CEOs Win (II)." Washington, DC: Institute for Policy Studies. [7]

ANDREWS, Kenneth R. (1984) *Trade, Plunder, and Settlement: Maritime Enterprise and the Genesis of the British Empire, 1480–1630*. New York: Cambridge University Press. [2]

ARBLASTER, Anthony. (1984) *The Rise and Decline of Western Liberalism*. New York: Basil Blackwell. [2]

ARNOLD, Andrew. (1993) "Rich Get Richer, Poor Get Poorer Under New Trade Pact." *Spotlight*, May 17. [7]

ARTHUR, Christopher J. (1987) "Hegel on Political Economy." In D. Lamb, ed., *Hegel and Modern Philosophy*, 102–118. London: Croom Helm. [4]

ASHLEY, Richard K. (1981) "Political Realism and Human Interest." *International Studies Quarterly* 25 (2) June: 204–236. [9]

———. (1983) "Three Modes of Economism." *International Studies Quarterly* 27 (4) December: 465–499. [2, 4]

———. (1984) "The Poverty of Neorealism." *International Organization* 38 (2) Spring: 225–286. [9]

———. (1988) "Untying the Sovereign State: A Double Reading of the Anarchy Problematique." *Millennium: Journal of International Studies* 17 (2) Summer: 227–262. [2]

———. (1989) "Living on Border Lines: Man, Poststructuralism, and War." In J. Der Derian and M. Shapiro, eds., *International/Intertextual Relations:*

Postmodern Readings of World Politics, 163–187. Lexington, MA: Lexington Books. [2]

ASTON, T., ed. (1965) *Crisis in Europe: 1560–1660.* London: Routledge and Kegan Paul. [2]

AUGELLI, Enrico, and Craig MURPHY. (1997) "Consciousness, Myth, and Collective Action: Sorel, Gramsci, and the Ethical State." Paper presented at the annual meeting of the International Studies Association, March, Toronto. [14]

AVINERI, Shlomo. (1972) *Hegel's Theory of the Modern State.* Cambridge: Cambridge University Press. [4]

AVINERI, Shlomo, and Avner de SHALIT, eds. (1992) *Communitarianism and Individualism.* Oxford: Oxford University Press. [3]

BAKER, Dean, and Lawrence MISHEL. (1995) "Profits Up, Wages Down: Worker Losses Yield Big Gains for Business." Washington, DC: Economic Policy Institute (http://epn.org/epi/eppuwd.html). [7]

BAKKER, Isabella, ed. (1994) *The Strategic Silence: Gender and Economic Policy.* London: Zed Books. [13]

BALL, Terence, James FARR, and Russell HANSON. (1989) "Editors' Introduction." In *Political Innovation and Conceptual Change,* 1–5. New York: Cambridge University Press. [2]

BARKUN, Michael. (1994) *Religion and the Racist Right.* Chapel Hill: University of North Carolina Press. [7]

BARNET, Richard, and John CAVANAGH. (1994) *Global Dreams: Imperial Corporations and the New World Order.* New York: Simon and Schuster. [8]

BARTELSON, Jens. (1995) *A Genealogy of Sovereignty.* New York: Cambridge University Press. [2]

BARTHELME, Donald. (1972) "The Rise of Capitalism." In D. Barthelme, *Sadness,* 143–148. New York: Farrar, Straus and Giroux. [10]

BEITZ, Charles. (1979) *Political Theory and International Relations.* Princeton, NJ: Princeton University Press. [3]

BENERIA, Lourdes, and Shelley FELDMAN, eds. (1992) *Unequal Burden: Economic Crises, Persistent Poverty and Women's Work.* Boulder, CO: Westview. [13]

BENNETT, David. (1995) *The Party of Fear: The American Far Right from Nativism to the Militia Movement.* New York: Vintage/Random House. [7]

BENNETT, James. (1995) "Buchanan in Unfamiliar Role . . ." *New York Times,* December 31. [7]

———. (1996) "Candidate's Speech Is Called Code for Controversy." *New York Times,* January 25. [7]

BERGER, P., and T. LUCKMANN. (1966) *The Social Construction of Knowledge: A Treatise on the Sociology of Knowledge.* Garden City, NJ: Anchor Books. [4]

BERLET, Chip. (1995) "Armed Militias, Right Wing Populism, and Scapegoating." Cambridge, MA: Political Research Associates (http://www.igc.apc.org/pra). [7]

BERLET, Chip, and Matthew LYONS. (1995) "Militia Nation." *The Progressive* (June). [7]

BERMAN, Marshall. (1982) *All That Is Solid Melts Into Air: The Experience of Modernity.* New York: Penguin Books. [8]

BERNSTEIN, Richard J. (1976) *The Restructuring of Social and Political Theory.* Philadelphia: University of Pennsylvania Press. [2]

———. (1983) *Beyond Objectivism and Relativism: Science, Hermeneutics, and Praxis.* Philadelphia: University of Pennsylvania Press. [2, 10]

BHASKAR, Roy. (1975) *A Realist Theory of Science.* Leeds, England: Leeds Books Ltd. [9]

BLACK, Don. (n.d.) "Pat Buchanan Stuns Establishment." Stormfront White Nationalist Resource Page: http://204.181.176.4/stormfront/Buchanan.html. [7]

BLACK, Max. (1958) "Notes on the Meaning of 'Rule.'" *Theoria* XXIV: 107–126. [9]

———. (1962). *Models and Metaphors: Studies in Language and Philosophy.* Ithaca, NY: Cornell University Press. [9]

BLANEY, D. L., and Naeem INAYATULLAH. (forthcoming) "IPE as a Culture of Competition." In D. Jacquin, A. Oros, and M. Verweij, eds., *Culture in World Politics.* London: Macmillan. [4]

BLUESTONE, Barry. (1995) *The Polarization of American Society.* New York: Twentieth Century Fund (http://epn.org/tcf/xxblue.html). [7]

BOURDIEU, Pierre. (1977) *Outline of a Theory of Practice.* New York: Cambridge University Press. [14]

BOWLES, Samuel, and Herbert GINTIS. (1987) *Democracy and Capitalism: Property, Community, and the Contradictions of Modern Social Thought.* New York: Basic Books. [2]

BOYER, Robert, and Daniel DRACHE, eds. (1996) *States Against Markets: The Limits of Globalization.* London: Routledge. [2]

BRAUER, Kinley J. (1984) "1821–1860: Economics and the Diplomacy of American Expansionism." In W. H. Becker and S. F. Wells, Jr., eds., *Economics and World Power: An Assessment of American Diplomacy Since 1789,* 55–118. New York: Columbia University Press. [6]

BRECHER, Jeremy, and Tim COSTELLO. (1994) *Global Village or Global Pillage.* Boston: South End Press. [7]

BRITTIN, Burdick H. (1986) *International Law for Seagoing Officers.* Annapolis, MD: Naval Institute Press. [9]

BUCHANAN for PRESIDENT. (1996) "Pat Buchanan—Setting the Record Straight on Anti-Semitism." Press release dated March 1: http://www.Buchanan.org/friend1.html. [7]

BUCHANAN, Patrick. (1993a) "America First—NAFTA Never." *Washington Post National Weekly Edition,* November 15–21. [7]

———. (1993b) "NAFTA Threatens US Sovereignty." *Human Events,* September 18. [7]

———. (1994) "The Rise of Sovereignty Fears," May 4. Reproduced at Buchanan for President web site: http://www.Buchanan.org. [7]

———. (1995a) "Where the Real Power Resides." *Washington Times,* February 8. [7]

———. (1995b) "An American Economy for Americans." *Wall Street Journal,* September 5. Reproduced at Buchanan for President web site: http://www.Buchanan.org. [7]

———. (1995c) Announcement Speech, Manchester, NH, March 20. Reproduced at Buchanan for President web site: http://www.Buchanan.org. [7]

———. (1996) "In Their Own Words." *New York Times,* March 8. [7]

BUCKE, Richard. (1947) *Cosmic Consciousness: A Study in the Evolution of the Human Mind.* New York: E. P. Dutton. [10]

BULL, Hedley. (1966) "International Theory: The Case for a Classical Approach." *World Politics* 18 (3) April: 361–377. [10]

BURAWOY, Michael. (1991) "Teaching Participant Observation." In M. Burawoy et al., eds., *Ethnography Unbound: Power and Resistance in the Modern Metropolis.* Berkeley: University of California Press. [10]

BURCH, Kurt. (1994) "The 'Properties' of the State System and Global Capitalism." In S. Rosow et al., eds., *The Global Economy as Political Space,* 37–59. Boulder, CO: Lynne Rienner. [2, 3]

———. (1997) *"Property" and the Making of the International System.* Boulder: Lynne Rienner. [2]

BURKE, Peter. (1988) "Republics of Merchants in Early Modern Europe." In J. Baechler, J. A. Hall, and M. Mann, eds., *Europe and the Rise of Capitalism.* Oxford: Basil Blackwell. [3]

BURNS, Tom. (1994). "Two Conceptions of Human Agency: Rational Choice Theory and the Social Theory of Action." In P. Sztompka, ed., *Agency and Structure: Reorienting Social Theory,* 197–249. Langhorne, PA: Gordon and Breach. [9]

CALLEO, David P., and Benjamin M. ROWLAND. (1973) *America and the World Political Economy: Atlantic Dreams and National Realities.* Bloomington: Indiana University Press. [6]

CAMILLERI, Joseph A., and Jim FALK. (1992) *The End of Sovereignty?: The Politics of a Shrinking and Fragmenting World.* Aldershot, England: Edward Elgar Publishing Limited. [2]

CAMPBELL, David. (1992) *Writing Security: United States Foreign Policy and the Politics of Identity.* Manchester, England: Manchester University Press. [10]

CAMPBELL, Linda. (1992) "Liberty Lobby in the Spotlight . . ." *Chicago Tribune,* January 12. [7]

CAPORASO, James. (1987) "International Political Economy: Fad or Field?" *ISNotes* 13 (1): 1–8. [2]

CAPORASO, J. A., and D. P. LEVINE. (1992) *Theories of Political Economy.* Cambridge: Cambridge University Press. [4]

CARR, Edward Hallett. (1939) *The Twenty Years' Crisis, 1919–1939: An Introduction to the Study of International Relations.* New York: Harper Torchbooks. [6]

CARTO, Willis. (1993) "The Global Plantation." *Spotlight,* special NAFTA issue, May 17. [7]

CARVER, T. (1995) "Ideology: Career of a Concept." In T. Ball and R. Dagger, eds., *Ideals and Ideologies,* 1–11. 2nd ed. New York: HarperCollins. [2]

CAVANAGH, John. (1992) "Free Trade as Opportunity." In J. Cavanagh et al., eds., *Trading Freedom: How Free Trade Affects Our Lives, Work and Environment.* San Francisco: Institute for Food and Development Policy. [7]

CENTER for DEMOCRATIC RENEWAL. (1994) *Willis Carto and the Liberty Lobby.* Atlanta: CDR. [7]

CHAPMAN, Charles F. (1983) *Piloting: Seamanship and Small Boat Handling.* 56th ed., revised by E. S. Maloney. New York: Hearst Marine Books. [9]

CHASE-DUNN, Christopher. (1981) "Interstate System and Capitalist World-Economy: One Logic or Two?" *International Studies Quarterly* 25 (1) March: 19–42. [2]

———. (1989) *Global Formation: Structures of the World-Economy.* Cambridge, MA: Basil Blackwell. [2]

CHASE-DUNN, Christopher, et al. (1994) "Hegemony and Social Change." *Mershon International Studies Review* 38 (Supplement) 2: 361–376. [6]

CHESNAIS, François. (1994) *La Mondialisation du Capital.* Paris: Syros. [8]

CHODOROW, Nancy. (1978) *The Reproduction of Mothering: Psychoanalysis and the Sociology of Gender.* Berkeley: University of California Press. [5]

COHEN, J. (1985) "Strategy or Identity: New Theoretical Paradigms and Contemporary Social Movements." *Social Research* 52: 663–714. [4]

COMMONWEALTH SECRETARIAT. (1989) *Engendering Adjustment for the 1990s.* London: Commonwealth Secretariat. [12]

CORBETT, Percy E. (1959) *Law in Diplomacy.* Princeton, NJ: Princeton University Press. [6]

COTTINGHAM, John. (1984) *Rationalism.* London: Paladin Books. [10]

COX, Robert. (1977) "Labor and Hegemony." *International Organization* 31 (3) Summer: 385–424. [6]

———. (1981). "Social Forces, States, and World Order." *Millennium: Journal of International Studies* 10 (2) Summer: 126–155. Reprinted in R. O. Keohane, ed. (1986), *Neorealism and Its Critics.* New York: Columbia University Press. [9]

———. (1987) *Production, Power, and World Order: Social Forces in the Making of History.* New York: Columbia University Press. [2, 6]

———. (1989) Review of *States and Markets* by Susan Strange. *Millennium: Journal of International Studies* 18 (1) Spring: 107–110. [2]

———. (1991) "The Global Political Economy and Social Choice." In D. Drache and M. S. Gertler, eds., *The New Era of Global Competition: State Policy and Market Power,* 335–349. Montreal: McGill-Queen's University Press. [8]

———. (1993) "Gramsci, Hegemony and International Relations: An Essay in Method." In S. Gill, ed., *Gramsci, Historical Materialism and International Relations,* 49–66. Cambridge: Cambridge University Press. [6]

———. (1996) "A Perspective on Globalization." In J. H. Mittelman, ed., *Globalization: Critical Reflections,* 21–30. Boulder, CO: Lynne Rienner. [8]

COX, Wayne S. (1994) "The Politics of Violence: Global Relations, Social Structures, and the Middle East." In C. T. Sjolander and W. S. Cox, eds., *Beyond Positivism: Critical Reflections on International Relations,* 59–80. Boulder, CO: Lynne Rienner. [8]

CROWLEY, John E. (1993) *The Privileges of Independence: Neomercantilism and the American Revolution.* Baltimore: Johns Hopkins University Press. [6]

Cuomo Commission Report: A New American Formula for a Strong Economy. (1988) New York: Simon and Schuster. [3]

DAVIDSON, Donald. (1963) "Actions, Reasons, and Causes." *Journal of Philosophy* 60 (23): 685–700. [9]

———. (1980) *Essays on Actions and Events.* Oxford: Clarendon Press. [9]

DAVIS, Mike. (1990) *City of Quartz: Excavating the Future City of Los Angeles.* New York: Verso. [8]

DEES, Morris, with James CORCORAN. (1996) *Gathering Storm: America's Militia Threat.* New York: Harper Collins. [7]

DE JOUVENEL, Bertrand. (1957) *Sovereignty: An Inquiry into the Political Good.* Translated by J. F. Huntington. Chicago: University of Chicago Press. [2]

DESCH, Michael C. (1996) "War and Strong States, Peace and Weak States." *International Organization* 50 (2) Spring: 237–268. [8]

DESSLER, David. (1989) "What's at Stake in the Agent-Structure Debate." *International Organization* 43 (3) Summer: 441–473. [9]

DIAMOND, Sara. (1995) *Roads to Dominion: Right-Wing Movements and Political Power in the United States.* New York: Guilford. [7]

DORAN, Charles F. (1971) *The Politics of Assimilation: Hegemony and Its Aftermath.* Baltimore: Johns Hopkins University Press. [6]

DORNBUSCH, Rudiger. (1991) "North American Free Trade: What It Means." *Columbia Journal of World Business* 26 (2) Summer (Focus Issue: Mexico): 72–76. [7]

DREYFUS, Hubert, and Stuart DREYFUS. (1987) "From Socrates to Expert Systems: The Limits of Calculative Rationality." In P. Rabinow and W. M. Sullivan, eds., *Interpretive Social Science: A Second Look, 327–350.* Berkeley: University of California Press. [10]

DRUCK, Dan. (1993) "Not a Fair Trade Agreement." From Council on Domestic Relations home page: http://www.logoplex.com/shops/cdr/cdr.html. [7]

DRYZEK, John S. (1995) "Critical Theory as a Research Program." In S. White, ed., *The Cambridge Companion to Habermas,* 97–119. New York: Cambridge University Press. [9]

DUNHAM, Arthur Louis. (1930) *The Anglo-French Treaty of Commerce of 1860 and the Progress of the Industrial Revolution in France.* Ann Arbor: University of Michigan Press. [6]

DURHAM, Martin. (1995) "The New Christian Right and the New World Order." Unpublished manuscript, University of Wolverhampton, England. [7]

Economic Development Quarterly. (1994) "Focus: Women and Economic Restructuring." 8 (1) May: 141–210. [13]

ECONOMIC POLICY INSTITUTE. (1995) "Introduction and Executive Summary to *The State of Working America 1994–95.*" Washington, DC: EPI (http://epn.org/epi/ep-swa01.html). [7]

The Economist. (1996) "Off-Piste in Davos," February 10. [7]

EDDLEM, Thomas. (1992) "NAFTA: The Misnamed Treaty." *The New American,* December 28. [7]

———. (1994) "Trading Away Our Sovereignty." *The New American,* March 7. [7]

EGAN, Timothy. (1995) "In Congress, Trying to Explain Contacts with Paramilitary Groups." *New York Times,* May 2. [7]

EINHORN, Barbara. (1993) *Cinderella Goes to Market: Citizenship, Gender and the Women's Movement in East Central Europe.* New York: Verso Books. [13]

ELIAS, Norbert. (1938/1978) *The Civilizing Process.* Translated by E. Jephcott. New York: Urizen Books. [3]

ELSON, Diane, ed. (1991) *Male Bias in the Development Process.* Manchester, England: Manchester University Press. [13]

———. (1995) "Alternative Visions." In W. Harcourt, L. Woestman, and L. Grogan, eds., *Towards Alternative Economics from a European Perspective,* 13–15. Brussels: Network Women in Development Europe (WIDE). [5]

ELSTER, Jon. (1985a) *Making Sense of Marx.* New York: Cambridge University Press.

———. (1985b) "The Nature and Scope of Rational-Choice Explanation." In E. LePore and F. McLaughlin, eds., *Actions and Events: Perspectives on the Philosophy of Donald Davidson,* 60–72. New York: Basil Blackwell. [9]

———. (1986) "Introduction." In J. Elster, ed., *Rational Choice,* 1–33. New York: New York University Press. [9]

ENGLAND, Paula, ed. (1993) *Theory on Gender, Feminism on Theory.* New York: Aldine de Gruyth. [13]

ETZOLD, Thomas H., and John Lewis GADDIS, eds. (1978) *Containment: Documents in American Policy and Strategy, 1945–1950.* New York: Columbia University Press. [6]

FEINER, Susan F. (1995) "Reading Neoclassical Economics: Toward an Erotic Economy of Sharing." In E. Kuiper and J. Sap, eds., *Out of the Margin: Feminist Perspectives on Economics,* 151–166. London: Routledge. [5]

FERBER, Marianne A., and Julie A. NELSON, eds. (1993) *Beyond Economic Man.* Chicago: University of Chicago Press. [13]

FINKLESTEIN, Lawrence. (1995) "What Is Global Governance?" *Global Governance* 1 (3) September–December: 367–372. [12]

FOUCAULT, Michel. (1977) "Nietzsche, Genealogy, History." In D. F. Bouchard, ed., *Language, Counter-Memory, Practice.* Ithaca, NY: Cornell University Press. [3]

FOWLER, Michael Ross, and Julie Marie BUNCK. (1995) *Law, Power, and the Sovereign State: The Evolution and Application of the Concept of Sovereignty.* University Park: Pennsylvania State University Press. [2]

FRANTZ, Douglas, and Michael JANOFSKY. (1996) "Buchanan Drawing Extremist Support . . ." *New York Times,* February 23. [7]

FREEMAN, John. (1989) *Democracy and Markets.* Ithaca, NY: Cornell University Press. [2]

FRIEDEN, Jeffry, and David A. LAKE. (1991) *International Political Economy: Perspectives on Global Power and Wealth.* 2nd ed. New York: St. Martin's Press. [2]

FRIEDMAN, Milton. (1996) "Hong Kong vs. Buchanan." *Wall Street Journal,* March 7. [7]

FUKUYAMA, Francis. (1992) *The End of History and the Last Man.* New York: Free Press. [3]

FUNK, Nanette, and Magda MUELLER. (1993) *Gender Politics and Post-Communism.* New York: Routledge. [13]

GALLAGHER, John, and Ronald ROBINSON. (1953) "The Imperialism of Free Trade." *Economic History Review* 6 (1): 1–15. [6]

GALLAGHER, Shaun. (1987) "Interdependence and Freedom in Hegel's Economics." In W. Maker, ed., *Hegel on Economics and Freedom,* 159–181. Macon, GA: Mercer University Press. [4]

GANZ, Joan Safran. (1971) *Rules: A Systematic Study.* The Hague: Mouton. [9]

GEERTZ, Clifford. (1973) *The Interpretation of Cultures.* New York: Basic Books. [2]

GEORGE, Jim. (1994) *Discourses on Global Politics: A Critical (Re)introduction to International Relations.* Boulder, CO: Lynne Rienner. [3, 10]

GIDDENS, A. (1979) *Central Problems in Social Theory: Action, Structure and Contradiction in Social Analysis.* Berkeley: University of California Press. [1, 4, 9]

———. (1981) *A Contemporary Critique of Historical Materialism, Vol. 1: Power, Property and the State.* Berkeley: University of California Press. [6]

———. (1984) *The Constitution of Society: Outline of the Theory of Structuration.* Berkeley: University of California Press. [4, 9]

———. (1990) *The Consequences of Modernity.* Stanford, CA: Stanford University Press. [2]

———. (1993) *New Rules of Sociological Methods: A Positive Critique of Interpretative Sociologies.* 2nd ed. Stanford, CA: Stanford University Press. [1]

GILBERT, Felix. (1961) *To the Farewell Address: Ideas of Early American Foreign Policy.* Princeton, NJ: Princeton University Press. [6]

GILL, Stephen, ed. (1993) *Gramsci, Historical Materialism, and International Relations.* Cambridge: Cambridge University Press. [3, 7]

GILL, Stephen, and David LAW. (1988) *The Global Political Economy: Perspectives, Problems, and Policies.* Baltimore: Johns Hopkins University Press. [2, 3]

GILLIGAN, Carol. (1982) *In a Different Voice: Psychological Theory and Women's Development.* Cambridge: Harvard University Press. [11]

GILPIN, Robert. (1975) *U.S. Power and the Multinational Corporation: The Political Economy of Direct Foreign Investment.* New York: Basic Books. [2, 4, 6]

————. (1976) "The Political Economy of the Multinational Corporations: Three Contrasting Perspectives." *American Political Science Review* 70 (1): 184–191. [6]

————. (1981) *War and Change in World Politics.* New York: Cambridge University Press. [2, 4]

————. (1984) "The Richness of the Tradition of Political Realism." *International Organization* 38 (2) Spring: 287–304. Reprinted in R. O. Keohane, ed. (1986), *Neorealism and Its Critics.* New York: Columbia University Press. [9]

————. (1987) *The Political Economy of International Relations.* Princeton, NJ: Princeton University Press. [2, 3, 4]

GLADWELL, Malcolm. (1996) "Patrick J. Buchanan: History-Conscious Fighter Focuses on Trade." *Washington Post,* January 26. [7]

GOLD, Edgar. (1981) *Maritime Transport: The Evolution of International Marine Policy and Shipping Law.* Lexington, MA: Lexington Books. [9]

GOLDSTEIN, Joshua. (1988) *Long Cycles: Prosperity and War in the Modern Age.* New Haven, CT: Yale University Press. [2]

————. (1996) *International Relations.* 2nd ed. New York: HarperCollins. [11]

GORDON, David. (1988) "The Global Economy: New Edifice or Crumbling Foundations?" *New Left Review* 168 (March/April): 24–64. [3]

GOTTLIEB, Gidon. (1968) *The Logic of Choice: An Investigation of the Concepts of Rule and Rationality.* New York: Macmillan. [9]

GOULD, Carol. (1978) *Marx's Social Ontology: Individuality and Community in Marx's Social Theory.* Cambridge: MIT Press. [4]

GRAMSCI, Antonio. (1971) *Selections from the Prison Notebooks.* Edited and translated by Quintin Hoare and Geoffrey Nowell Smith. New York: International Publishers. [1, 6, 7, 14]

GRAY, Colin. (1996) "The Continued Primacy of Geography." *Orbis* 40 (2) Spring: 247–259. [8]

GRAY, John. (1986) *Liberalism.* Minneapolis: University of Minnesota Press. [2, 3]

GREEN, Philip. (1966) *Deadly Logic: The Theory of Nuclear Deterrence.* Columbus: Ohio State University Press. [12]

GREIDER, William. (1993) "The Global Marketplace: A Closet Dictator." In R. Nader et al., *The Case Against Free Trade,* 195–217. San Francisco: Earth Island Press. [7]

HABERMAS, Jürgen. (1971) *Knowledge and Human Understanding.* Boston: Beacon Press. [9]

————. (1973) *Theory and Practice.* Translated by J. Viertel. Boston: Beacon Press. [2]

————. (1978) *Knowledge and Human Interests.* London: Heineman. [10]

————. (1987) *The Philosophical Discourse of Modernity: Twelve Lectures.* Translated by Frederick Lawrence. Cambridge: MIT Press. [2]

HAMILTON, Malcolm B. (1987) "The Elements of the Concept of Ideology." *Political Studies* 35 (1): 18–38. [2]

HANNUM, Hurst. (1990) *Autonomy, Sovereignty, and Self-Determination: The Accommodation of Conflicting Rights.* Philadelphia: University of Pennsylvania Press. [2]

Harper's. (1996) "Forum: Does America Still Work?" 292 (1752) May: 35–47. [8]

HARRIS, William, and Judith LEVEY, eds. (1975) *The New Columbia Encyclopedia.* New York: Columbia University Press. [7]

HART, Jeffrey A. (1992) *Rival Capitalists: International Competitiveness in the United States, Japan and Western Europe.* Ithaca, NY: Cornell University Press. [3]

HARTZ, Louis. (1955) *The Liberal Tradition in America: An Interpretation of American Political Thought Since the Revolution.* New York: Harcourt, Brace and World. [6]

HARVEY, David. (1989) *The Condition of Postmodernity: An Enquiry into the Origins of Cultural Change.* Cambridge, MA: Basil Blackwell. [2]

HEGEL, G. W. F. (1991) *Elements of the Philosophy of Right.* Translated by H. B. Nisbet. Cambridge: Cambridge University Press. [4]

HEIDEGGER, Martin. (1987a) "The Age of the World Picture." In M. Heidegger, *The Question Concerning Technology and Other Essays,* 115–154. New York: Harper Torchbooks. [10]

———. (1987b) "Science and Reflection." In M. Heidegger, *The Question Concerning Technology and Other Essays,* 155–182. New York: Harper Torchbooks. [10]

HEILBRUNN, Jacob. (1995) "On Pat Robertson: His Anti-Semitic Sources." *New York Review of Books,* April 20: 68–71. [7]

HEIMAN, G. (1971) "The Sources and Significance of Hegel's Corporate Doctrine." In Z. A. Pelczynski, ed., *Hegel's Political Philosophy: Problems and Perspectives,* 111–135. Cambridge: Cambridge University Press. [4]

HELD, David. (1991) "Democracy, the Nation-State, and the Global System." In D. Held, ed., *Political Theory Today,* 197–235. Cambridge: Polity Press. [3]

HERZ, John. (1981) "Political Realism Revisited." *International Studies Quarterly* 25 (2) June: 182–197. [9]

HINSLEY, F. H. (1986) *Sovereignty.* 2nd ed. New York: Cambridge University Press. [2]

HIRSCHMAN, A. O. (1977) *The Passions and the Interests: Political Arguments for Capitalism Before Its Triumph.* Princeton, NJ: Princeton University Press. [3, 4]

HOLLIS, Martin. (1994) *The Philosophy of Social Science: An Introduction.* Cambridge: Cambridge University Press. [1]

HOLSTI, K. J. (1992) "Governance Without Government: Polyarchy in Nineteenth-Century European International Politics." In J. N. Rosenau and E.-O. Czempiel, eds., *Governance Without Government: Order and Change in World Politics,* 30–57. Cambridge: Cambridge University Press. [6]

HORMATS, Robert. (1996) "The High Price of Economic Isolationism." *Washington Post National Weekly Edition,* March 18–24. [7]

HORNE, Thomas A. (1990) *Property Rights and Poverty: Political Argument in Britain, 1605–1834.* Chapel Hill: University of North Carolina Press. [2]

HOWAT, G. M. D. (1974) *Stuart and Cromwellian Foreign Policy.* New York: St. Martin's Press. [2]

HUDSON, David. (1993) "American Dream Dead for People Out of Work." *Spotlight,* special NAFTA issue, May 17. [7]

HUFBAUER, Gary Clyde, and Jeffrey SCHOTT. (1993–1994) "Prescription for Growth." *Foreign Policy* 93 (Winter): 104–114. [7]

HYAM, Ronald. (1993) *Britain's Imperial Century, 1815–1914: A Study of Empire and Expansion.* 2nd ed. Lanham, MD: Barnes and Noble. [6]

HYMER, Stephen. (1979) *The Multinational Corporation: A Radical Approach.* Cambridge: Cambridge University Press. [3]

IKENBERRY, G. John. (1988) "Conclusion: An Institutional Approach to American Foreign Economic Policy." *International Organization* 42 (1): 219–243. [6]

IMLAH, Albert H. (1958) *Economic Elements in the Pax Britannica: Studies in British Foreign Trade in the Nineteenth Century.* Cambridge: Harvard University Press. [6]

INAYATULLAH, Naeem, and David BLANEY. (1995) "Realizing Sovereignty." *Review of International Studies* 21 (1): 3–20. [2, 4]

JACKSON, Robert. (1990) *Quasi-States: Sovereignty, International Relations, and the Third World.* New York: Cambridge University Press. [2]

JAMES, Alan. (1986) *Sovereign Statehood: The Basis for International Society.* London: Allen and Unwin. [2]

JAMES, Scott C., and David A. LAKE. (1989) "The Second Face of Hegemony: Britain's Repeal of the Corn Laws and the American Walker Tariff of 1846." *International Organization* 43 (1) Winter: 1–29. [6]

JANOFSKY, Michael. (1995) "Demons and Conspiracies Haunt a 'Patriot' World." *New York Times,* May 31. [7]

JASPER, William. (1992) *Global Tyranny . . . Step by Step.* Appleton, WI: Western Islands Publishers. [7]

———. (1993) "The Free Trade Charade." *The New American,* December 27. [7]

JENNINGS, Ann L. (1993) "Public or Private? Institutional Economics and Feminism." In M. A. Ferber and J. A. Nelson, eds., *Beyond Economic Man: Feminist Theory and Economics,* 111–129. Chicago: University of Chicago Press. [5]

JOEKES, Susan P. (1987) *Women in the World Economy.* New York: Oxford University Press. [13]

JOHN BIRCH SOCIETY. (various dates) *The New American.* Various issues from the collection of Political Research Associates, Cambridge, MA. [7]

———. (1985) *Back to Basics.* Appleton, WI: JBS. [7]

JOHNSON, James. (1991) "Rational Choice as Reconstructive Theory." In K. R. Monroe, ed., *The Economic Approach to Politics,* 112–142. New York: HarperCollins. [9]

KADIOGLÜ, Ayse. (1996) "The Paradox of Turkish Nationalism and the Construction of Official Identity." *Middle Eastern Studies* 32 (2) April: 177–193. [8]

KAH, Gary. (1991) *En Route to Global Occupation.* Lafayette, LA: Huntington House. [7]

KARATANI, Kojin. (1995) *Architecture as Metaphor: Language, Number, Money.* Cambridge: MIT Press. [1]

KATSON, Trisha. (1994) *The Disaster That Is GATT 1994: The Ruling Elite's Plan for the Global Plantation.* Washington, DC: Liberty Lobby. [7]

KEANE, John. (1988) *Democracy and Civil Society.* New York: Verso Books. [3]

———. (1991) *The Media and Democracy.* Cambridge, England: Polity Press. [3]

KELLEY, Kevin. (1988) *The Home Planet: Images and Reflections of Earth from Space Explorers.* Reading, MA: Addison-Wesley. [10]

KELLER, Evelyn Fox. (1985) *Reflections on Gender and Science.* New Haven, CT: Yale University Press. [11]

KELSEN, Hans. (1961) *General Theory of Law and the State.* New York: Russell and Russell. [1]

KENYON, J. P. (1978) *Stuart England.* New York: Penguin Books. [2]

KEOHANE, Robert O. (1980) "The Theory of Hegemonic Stability and Changes in International Economic Regimes, 1967–1977." In O. R. Holsti, R. M. Siverson, and A. L. George, eds., *Change in the International System,* 131–162. Boulder, CO: Westview. [6]

———. (1983) "Theory of World Politics: Structural Realism and Beyond." In A. Finifter, ed., *The State of the Discipline,* 503–540. Washington, DC: American Political Science Association. [9]

———. (1986) "Theory of World Politics: Structural Realism and Beyond." In R. O. Keohane, ed., *Neorealism and Its Critics,* 158–203. New York: Columbia University Press. [2]

———. 1989. "International Relations Theory: Contributions of a Feminist Standpoint." *Millennium: Journal of International Studies* 18 (2): 245–254. [5, 11]

KEOHANE, Robert O., and Joseph S. NYE. (1977) *Power and Interdependence: World Politics in Transition.* Boston: Little, Brown. [6]

KIM, Jaegwon. (1985) "Psychophysical Laws." In E. LePore and B. McLaughlin, eds., *Actions and Events: Perspectives on the Philosophy of Donald Davidson,* 369–386. New York: Basil Blackwell. [9]

KINDLEBERGER, Charles. (1970) *Power and Money: The Politics of International Economics and the Economics of International Politics.* New York: Basic Books. [2]

———. (1973) *The World in Depression, 1929–1939.* Berkeley: University of California Press. [6]

———. (1975) "The Rise of Free Trade in Western Europe, 1820–1875." *Journal of Economic History* 35 (1): 20–55. [6]

KLANWATCH. (1996) *False Patriots.* Montgomery, AL: Southern Poverty Law Center. [7]

KLINK, Frank F. (1993) "Core and Periphery States Make Choices—But Not Under Circumstances of Their Own Choosing: Postcolonial Imperialism and the Agent-Structure Problem." Paper presented at the annual meeting of the International Studies Association, March, Acapulco. [9]

———. (1994) "Making Room for Rule Without Forsaking Agency (and Vice Versa): Sovereignty and the Macrofoundations of Postcolonial Imperialism." Paper presented at the annual meeting of the International Studies Association, March, Washington, DC. [9]

KRAFT, Charles. (1992) "A Preliminary Socio-Economic and State Demographic Profile of the John Birch Society." Cambridge, MA: Political Research Associates. [7]

KRASNER, Stephen D. (1976) "State Power and the Structure of International Trade." *World Politics* 28 (3): 317–347. [6]

———. (1982) "Structural Causes and Regime Consequence: Regimes as Intervening Variables." *International Organization* 36 (2) Spring: 185–205. [1]

———. (1988) "Sovereignty: An Institutional Perspective." *Comparative Political Studies* 21 (1) April: 66–94. [2]

———. (1996) "The Accomplishments of International Political Economy." In S. Smith et al., eds., *International Theory: Positivism and Beyond,* 108–127. Cambridge: Cambridge University Press. [14]

KRATOCHWIL, Friedrich V. (1989) *Rules, Norms, and Decisions: On the*

Conditions of Practical and Legal Reasoning in International Relations and Domestic Affairs. Cambridge: Cambridge University Press. [9]

———. (1995) "Sovereignty as *Dominium.*" In G. Lyons and M. Mastanduno, eds., *Beyond Westphalia?* 21–42. Baltimore: Johns Hopkins University Press. [2]

KRUGMAN, P. (1993) "The Uncomfortable Truth about NAFTA." *Foreign Affairs* 72 (5) November/December: 13–19. [7]

KUEHLS, Thom. (1996) *Beyond Sovereign Territory: The Space of Ecopolitics.* Minneapolis: University of Minnesota Press. [2]

KURTH, James R. (1973) "United States Foreign Policy and Latin American Military Rule." In P. C. Schmitter, ed., *Military Rule in Latin America: Functions, Consequences and Perspectives,* 244–322. Beverly Hills, CA: Sage. [6]

LACLAU, Ernesto, and Chantal MOUFFE. (1985) *Hegemony and Socialist Strategy: Towards a Radical Democratic Politics.* New York: Verso Books. [3]

LAFFEY, Mark A. (1992) "Ideology and the Limits of Gramscian Theory in International Relations." Paper presented at the annual meeting of the International Studies Association, April, Atlanta, GA. [8]

LAIRSON, Thomas, and David SKIDMORE. (1993) *International Political Economy: The Struggle for Power and Wealth.* Fort Worth, TX: Harcourt Brace Jovanovich. [2]

LAKATOS, Imre. (1978) "Falsification and the Methodology of Scientific Research Programmes." Reprinted in J. Worrall and F. Currie, eds., *The Methodology of Scientific Research Programmes, Philosophical Papers.* Vol. I. Cambridge: Cambridge University Press. [9]

LAKE, David A. (1988) "The State and American Trade Policy in the Pre-Hegemonic Era." *International Organization* 42 (1) Winter: 33–58. [6]

———. (1993) "Leadership, Hegemony, and the International Economy: Naked Emperor or Tattered Monarch with Potential?" *International Studies Quarterly* 37 (4) December: 459–489. [6]

———. (1996) "Anarchy, Hierarchy, and the Variety of International Relations." *International Organization* 50 (1) Winter: 1–33. [1, 6]

LAMB, D. (1979) *Language and Perception in Hegel and Wittgenstein.* London: Avebury. [4]

LANDRY, Donna, and Gerald MACLEAN. (1993) *Materialist Feminisms.* Cambridge, MA: Blackwell. [13]

LARUDEE, Mehrene. (1993) "Trade Policy: Who Wins? Who Loses?" In G. Epstein et al., eds., *Creating a New World Economy,* 47–63. Philadelphia: Temple University Press. [7]

LEAPER, Campbell. (1991) "Influence and Involvement in Children's Discourse: Age, Gender, and Partner Effects." *Child Development* 62: 797–811. [11]

LEVI, Margaret. (1987) *Of Rule and Revenue.* Berkeley: University of California Press. [2]

LEVINE, D. P. (1977) *Economic Studies: Contributions to the Critique of Economic Theory.* London: Routledge and Kegan Paul. [4]

———. (1988) *Needs, Rights and the Market.* Boulder, CO: Lynne Rienner. [4]

———. (1995) *Freedom and Wealth: An Introduction to Political Economy.* Cambridge: Cambridge University Press. [4]

LIBERTY LOBBY. (various dates) *The Spotlight.* Various issues from the collection of Political Research Associates, Cambridge, MA. [7]

LIBICKI, Martin. (1996) "The Emerging Primacy of Information." *Orbis* 40 (2) Spring: 261–274. [8]

LIND, Michael. (1995a) "Rev. Robertson's Grand International Conspiracy Theory." *New York Review of Books,* February 2: 21–25. [7]
———. (1995b) "On Pat Robertson: His Defenders." *New York Review of Books,* April 20: 67–68. [7]
LINDBLOM, Charles. (1977) *Politics and Markets.* New York: Basic Books. [2]
LING, L. H. M. (1996) "Hegemony and the Internationalizing State: A Post-Colonial Analysis of China's Integration into Asian Corporatism." *Review of International Political Economy* 3 (1) Spring: 1–26. [8]
LITTLE, David. (1969/1984) *Religion, Order, and Law: A Study in Pre-Revolutionary England.* With a new preface. Foreword by R. N. Bellah. Chicago: University of Chicago Press. [2]
LOCKE, John. (1690/1965) *Two Treatises of Government.* Revised ed., with an introduction and notes by Peter Laslett. New York: Mentor/New American Library. [3]
LODGE, David. (1980) "My First Job." *London Review of Books* 2 (17) September 4–17: 23–24. (Also in R. Pettman, 1996.) [10]
LYONS, Gene M., and Michael MASTANDUNO, eds. (1995) *Beyond Westphalia?: State Sovereignty and International Intervention.* Baltimore: Johns Hopkins University Press. [2]
MACCOBY, Eleanor E. (1990) "Gender and Relationships: A Developmental Account." *American Psychologist* 45 (April): 513–520. [11]
MACPHERSON, C. B. (1962) *The Political Theory of Possessive Individualism.* New York: Oxford University Press. [2]
MARCUS, George E., and Michael M. J. FISCHER. (1986) *Anthropology as Cultural Critique.* Chicago: University of Chicago Press. [2]
MARSH, J. L. (1974) "Political Radicalism: Hegel's Critique and Alternative." *Idealistic Studies* IV: 189–199. [4]
MARX, Karl. (1934) *The Eighteenth Brumaire of Louis Bonaparte.* Moscow: Progress Publishers. [1]
———. (1964) *Economic and Philosophic Manuscripts of 1844.* Edited, with an introduction, by D. J. Struik. Translated by M. Milligan. New York: International Publishers. [2]
———. (1973) *Grundrisse.* Translated by M. Nicolaus. New York: Vintage. [4]
———. (1977) *Capital.* Vol. I. Translated by B. Fowkes. New York: Vintage. [4]
MARX, Karl, and Friedrich ENGELS. (1964) *The German Ideology.* 3rd rev. ed. Moscow: Progress Publishers.
MASUR, Sandra. (1991) "The North American Free Trade Agreement: Why It's in the Interest of U.S. Business." *Columbia Journal of World Business* 26 (2) Summer (Focus Issue: Mexico): 98–103. [7]
MATHEWS, Jessica Tuchman. (1994) "The Environment and International Security." In M. T. Klare and D. C. Thomas, eds., *World Security: Challenges for a New Century,* 274–289. New York: St. Martin's Press. [8]
MCFEE, William. (1950) *The Law of the Sea.* Philadelphia: J. B. Lippincott. [9]
MCKENDRICK, Neil, John BREWER, and J. H. PLUMB. (1982) *The Birth of a Consumer Society: The Commercialization of Eighteenth-Century England.* Bloomington: Indiana University Press. [3]
MCKEOWN, Timothy J. (1983) "Hegemonic Stability Theory and 19th Century Tariff Levels in Europe." *International Organization* 37 (1) Winter: 73–91. [6]
MCLELLAN, David. (1986) *Ideology.* Minneapolis: University of Minnesota Press. [2]

MCMANUS, John. (1995a) *The Insiders: Architects of the New World Order.* Appleton, WI: John Birch Society. [7]

————. (1995b) "More 'Free Trade' Follies." *The New American,* January 9. [7]

————. (1996) "Targeted for Destruction: Pat Buchanan's Campaign Has Raised the Ire of the Establishment." *The New American,* March 18. [7]

MCNEILL, William. (1982) *The Pursuit of Power.* Chicago: University of Chicago Press. [2]

MEARSHEIMER, John. (1990) "Why We Will Soon Miss the Cold War." *Atlantic* 266 (August). [8]

MERCER, Jonathan. (1995) "Anarchy and Identity." *International Organization* 49 (2) Spring: 229–252. [9]

MERRIAM, Jr., C. E. (1900) *History of the Theory of Sovereignty Since Rousseau.* New York: Columbia University Press. [2]

MIES, Maria. (1986) *Patriarchy and Accumulation on a World Scale: Women and the International Division of Labour.* London: Zed Books. [13]

MIES, Maria, Veronika BENNHOLDT-THOMSEN, and Claudia VON WERLHOF. (1988) *Women: The Last Colony.* London: Zed Books. [13]

MINTZ, Frank. (1985) *The Liberty Lobby and the American Right.* Westport, CT: Greenwood Press. [7]

MISHEL, Lawrence, and Jared BERNSTEIN. (1993) *The State of Working America, 1992–93.* Armonck, NJ: M. E. Sharpe. [7]

MITTELMAN, James H. (1996) "The Dynamics of Globalization." In J. H. Mittelman, ed., *Globalization: Critical Reflections,* 1–19. Boulder, CO: Lynne Rienner. [8]

MITTELMAN, James H., ed. (1996) *Globalization: Critical Reflections.* Boulder, CO: Lynne Rienner. [14]

MOGHADAM, Valentine M., ed. (1994) *Democratic Reform and the Position of Women in Transitional Economies.* Oxford: Oxford University Press. [13]

MOODY, K., and MCGINN, M. (1992) *Unions and Free Trade: Solidarity vs. Competition.* Detroit: Labor Notes Books. [7]

MORGENSTERN, Oskar. (1968) "Game Theory: Theoretical Aspects." *International Encyclopedia of the Social Sciences.* Vol. 6. New York: Macmillan. [9]

MORGENTHAU, Hans J. (1956) *Politics Among Nations.* 2nd ed., revised and enlarged. New York: Alfred Knopf.

MOUFFE, Chantal, ed. (1992) *Dimensions of Radical Democracy.* New York: Verso Books. [3]

MULLINS, Eustace. (1992) *The World Order: Our Secret Rulers.* 2nd ed. Staunton, VA: Ezra Pound Institute of Civilization. [7]

————. (1993) "Secret of Rockefeller Fortune Is Part of Our Hidden History." *Spotlight,* January 4. [7]

MURPHY, Craig N., and Roger TOOZE. (1991a) "Introduction." In C. Murphy and R. Tooze, eds., *The New International Political Economy,* 1–7. Boulder, CO: Lynne Rienner Publishers. [2]

————. (1991b) "Getting Beyond the 'Common Sense' of the IPE Orthodoxy." In C. Murphy and R. Tooze, eds., *The New International Political Economy,* 11–31. Boulder, CO: Lynne Rienner Publishers. [2]

NADER, Ralph, et al. (1993) *The Case Against Free Trade: GATT, NAFTA, and the Globalization of Corporate Power.* San Francisco: Earth Island Press. [7]

NAGEL, Thomas. (1986) *The View from Nowhere.* New York: Oxford University Press. [10]

NATIONAL ALLIANCE. (n.d.) *What Is the National Alliance?* Hillsboro, WV: National Alliance web page (http://www.natvan.com/what/what.html). [7]

NEFF, Stephen C. (1990) *Friends but No Allies: Economic Liberalism and the Law of Nations.* New York: Columbia University Press. [6]

NENNER, Howard A. (1977) *By Colour of Law: Legal Culture and Constitutional Politics in England, 1660–1689.* Chicago: University of Chicago Press. [2]

NEUFELD, Mark. (1993a) "Interpretation and the 'Science' of International Relations." *Review of International Studies* 19 (1) January: 39–61. [10]

———. (1993b) "Reflexivity and International Relations Theory." *Millennium: Journal of International Studies* 22 (1) Spring: 53–76. [10]

New York Times. (1996) *Special Report: The Downsizing of America.* New York: Times Books. Reprinted from *New York Times,* March 3–9, 1996. [7]

NICHOLSON, Linda. (1986) *Gender and History: The Limits of Social Theory in the Age of the Family.* New York: Columbia University Press. [5]

NORDHEIMER, Jon. (1996) "Buchanan Threatens Longtime Bipartisan Policy, Official Warns." *New York Times,* February 25. [7]

NORTH, Douglass C., and Robert Paul THOMAS. (1973) *The Rise of the West: A New Economic History.* New York: Cambridge University Press. [2]

NORTH, Gary. (1985) "Prologue" and "Epilogue." In L. Abraham, ed., *Call It Conspiracy.* Wauna, WA: Double A Publications. [7]

NUSSBAUM, Arthur. (1954) *A Concise History of the Law of Nations.* Rev. ed. New York: Macmillan. [6]

O'HEAR, Anthony. (1989) *Introduction to the Philosophy of Science.* Oxford: Clarendon Press. [9]

OLSON, Mancur. (1965) *The Logic of Collective Action: Public Goods and the Theory of Groups.* Cambridge: Harvard University Press. [6]

ONUF, Nicholas G. (1989) *World of Our Making: Rules and Rule in Social Theory and International Relations.* Columbia: University of South Carolina Press. [1, 2, 6, 9, 12]

———. (1991) "Sovereignty: Outline of a Conceptual History." *Alternatives* 16 (4) Fall: 425–446. [2]

———. (1994a) *"Civitas Maxima:* Wolff, Vattel and the Fate of Republicanism." *American Journal of International Law* 88 (2): 280–303. [6]

———. (1994b) "The Constitution of International Society." *European Journal of International Law* 5 (1): 1–19. [2, 9]

———. (1995) "Intervention for the Common Good." In G. M. Lyons and M. Mastanduno, eds., *Beyond Westphalia?: State Sovereignty and International Intervention,* 43–58. Baltimore: Johns Hopkins University Press. [1]

———. (1997) *The Republican Legacy in International Thought.* New York: Cambridge University Press. [3]

ONUF, Nicholas G., and Frank F. KLINK. (1989) "Anarchy, Authority, Rule." *International Studies Quarterly* 33 (2) June: 149–173. [1]

ONUF, Peter, and Nicholas ONUF. (1993) *Federal Union, Modern World: The Law of Nations in an Age of Revolutions.* Madison, WI: Madison House. [6]

PATEMAN, Carole. (1988) *The Sexual Contract.* Stanford, CA: Stanford University Press. [13]

———. (1989) *The Disorder of Women.* Stanford, CA: Stanford University Press. [13]

PELCZYNSKI, Z.A., ed. (1971) *Hegel's Political Philosophy: Problems and Perspectives.* Cambridge: Cambridge University Press. [4]

PENDERGRAST, Mark. (1993) *For God, Country, and Coca-Cola.* New York: Macmillan. [8]

PERLOFF, James. (1988) *The Shadows of Power.* Appleton, WI: Western Islands Publishers. [7]

PETERSON, Janice, and Doug BROWN, eds. (1994) *The Economic Status of Women Under Capitalism.* Aldershot, England: Edward Elgar. [13]

PETERSON, V. Spike. (1992) "Transgressing Boundaries: Theories of Knowledge, Gender, and International Relations." *Millennium: Journal of International Studies* 21 (2) Summer: 183–206. [13]

———. (1996) "The Politics of Identification in the Context of Globalization." *Women's Studies International Forum* 19 (1–2) January–April: 5–15. [13]

———. (1997) "Whose Crisis?: Early and Postmodern Masculinism." In S. Gill and J. H. Mittelman, eds., *Innovation and Transformation in International Studies.* Cambridge, England: Cambridge University Press. [13]

PETERSON, V. Spike, and Anne Sisson RUNYAN. (1993) *Global Gender Issues.* Boulder, CO: Westview. [3]

PETTMAN, Ralph. (1996) *Understanding International Political Economy, with readings for the fatigued.* Boulder, CO: Lynne Rienner. [10]

PHILPOTT, Daniel. (1995) "Sovereignty: An Introduction and Brief History." *Journal of International Affairs.* 48 (2) Winter: 353–368. [2]

PIERCE, William. (n.d.) *The New World Order, "Free Trade," and the Deindustrialization of America.* Hillsboro, WV: National Alliance web page (http://www.natvan.com/natvan/n-wd-ord.html). [7]

———. (1992) "Free Trade and the U.S. Economy." Audio recording of *American Dissident Voices* radio program. Hillsboro, WV: National Vanguard Books/ National Alliance. [7]

PIPER, Michael. (1995) "Broad-Spectrum Push for Populist Candidate." *Spotlight,* July 24. [7]

PLANT, R. (1987) "Hegel and the Political Economy." In W. Maker, ed., *Hegel on Economics and Freedom,* 95–126. Macon, GA: Mercer University Press. [4]

POCOCK, J. G. A. (1957) *The Ancient Constitution and the Feudal Law.* New York: Cambridge University Press. [2]

———. (1975) *The Machiavellian Moment.* Princeton, NJ: Princeton University Press. [2, 3]

———. (1977) "Historical Introduction." In J. G. A. Pocock, ed., *The Political World of James Harrington,* 1–152. New York: Cambridge University Press. [2]

———. (1980) "Introduction." In J. G. A. Pocock, ed., *Three British Revolutions: 1641, 1688, 1776,* 3–20. Princeton, NJ: Princeton University Press. [2]

———. (1985) *Virtue, Commerce, and History.* New York: Cambridge University Press. [2]

POLANYI, Karl. (1957) *The Great Transformation: The Political and Economic Origins of Our Time.* Boston: Beacon Press. [2, 3, 4, 5, 6]

PRZEWORSKI, Adam. (1986) *Capitalism and Social Democracy.* Cambridge: Cambridge University Press. [9]

RAPACZYNSKI, Andrzej. (1987) *Nature and Politics: Liberalism in the Philosophies of Hobbes, Locke, and Rousseau.* Ithaca, NY: Cornell University Press. [2]

RAPKIN, David P. (1990) "The Contested Concept of Hegemonic Leadership." In D. Rapkin, ed., *World Leadership and Hegemony,* 1–19. Boulder, CO: Lynne Rienner. [6]

RAWLS, John. (1955) "Two Concepts of Rules." *Philosophical Review* 64 (1) January: 3–32. [9]

RAZ, Joseph. (1975) "Reasons for Actions, Decisions and Norms." *Mind* 84 (336) October: 481–499. [9]

REEVE, Andrew. (1986) *Property.* Atlantic Highlands, NJ: Humanities Press International, Inc. [2]

RIEDEL, Manfred. (1984) *Between Tradition and Revolution: The Hegelian Transformation of Political Philosophy.* Cambridge: Cambridge University Press. [4]

RIKER, William. (1990) "Political Science and Rational Choice." In J. Alt and K. Shepsle, eds., *Perspectives on Positive Political Economy,* 163–181. New York: Cambridge University Press. [9]

ROBERTSON, Pat. (1991) *The New World Order.* Dallas: Word Publishing. [7]

ROBERTSON, Roland. (1992) *Globalization: Social Theory and Global Culture.* London: Sage Publications Ltd. [8]

ROSENAU, James. (1995) "Governance in the Twenty-first Century." *Global Governance* 1 (1) Winter: 13–44. [12]

ROSENBERG, Justin. (1994) *The Empire of Civil Society: A Critique of the Realist Theory of International Relations.* London: Verso Books. [4]

ROSENBLUM, Nancy, ed. (1989) *Liberalism and the Moral Life.* Cambridge: Harvard University Press. [3]

ROSOW, Stephen. (1994) "Nature, Need, and the Human World: 'Commercial Society' and the Construction of the World Economy." In S. J. Rosow, N. Inayatullah, and M. Rupert, eds., *The Global Economy as Political Space,* 17–36. Boulder, CO: Lynne Rienner. [3]

ROSOW, Stephen, Naeem INAYATULLAH, and Mark RUPERT, eds. (1994) *The Global Economy as Political Space.* Boulder, CO: Lynne Rienner. [2]

ROSS, Robert J. S., and Kent C. TRACHTE. (1990) *Global Capitalism: The New Leviathan.* Albany: State University of New York Press. [8]

ROWBOTHAM, Sheila, and Swasti MITTER, eds. (1994) *Dignity and Daily Bread: New Forms of Economic Organization in the Third World and the First.* London: Routledge. [13]

RUGGIE, John G. (1972) "Collective Goods and Future International Collaboration." *American Political Science Review* 66 (3): 874–893. [6]

———. (1983) "Continuity and Transformation in the World Polity: Toward a Neorealist Synthesis." *World Politics* 35 (2) January: 261–285. [2, 9]

RUNYAN, Anne Sisson. (1996) "Trading Partners: Gender Regimes and Gendered Regimes." *ICDA Journal: Focus on Trade and Development* 4 (1) Fall: 5–9. [5]

RUPERT, Mark. (1995a) *Producing Hegemony.* New York: Cambridge University Press. [7]

———. (1995b) "(Re)Politicizing the Global Economy: Liberal Common Sense and Ideological Struggle in the U.S. NAFTA Debate." *Review of International Political Economy* 2 (4) Autumn: 658–692. [7]

———. (1997) "Globalization and the Reconstruction of Popular Common Sense in the U.S." In S. Gill and J. Mittelman, eds., *Innovation and Transformation in International Studies.* New York: Cambridge University Press. [7]

RYLE, Gilbert. (1949) *The Concept of Mind.* New York: Barnes and Noble. [9]

SAHLINS, M. (1976a) *Culture and Practical Reason.* Chicago: University of Chicago Press. [4]

———. (1976b) *The Use and Abuse of Biology.* Ann Arbor: University of Michigan Press. [4]

SAID, Edward. (1978) *Orientalism.* New York: Vintage Books. [8]

SAMPSON, Anthony. (1973) *The Sovereign State: The Secret History of ITT.* London: Hodder and Stoughton. (Chapter 1 also in R. Pettman, 1996). [10]

SANGER, David. (1995) "Buchanan's Tough Tariff Talk Rattles GOP." *New York Times,* October 8. [7]

SATZ, Debra, and John FEREJOHN. (1994) "Rational Choice and Social Theory." *Journal of Philosophy* 91 (2): 71–87. [9]

SAYER, D. (1991) *Capitalism and Modernity: An Excursus on Marx and Weber.* London: Routledge. [4]

SCHAUER, Frederick. (1991) *Playing by the Rules: A Philosophical Examination of Rule-Based Decision-Making in Law and in Life.* Oxford: Clarendon Press. [9]

SCHELLING, Thomas. (1960) *The Strategy of Conflict.* Cambridge: Harvard University Press. [12]

SCHRAM, Sanford F. (1995) *Words of Welfare: The Poverty of Social Science and the Social Science of Poverty.* Minneapolis: University of Minnesota Press. [5]

SCHROEDER, Paul W. (1992) "Did the Vienna System Rest upon a Balance of Power?" *American Historical Review* 97 (3): 683–706. [6]

SCHWAB, Klaus, and Claude SMADJA. (1996) "Start Taking the Backlash Against Globalization Seriously." *International Herald Tribune,* February 1. [7]

SCHWARTZ, Herman M. (1994) *States versus Markets: History, Geography, and the Development of the International Political Economy.* New York: St. Martin's. [2]

SCOTT, William Robert. (1912/1968) *The Constitution and Finance of English, Scottish, and Irish Joint-Stock Companies to 1720.* Vols. I–III. Gloucester, MA: Peter Smith. (Originally published by Cambridge University Press.) [2]

SEARLE, John R. (1969) *Speech Acts: An Essay in the Philosophy of Language.* Cambridge: Cambridge University Press. [9]

———. (1979) *Expression and Meaning: Studies in the Theory of Speech Acts.* Cambridge: Cambridge University Press. [1]

SEIDMAN, Steven. (1983) *Liberalism and the Origins of European Social Theory.* Berkeley: University of California Press. [2]

SELIGMAN, Adam. (1992) *The Idea of Civil Society.* New York: The Free Press. [3]

SEMMEL, Bernard. (1970) *The Rise of Free Trade Imperialism: Classical Political Economy, the Empire of Free Trade and Imperialism 1750–1850.* Cambridge: Cambridge University Press. [6]

SETSER, Vernon G. (1937) *The Commercial Reciprocity Policy of the United States, 1774–1829.* Philadelphia: University of Pennsylvania Press. [6]

SHAPIRO, Ian. (1986) *The Evolution of Rights in Liberal Theory.* New York: Cambridge University Press. [2]

SHAPIRO, Michael J. (1994) *Reading "Adam Smith": Desire, History, Value.* Newbury Park, CA: Sage Publications. [3]

SHERMAN, H. J. (1987) *Foundations of Radical Political Economy.* Armonk, NY: M. E. Sharpe, Inc. [2]

SHIVA, Vandana. (1995) *Trading Our Lives Away: An Ecological and Gender Analysis of "Free Trade" and the WTO.* Penang, Malaysia: Pesticide Action Network (PAN) for Asia and the Pacific and the Research Foundation for Science, Technology and Natural Resource Policy. [5]

SMITH, Steve. (1995) "The Self-Images of a Discipline: A Genealogy of International Relations Theory." In K. Booth and S. Smith, eds., *International Relations Theory Today*, 1–37. University Park: Pennsylvania State University Press. [Intro]

———. (1996) "Positivism and Beyond." In S. Smith et al., eds., *International Theory: Positivism and Beyond*, 11–44. Cambridge: Cambridge University Press. [14]

SMITH, Steve, Ken BOOTH, and Marysia ZALEWSKI, eds. (1996) *International Theory: Positivism and Beyond*. Cambridge: Cambridge University Press. [14]

SNIDAL, Duncan. (1985) "The Limits of Hegemonic Stability Theory." *International Organization* 39 (4) Autumn: 579–614. [6]

SPRADLEY, James. (1980) *Participant Observation*. New York: Holt, Rinehart and Winston. [10]

SPRUYT, Hendrik. (1994) *The Sovereign State and Its Competitors: An Analysis of Systems Change*. Princeton, NJ: Princeton University Press. [2]

STANFIELD, J. R. (1986) *The Economic Thought of Karl Polanyi: Lives and Livelihood*. London: Macmillan. [4]

STANILAND, Martin. (1985) *What Is Political Economy?* New Haven, CT: Yale University Press. [2]

STEIN, Arthur A. (1984) "The Hegemon's Dilemma: Great Britain, the United States, and the International Economic Order." *International Organization* 38 (2) Spring: 355–386. [6]

STERN, Kenneth. (1996) *A Force upon the Plain: The American Militia Movement and the Politics of Hate*. New York: Simon and Schuster. [7]

STILLMAN, P. G. (1987) "Partiality and Wholeness: Economic Freedom, Individual Development, and Ethical Institutions in Hegel's Political Thought." In W. Maker, ed., *Hegel on Economics and Freedom*, 65–93. Macon, GA: Mercer University Press. [4]

STOPFORD, John, and Susan STRANGE. (1991) *Rival States, Rival Firms: Competition for World Market Shares*. New York: Cambridge University Press. [2]

STRANGE, Susan. (1986) *Casino Capitalism*. New York: Basil Blackwell. [3]

——— (1988) *States and Markets: An Introduction to International Political Economy*. London: Pinter. [2]

STRANGE, Susan, ed. (1984) *Paths to International Political Economy*. London: George Allen and Unwin. [2]

SYLVESTER, Christine. (1994) *Feminist Theory and International Relations in a Postmodern Era*. New York: Cambridge University Press. [5]

TAYLOR, Charles. (1985) *Philosophy and the Human Sciences*. New York: Cambridge University Press. [9]

———. (1987) "Interpretation and the Sciences of Man." In P. Rabinow and W. Sullivan, eds., *Interpretive Social Science: A Second Look*. Berkeley: University of California Press. [10]

THOMASON, B. C. (1982) *Making Sense of Reification: Alfred Schutz and Constructionist Theory*. Atlantic Highlands, NJ: Humanities Press. [4]

THOMPSON, John B. (1984) *Studies in the Theory of Ideology*. Berkeley: University of California Press. [2]

THOMSON, Janice. (1994) *Mercenaries, Pirates, and Sovereigns: State-building and Extraterritorial Violence in Early Modern Europe*. Princeton, NJ: Princeton University Press. [2]

THRIFT, Nigel. (1983) "On the Determination of Social Action in Space and Time." *Society and Space* 1 (March): 23–57. [9]

TICKNER, J. Ann. (1991) "On the Fringes of the World Economy: A Feminist Perspective." In C. N. Murphy and R. Tooze, eds., *The New International Political Economy,* 191–206. Boulder, CO: Lynne Rienner. [5]

———. (1992a) "Foreword." In V. S. Peterson, ed., *Gendered States: Feminist (Re)Visions of International Relations Theory,* ix–xi. Boulder, CO: Lynne Rienner. [9]

———. (1992b) *Gender in International Relations: Feminist Perspectives on Achieving Global Security.* New York: Columbia University Press. [3, 11]

TIGAR, Michael E., and Madeleine R. LEVY. (1977) *Law & the Rise of Capitalism.* New York: Monthly Review Press. [3]

TILLY, Charles, ed. (1975) *The Formation of National States in Western Europe.* Princeton, NJ: Princeton University Press. [2]

TOOZE, Roger. (1984) "Perspectives and Theory: A Consumers' Guide." In S. Strange, ed., *Paths to International Political Economy,* 1–22. London: George Allen and Unwin. [2]

TOOZE, Roger, and Craig MURPHY. (1996) "The Epistemology of Poverty and the Poverty of Epistemology in IPE: Mystery, Blindness and Invisibility." *Millennium: Journal of International Studies* 25(3) Winter:681–707. [14]

TOULMIN, Stephen. (1990) *Cosmopolis: The Hidden Agenda of Modernity.* New York: The Free Press. [2]

TUCK, Richard. (1979) *Natural Rights Theories: Their Origin and Development.* New York: Cambridge University Press. [2]

TUCKER, James. (1993) "Globalists Celebrate Too Soon." *Spotlight,* December 6. [7]

———. (1994) "One World Closer with GATT." *Spotlight,* January 10. [7]

———. (1995) "Bought Think Tankers Beat Drums for One Worlders." *Spotlight,* May 15. [7]

UNITED STATES, STATE DEPARTMENT. (1890). *International Marine Conference.* Vol. II, *Protocol of Proceedings and Final Act.* Washington, DC: Government Printing Office. [9]

VAN DER PJIL, Kees. (1984) *The Making of an Atlantic Ruling Class.* London: Verso Books. [3]

VAN STAVEREN, Irene. (1995) "Trade: A Gendered Business." *ICDA Journal: Focus on Trade and Development* 3 (2): 101–104. [5]

VERDIER, Daniel. (1994) *Democracy and International Trade: Britain, France, and the United States, 1860–1990.* Princeton, NJ: Princeton University Press. [6]

VER EECKE, W. (1980) "Relation Between Economics and Politics in Hegel." In D. P. Verene, ed., *Hegel's Social and Political Thought: The Philosophy of Objective Spirit,* 91–101. New York: Humanities Press. [4]

———. (1987) "Hegel on Freedom, Economics, and the State." In W. Maker, ed., *Hegel on Economics and Freedom,* 127–157. Macon, GA: Mercer University Press. [4]

VICKERS, Jean. (1991) *Women and the World Economic Crisis.* London: Zed Books. [13]

VINCENT, Isabel. (1996) "Rebel Dispatches Find Home on Net." *The Globe and Mail* (Toronto), June 11. [8]

WALDRON, Jeremy. (1988) *The Right to Private Property.* New York: Clarendon Press. [2]

WALKER, R. B. J. (1988) *One World/Many Worlds*. Boulder, CO: Lynne Rienner. [10]
———. (1993) *Inside/Outside: International Relations as Political Theory*. New York: Cambridge University Press. [2]
WALKER, R. B. J., and Saul H. MENDLOVITZ, eds. (1990) *Contending Sovereignties: Redefining Political Community*. Boulder, CO: Lynne Rienner. [2]
WALLERSTEIN, Immanuel. (1974a) *The Modern World-System: Capitalist Agriculture and the Origins of the European World-Economy in the Sixteenth Century*. New York: Academic Press. [6]
———. (1974b) "The Rise and Future Demise of the World Capitalist System: Concepts for Comparative Analysis." *Comparative Studies in Society and History* 16 (4): 387–415. [6]
———. (1979) *The Capitalist World-Economy*. New York: Cambridge University Press. [3]
———. (1980) *The Modern World-System II: Mercantilism and the Consolidation of the European World-Economy, 1600–1750*. New York: Academic Press. [6]
———. (1983) *Historical Capitalism*. New York: Verso Books. [3]
———. (1984) *The Politics of the World Economy: The States, the Movements, and the Civilizations*. New York: Cambridge University Press. [6]
WALTZ, Kenneth. (1979) *Theory of International Politics*. Reading, MA: Addison-Wesley. [2, 9, 12]
WALZER, Michael. (1984) "Liberalism and the Art of Separation." *Political Theory* 12 (3) August: 315–330. [2]
———. (1988) *The Company of Critics: Social Criticism and Political Commitment in the Twentieth Century*. New York: Basic Books. [4]
WARD, Kathryn B., ed. (1990) *Women Workers and Global Restructuring*. Ithaca, NY: ILR Press of Cornell University. [13]
WARING, Marilyn. (1988) *If Women Counted: A New Feminist Economics*. San Francisco: Harper. [13]
WARREN, Mark E. (1995) "Marx and Methodological Individualism." In T. Carver and P. Thomas, eds., *Rational Choice Marxism*, 231–257. University Park: Pennsylvania State University Press. [9]
WEBER, Cynthia. (1995) *Simulating Sovereignty: Intervention, the State, and Symbolic Exchange*. New York: Cambridge University Press. [2]
WEBER, Max. (1958) *The Protestant Ethic and the Spirit of Capitalism*. New York: The Free Press. [2]
———. (1978) *Economy and Society: An Outline of Interpretive Sociology*. Berkeley: University of California Press. [1]
WELCH, Robert. (1986) *Republics and Democracies*. Appleton, WI: John Birch Society. [7]
WENDT, Alexander. (1987) "The Agent-Structure Problem in International Relations Theory." *International Organization* 41 (3) Summer: 335–370. [1, 2, 9, 12]
———. (1991) "Bridging the Theory/Meta-Theory Gap in International Relations." *Review of International Studies* 17 (4): 383–392. [1]
———. (1992) "Anarchy Is What States Make of It: The Social Construction of Power Politics." *International Organization* 46 (2) Spring: 395–421. [2, 9]
———. (1994) "Collective Identity Formation and the International State." *American Political Science Review* 88 (2) June: 384–396. [1, 2]

————. (1995) "Constructing International Politics." *International Security* 20 (1) Summer: 71–81. [2]

WESTPHAL, M. (1987) "Hegel, Human Rights, and the Hungry." In W. Maker, ed., *Hegel on Economics and Freedom,* 209–228. Macon, GA: Mercer University Press. [4]

WHITWORTH, Sandra. (1994) "Theory as Exclusion: Gender and International Political Economy." In R. Stubbs and G. R. D. Underhill, eds., *Political Economy and the Changing Global Order,* 116–129. Toronto: McClelland and Stewart. [8]

WIENER, Jarrod. (1995) "'Hegemonic' Leadership: Naked Emperor or the Worship of False Gods." *European Journal of International Relations* 1 (2): 219–243. [6]

WILKINSON, David. (1994) "Reconceiving Hegemony." Paper presented at the annual meeting of the International Studies Association, March, Washington, DC. [6]

WILLS, Gary. (1995) "The New Revolutionaries." *The New York Review of Books,* August 10. [7]

WILSON, Charles. (1977) "The British Isles." In C. Wilson and G. Parker, eds., *An Introduction to the Sources of European Economic History 1500–1800,* 115–154. Ithaca, NY: Cornell University Press. [2]

WINCH, Donald. (1978) *Adam Smith's Politics: An Essay in Historiographic Revision.* New York: Cambridge University Press. [3]

WITTGENSTEIN, Ludwig. (1958) *Philosophical Investigations.* Translated by G. E. M. Anscombe. New York: Macmillan. [4, 9]

WOLF, Naomi. (1990) *The Beauty Myth.* Toronto: Vintage. [8]

WOLFF, Edward N. (1995) "How the Pie Is Sliced." *The American Prospect* 22 (Summer) (http://epn.org/prospect/22/22wolf.html). [7]

World Development. (1995) Special Issue: Gender, Adjustment and Macroeconomics 23 (11) November. [13]

XENOS, Nicholas. (1989) *Scarcity and Modernity.* New York: Routledge. [3]

YARBROUGH, Beth V., and Robert M. YARBROUGH. (1992) *Cooperation and Governance in International Trade: The Strategic Organization Approach.* Princeton, NJ: Princeton University Press. [6]

YOUNGS, Gillian. (1994) "The Knowledge Problematic: Richard Ashley and Political Economy." Unpublished manuscript, Nottingham Trent University Park, Nottingham. [4]

ZESKIND, Leonard. (1996) "White-Shoed Supremacy." *The Nation,* June 10. [7]

Contributors and Commentators

David L. Blaney is an associate professor in the Department of Political Science at Macalester College (1600 Grand Avenue, St. Paul, MN, USA, 55105; e-mail: blaney@macalester.edu). His research focuses on the roles of culture and sovereignty in international political theory. Recent work with Naeem Inayatullah appears in *Review of International Political Economy.*

Kurt Burch is an associate professor in the Department of Political Science and International Relations at the University of Delaware (Newark, DE, USA, 19716; e-mail: kurt@udel.edu). His research addresses the social construction of ethics and political economy. His book *"Property" and the Making of the International System: Constituting Sovereignty, Political Economy, and the Modern Era* will appear in 1997.

Wayne S. Cox is an assistant professor in the Department of Politics and Economics at the Royal Military College of Canada (Kingston, Ontario, Canada, K7K 5L0; e-mail: 3wsc2@qlink.queensu.ca). His interests include globalization and the construction of ethnic and national identities, Kurdish ethnonationalism, and Middle Eastern politics. He recently coedited with Claire Turenne Sjolander the volume *Beyond Positivism: Critical Reflections on International Relations.*

Naeem Inayatullah is an assistant professor at Ithaca College (Ithaca, NY, USA, 14850; e-mail: naeem@ithaca.edu). His research addresses the history of political economic thought and the role of the Third World in the construction of the global political economy. Recent work with David L. Blaney appears in *Review of International Studies.*

Nicholas Onuf is a professor in the International Relations Department at Florida International University–University Park (Miami, FL, USA, 33199; e-mail: onufn@servax.fiu.edu). His interests include social, legal, and political theory bearing on international relations. His latest book, *The Republican Legacy in International Thought,* will appear in 1997.

Ralph Pettman holds the Foundation Chair of International Relations in the Department of Politics at Victoria University of Wellington (P.O. Box 600, Wellington, New Zealand; e-mail: ralph.pettman@vuw.ac.nz). His current research explores the limits of rationalism in the study of world affairs and considers contemporary attempts in Asia to articulate alternative forms of globalism. He most recently published *Understanding International Political Economy, with readings for the fatigued* (1996).

James C. Roberts is the coordinator of International Studies and an associate professor in the Department of Political Science at Towson State University (Towson, MD, USA, 21204; e-mail: roberts-j@toe.towson.edu).

Stephen J. Rosow is a professor in the Department of Political Science at the State University of New York at Oswego (Oswego, NY, USA, 13126; e-mail: rosow@oswego.edu). His research addresses questions of democratic theory and political theory in the world economy. His research interests include international political economy and rational choice theory. He has published in *Polity, Review of Politics, RIPE,* and *Alternatives,* and he is completing a book on Western democratic theory.

Anne Sisson Runyan is an associate professor and the director of the Women's Studies program in the Department of Political Science at Wright State University (Dayton, OH, USA, 45435-0001; e-mail: arunyan@ wright.edu). She has written extensively on gender and IR/IPE, including coauthoring, with V. Spike Peterson, *Global Gender Issues* (1993; second edition forthcoming 1999). She is currently coediting *Gender and Global Restructuring* (forthcoming 1998 with Marianne Marchand).

Mark Rupert is an associate professor in the Department of Political Science at Syracuse University's Maxwell School of Citizenship and Public Affairs (Syracuse, NY, USA, 13210; e-mail: merupert@syr.edu). He is interested in international political economy, broadly defined, and is the author of *Producing Hegemony: The Politics of Mass Production and American Global Power* (1995).

Claire Turenne Sjolander is an associate professor in the Department of Political Science at the University of Ottawa (75 Laurier E, P.O. Box 450, Station A, Ottawa, Ontario, Canada, K1N 6N5; e-mail: cturenne@ uottawa.ca). Her interests include the consequences of globalization, especially for the aviation industry and international trade policy. She has recently coedited with Wayne S. Cox the volume *Beyond Positivism: Critical Reflections on International Relations.*

COMMENTATORS

Joshua S. Goldstein is a professor in the School of International Service at the American University (Washington, DC, USA, 20016-8071; e-mail: jgoldst@american.edu). His interests bridge international security, political economy, and data analysis. He is working on a book about war and gender.

James K. Oliver is a Unidel Professor in the Department of Political Science and International Relations at the University of Delaware (Newark, DE, USA, 19716; e-mail: jkoliver@udel.edu). His interests include U.S. foreign policy, international organization, and IR theory. His most recent book is *Foreign Policy Making and the American Political System.*

V. Spike Peterson is an associate professor in the Department of Political Science at the University of Arizona (Tucson, AZ, USA, 85721; e-mail: spikep@u.arizona.edu). Her research focuses on the relationship of globalization to social hierarchies and sexualities. She is the editor of *Gendered States* (1992) and, with Anne Sisson Runyan, coauthor of *Global Gender Issues* (1993). She recently received a MacArthur Foundation grant to conduct research on globalization, democratization, and gender.

Roger Tooze is a reader in political economy in the Department of International Politics at the University of Wales, Aberystwyth (Penglais, Aberystwyth, Dyfed, UK, SY23 3DA; e-mail: rit@aber.ac.uk). His interests include the theorization of IPE, the theory of International Relations, and the construction of foreign economic policy and economic security. He is currently completing a study on theory and IPE. He wrote his commentary for this book while on sabbatical leave from Aberystwyth as visiting professor of international relations in the Department of Political Science at Northern Arizona University.

Index

Activists, 114, 118–119

Adams, Douglas, 185n2

Adams, John, 103

Advertisements, advertising, 56n3, 150

Agency, 7, 8, 61, 113, 195; agent-structure relations, 7, 60; cognitive competence and choice-making, 9, 151, 157, 164, 165; collective, 9, 17, 116, 128; far-right ideology, 121, 128; identity, 9, 147, 166; intentional, purposeful, 8–9, 11, 60, 159, 160, 162–163; limitations, 9, 152; preferences, 157–158, 161, 163; racial, 129; rational choice, 9, 10, 12, 163, 164; reconstructed by globalization, 140, 204; rules and, 8, 11, 12, 13–14, 15, 60, 93, 103, 156–157, 159, 164–166; tension between autonomy and heteronomy, 17, 166, 190–191, 192. *See also* Agent-structure problem, Political action, Unintended consequences

Agent-structure problem, 157, 158, 159, 166, 167n1, 195; constructivism and, 7, 155, 157; progressive rational agent as solution, 166–167; rational choice theory, 161–164; realism and, 158–159; rules as solution, 7–8, 159

Alienation, 70, 71, 72, 76, 197

Alliances, 12, 28, 97, 109, 122–124, 126, 127, 129, 137n9, 138n17

Anarchy, 17, 64; constraining actors, 65, 158, 191; yields system structure, 62, 65, 158

Anti-Semitism. *See* Far-right politics, White supremacy groups

Arbitration, 105–106, 107

Arblaster, Anthony, 26, 40n7

Arthur, Christopher J., 77n3

Aryan World Order, 129–130. *See also* Far-right politics, Neo-Nazi groups

Ashley, Richard, 74, 167, 167n2, 196, 210; constructing politics, 66, 67, 70, 76; economic anxiety, 59–60, 62, 66–69, 72; knowledgeable practice, 40n7, 66, 67–68, 75; logic of economy, 66–68, 70, 73, 75; politics as salvation, 69; politics/economics split, 40n7, 67, 69

Asian Pacific Economic Cooperation forum (APEC), 125

Associations, 13, 17

Atlantic republicanism, 46

Austin, John, 38

Authority, 27–32; exercise of property rights, 28–29, 34; hegemony and, 16; sovereignty and, 22, 27, 28

Autonomy, 76, 88, 190–191; challenged by interdependence, 119–120; heteronomy, 17, 93–94, 103; sovereignty and, 158–159; yields anarchy, 17, 158. *See also* Individualism

Avineri, Shlomo, 76n2

Bacchus, James, 133

Bakker, Isabella, 205n2

Balance of power, 12, 13, 141

Barkun, Michael, 137n14, 138n18

Bartelson, Jens, 40n5

Barthelme, Donald, 185n1

Behavioralism. *See* Scientific rationalism

Beitz, Charles, 55

Beneria, Lourdes, 205n2

Bennett, David, 137nn8–12, 138n18

Bentham, Jeremy, 45, 71

Berlet, Chip, 124, 137n8, 10, 14–16

Berman, Marshall, 149

Bernstein, Richard, 26

Bhaskar, Roy, 160

Bilderberg Group, 123, 127

Black, Don, 138n20

239

science and, 8, 207–208; threats to IPE, 209–210
Convention. *See* Rules
Conventional IPE. *See* Mainstream international political economy; *see also* International political economy
Corn Laws. *See* Great Britain
Council on Domestic Relations (far-right organization), 124, 125, 137n7
Council on Foreign Relations (CFR), 123, 125, 126, 127, 130
Cox, Robert, 40n4, 99–100, 145, 146
Cox, Wayne, 190, 204–205
CPI (Consumer Price Index), 87
Cross-hairs, 21–22, 24, 25, 36, 37, 38
Crowley, John, 104
Culture, 23
Cuomo Commission Report, 53

Davidson, Don, 162
Dees, Morris, 137n10, 138n18
Democracy: cosmopolitan, 114, 119; industrial, 116; tensions with property, 118
Democratization, 54, 119; workplace, 53
Dependency theory, 99
De-reification. *See* Reification
Descartes, Rene, 175, 176
Dessler, David, 158, 167n1
Diamond, Sara, 137nn8, 9, 11, 12, 16
Dichotomies. *See* Domestic/international, Family/economy, Family/society, Home/market, Objective/subjective, Politics/economics, Public/private, Rational/irrational, Reproduction/production, State/society, Us/other; Double dualism, Economics, Politics, Production, Reproduction
Directive-rules, 10, 13, 14, 160; forming an organization, 13, 93; related to offices, 13, 16
Domestic/international conceptual split, 22, 37–38, 55n1, 119, 190, 196, 203, 211
Domination, 23–24, 38, 72, 74, 100, 191, 196; capitalist, 69, 71, 119; *dominium,* 27, 28–29, 32; as element of rule, 22–23, 36, 93, 201; hegemony and, 65, 75; language and, 23, 191; liberal-modern version, 32, 36, 38; logic of economy, 67–68, 71; structures of, 60–61; via property rights, 33, 36, 37
Double dualism, double movement, 72–74, 84

Downward harmonization, 118
Druck, Dan, 125
Dryzek, John S., 161
Dualisms. *See* Dichotomies
Durham, Martin, 137n8, 12

Eastman Kodak, 117
Economic anxiety, 62–69, 74–76; alternatives to, 69–74
Economic liberalism: dominance (as commercial society) in IPE, 42–48, 49, 51–54, 190, 203; institutional setting, 109; interpretations of Adam Smith, 44–48; marginalizes alternative versions, 43; neorealism and, 51; political versions, 48–54; prehistory, 44–46; rules and, 95. *See also* Commercial society, International political economy, Liberalism
Economics, the economy, 23; capital accumulation, 45; care work, 83–84, 88; commercial society, 45; emergence as apparently distinct system, 33, 35, 37, 45, 63, 203; ethics, 69; etymology, 83; family and, 80, 82, 84; feminist, 81–85, 204, 205n2; free trade, 101; gendered constructions, 79–85; Gilpin's views, 62; Hegel's views, 69–71; International Relations and, 25; as "iron laws," 63; Marx's views, 71–72; as natural, naturalized, 47–48, 65, 203; neglect of women, 81–84; neoclassical characterizations, critiques, 41, 69, 81–85, 87; Polanyi's views, 72–74; property, property rights and, 32–36, 46; psychoanalytical critique, 85–88; rationality premises, 161; as social practices, 60; as social practices, autonomous, 32–36, 45, 63; as social practices, denying knowledgeable activities, 64–66, 68, 72; as social practices, disruptive, 63–64, 69; as social practices, embedded, 70, 72–74, 82; as social practices, promoting knowledgeable activities, 69–70, 71, 74, 75, 81; as social practices, separated, 32–36, 45, 63, 82, 196, 203; as social practices, universalizing, 140. *See also* Capitalism, Commercial society, Logic of economy, Market
Eddlem, Thomas, 126
Einhorn, Barbara, 205n2
Elias, Norbert, 44
Elshtain, Jean, 192

About the Book

International political economy is both a discipline and a set of global practices and conditions. This volume explores how disciplinary frameworks and social practices are related. This volume also explores the changing character of the global political economy and changing perspectives on that character.

The authors first consider how social issues, policy concerns, and philosophical judgments help constitute IPE both as a worldview and as a discipline. A central theme is the reciprocal creation of the discipline and the social practices said to comprise it and its subjects.

Subsequent chapters illustrate the incongruence between the nature of the social world as alleged in IPE's premises—which often distortedly frame issues—and the alternative characterizations available from other social groups, behaviors, and approaches. The authors also draw conclusions about the tensions between "conventional" and "alternative" framings of the international political economy, raising questions about the nature, consequences, and insights of diverse approaches to IPE.

In a commentary section, four notable scholars share their reactions to the volume as a whole and to select themes. The editors invited their comments to exemplify the view that (self-)critique is an essential element of scholarly life. These commentaries help engage readers, build bridges between subfields, and spark scholarly conversations.